AF527901

Mapping Indian Diaspora

Mapping Indian Diaspora

Contestations and Representations

Edited by
Ajaya K. Sahoo

RAWAT PUBLICATIONS
Jaipur • New Delhi • Bangalore • Guwahati • Kolkata

ISBN 978-81-316-0897-5

© Contributors, 2017

No part of this book may be reproduced or transmitted in any form or by any means, electronic or mechanical, including photocopying, recording or by any information storage and retrieval system, without permission in writing from the publishers.

Published by
Prem Rawat for **Rawat Publications**
Satyam Apts, Sector 3, Jawahar Nagar, Jaipur 302 004 (India)
Phone: 0141 265 1748 / 7006 Fax: 0141 265 1748
E-mail: info@rawatbooks.com
Website: www.rawatbooks.com

New Delhi Office
4858/24, Ansari Road, Daryaganj, New Delhi 110 002
Phone: 011 2326 3290

Also at *Bangalore, Guwahati* and *Kolkata*

Typeset by Rawat Computers, Jaipur
Printed at Chaman Enterprises, New Delhi

Contents

Acknowledgements

This volume grows out of the international conference on Indian diaspora organized by the Centre for Study of Indian Diaspora, University of Hyderabad, in November 2014. I would like to thank all the contributors for sending their revised papers on time, without which this volume would not have been possible.

The conference was financially supported by the Centre for the Study of Indian Diaspora (UGC Area Studies Programme), University of Hyderabad, and the Indian Council of Social Science Research (ICSSR), Southern Regional Centre, Hyderabad.

I would like to specially thank Mr Pranit Rawat of Rawat Publications for his guidance and support throughout in bringing out the volume.

Ajaya Kumar Sahoo

Contributors

Ajaya K. Sahoo teaches at the Centre for Study of Indian Diaspora, University of Hyderabad. His research interests include international migration, South Asian diaspora, transnationalism and religion. He has co-edited *Diaspora, Development and Distress: Indians in the Persian Gulf* (2015), *Indian Transnationalism Online: New Perspective on Diaspora* (2014), *Indian Diaspora and Transnationalism* (2012), *Transnational Migrations: The Indian Diaspora* (2009) and *Tracing an Indian Diaspora: Contexts, Memories, Representations* (2008).

Angshuman Kar is an Associate Professor and former Head, Department of English and Culture Studies, the University of Burdwan, West Bengal, India. He has also served in the Sahitya Akademi as the Secretary of the Eastern Region. He has published his works in India and abroad and has co-edited *The Politics of Social Exclusion in India: Democracy at the Crossroads* (Routledge 2010) and edited *Contemporary Indian Diaspora: Literary and Cultural Representations* (Rawat 2015). He is also the recipient of the Australia-India Council Fellowship (2006) and a well-known Bengali poet.

Anindita Shome is a Ph.D. Research Scholar at the UGC Centre for Study of Indian Diaspora, School of Social Sciences, University of Hyderabad, India.

Arnab Kumar Sinha is an Assistant Professor in the Department of English and Culture Studies, the University of Burdwan, West Bengal. He has done his Ph.D. on the novels of Chinua Achebe. He has published articles in several journals and books and also presented papers at many national and international conferences/seminars. He has co-edited the book, *Indian Fiction in English: Mapping the Contemporary Literary Landscape* (2014). His areas of interest include Nigerian literature, South Asian diasporic literature and postcolonial criticism.

Diksha Jha is a Ph.D. Research Scholar at the Centre for the Study of Law and Governance, Jawaharlal Nehru University, New Delhi, India.

Joanna P. Coelho is an Assistant Professor, Department of Sociology, Goa University, Goa, India. Her areas of research interest include Sociology of Indian Society, Sociology of Language, Environment and Society.

Karen Leonard has published her works on the history and culture of India, especially the former Hyderabad State, and on Asian American and Muslim American history and culture. Her latest book, *Hyderabad and Hyderabadis*, reprints her 14 best articles on Hyderabad, Deccan. *Locating Home: India's Hyderabadis Abroad* (2007) was a multisite ethnography of the diaspora from Hyderabad to Pakistan, the United Kingdom, Australia, Canada, the United States, and the Gulf states of the Middle East. *Muslims in the United States: The State of Research* (2003) led to many speaking engagements and consultations. Leonard retired in 2014, after Chairing the Anthropology Department at the University of California, Irvine.

Kishore Kumar Aleti is a Ph.D. Research Scholar at the UGC Centre for Study of Indian Diaspora, School of Social Sciences, University of Hyderabad, India. His recent publications include 'Migration, Diaspora and Return: A Study on Information Technology (IT) Professionals in Hyderabad', *International Journal of Global Diaspora Studies*, 2 (2), 2016.

Neetu Devi is a Ph.D. Research Scholar at the UGC Centre for Study of Indian Diaspora, School of Social Sciences, University of Hyderabad, India.

Rakesh Ranjan is a Ph.D. Research Scholar at the Centre for the Study of Social Systems, Jawaharlal Nehru University, Delhi. He is a founding member of Global Research Forum on Diaspora and Transnationalism (GRFDT), an international think tank based in New Delhi, India. Mr Ranjan has research interest in Diaspora, Entrepreneurship, International Migration, Labour and Development, Gender Studies, Media Studies, and so on. He has contributed several articles and chapters in national and international referred publications.

Sanjoy Malik is an Assistant Professor of English in the Department of English and Culture Studies at the University of Burdwan, West Bengal. He is currently working on the poetry of Imtiaz Dharker for his Ph.D. thesis. He has published many articles in various journals. He has also presented papers in several national and international conferences. His areas of interest include gender studies, diaspora studies and postcolonial studies.

Sridhar Bhagavatula is currently an Executive Officer at the Confederation of Indian Industry (CII), Hyderabad, and also a doctoral research scholar with Zakir Husain Centre for Educational Studies (ZHCES), Jawaharlal Nehru University (JNU), New Delhi. Previously, he was associated with Ministry of Overseas Indian Affairs (MOIA), National University of Educational Planning and Administration (NUEPA) and Society for Educational and Economic Development (SEED). A master's degree in political science from JNU and graduation in economics from Kerala University helped him evolve a multidisciplinary approach towards diaspora studies and migration research.

Subhadeep Kumar is a Ph.D. Research Scholar at the UGC Centre for Study of Indian Diaspora, School of Social Sciences, University of Hyderabad, India. He has contributed to UGC e-Pathsala course module on Literary Theory, Indian Drama and Literature and Migration.

Introduction

Mapping Indian Diaspora: Contestations and Representations

Ajaya K. Sahoo

The emergence of diaspora studies goes back to the launch of an interdisciplinary journal titled *Diaspora: A Journal of Transnational Studies* in 1991 by Professor Khachig Tololyan under the University of Toronto Press. This journal provided a very significant platform for scholars and researchers to experiment their new research on various dimensions of diasporas, their patterns and practices, emergences and growth, homogeneity and diversity, locality and transnationality, presentations and representations. In doing so, it was observed that by the end of the twentieth century, within a decade, the study of diasporas had become endemic globally. The diaspora studies today is not only studied within the traditional disciplines of social sciences and humanities but has also established itself as an important area of academic discipline.

The use of the word 'diaspora' applied to the case of Indians came in prominent use by the mid-1990s. Though several scholars have already worked on Indian communities living outside their homeland prior to mid-1990s, none of them used the word diaspora rather they use words such as 'Indian overseas' or 'Indian immigrants'. In 1989 for instance, *Sociological Bulletin,* the official journal of the Indian Sociological Society, brought out a special issue on the theme 'Indians Abroad' (Vol. 38, No. 1, March 1989) in which eight out of nine special issue papers focused on Indian communities abroad, but not a single paper referred to them as diasporic (Raghuram and Sahoo 2008: 6). Thanks to the journal *Diaspora: A Journal of Transnational Studies* that not only opened up debates among scholars and early researchers but also provided solid grounds for quality research to come up in the future, as these scholars were acquainted with research on 'other diasporas' and most importantly the use of methodological tools to study the diasporic phenomenon.

This volume grows out of the international conference, which was held at University of Hyderabad and organized by the Centre for the Study of Indian Diaspora. Being one of the earliest centres in India focusing exclusively on Indian diaspora from an interdisciplinary perspective, this conference also focuses on a broader theme on Indian diaspora, that is, contestations and representations.

The Indian Diaspora

Historically, Indians have been migrating to different parts of the world under different circumstances. In terms of sheer numbers, today they constitute the third largest group of diasporics living outside their homeland, next to the British and the Chinese. The people of Indian origin, with nearly 25 million plus populations settled in more than 100 countries, constitute more than 40 per cent of the population in Fiji, Mauritius, Trinidad, Guyana and Surinam. They are smaller minorities in Malaysia, South Africa, Sri Lanka, Uganda, United Kingdom, United States and Canada. There are broadly three periods of Indian emigration evidenced from the literature on Indian diaspora (see Dubey 2003; Jain 1993; Sahoo 2006).

Precolonial Migration

As far as historical and archival data is concerned, Indian emigration goes back to the first century AD, when Indian merchants, princes, priests, poets and artisans migrated to East Africa and Southeast Asian countries (see MEA 2002; Shanmugam 2009) and made vibrant cultural relations with these countries. The maritime history of precolonial India shows evidence of continuous contact between the Kingdoms of the Coromandel Coast and the islands of South East Asia (Jayaram 2004; Tinker 1977). As Shanmugam (2009: 210) traces through archaeological evidence that during the Chola period (the ninth to thirteenth century AD), Southeast Asian countries become a good market for traders especially from South India. The Cholas, one of the most powerful kingdoms in South India, controlled the most extensive shipping from the Coromandel Coast across the Indian Ocean and the Arabian Sea. The two flourishing port towns of South Indian that provided impetus for the trade and commerce during this period were Kaveripattinam and Nagapattinam (Devare 2009: 179). The trade contacts slowly developed and thereby small colonies established themselves in Southeast Asia. It is observed that merchants from Gujarat, Bengal and Tamil Nadu settled down in the great port cities of Southeast Asia. It is through the trade that the merchants carried with them the Indian beliefs and customs and made significant cultural influence in Southeast Asia. Claude Markovits (2000) provided an excellent analysis of diasporic trading networks of Hindu merchants from the towns of Shikarpur and Hyderabad in the province of Sind, describing how they came to control the trading networks throughout the world. According to Peter van der Veer (1995: 4), 'the pervasiveness of precolonial migration inside and outside of India may at least lead us to question the radical modernity of the experience of displacement, disjuncture, and diaspora'.

Colonial Migration

It was only in the nineteenth and twentieth century that further conditions for emigration of large numbers of Indians to different parts of the world were created, in the wake of European imperialist expansion (van der Veer 1995). New plantations, and industrial and commercial ventures in European colonies, furthered by swifter travel and communication, [1] created the need for large supplies of labour, and, with the abolition of slavery in the British, French and Dutch colonies respectively in 1834, 1846 and 1873, there were severe shortages of labour to work in the sugar, tea, coffee, cocoa and rubber plantations in the colonies. The emancipation of slavery made the colonial planters in crisis, as they 'perceived their success as being founded upon a critical ratio between abundant land and cheap labor – a ratio which slavery had served well and which after abolition needed to be replaced' (Mahmud 2012: 16). Looking for alternative sources of labour, aside from the African ex-slaves and European immigrants, the colonial government imported Indians under the designation of indentured labour. The indentured labour system[2] 'took a variety of forms, typically articulating with indigenous social relations, but generally was a contractual arrangement with penal sanctions whereby workers agreed to passage to and employment in a foreign country under specified terms, usually for five to ten years' (Goss and Lindquist 2000: 389). The emigration of indentured labour continued up to the early twentieth century. Approximately 1.5 million Indians crossed the oceans under the contracts of indenture (Clarke et al. 1990). There are several factors pushed Indian migrants into seeking employment under the indenture. The first was the poor condition that prevailed at that time in India because of the killing of the Indian village due to famine and natural calamities and the shrinking of cottage industry resulting in extreme poverty and unemployment. The West, on the other hand, was getting affluent because of the industrial development. Second, all colonial masters found Indians skilful, hardworking and useful, as a result of which the British, the French, the Dutch and the Portuguese all took Indian skilled labour for development of plantations and agricultural economies for their territories.

Upon their arrival in the colonies, the immigrants were assigned to plantations to which they were 'bound' for five or more years. As the Indians signed the indentured contract, the colonial government restricted their movement outside the plantations in which they were assigned. That apart, 'it not only regulated their labor power but also isolated them on plantations. Planters deployed many formal and informal systems of control not only to confine workers on the estates but also to keep them under indenture' (Mahmud 2012: 22). Although they were promised fair wages and a return voyage to India in exchange for a predetermined number of years spent working in the colonies, poverty and the desire to build a new life ensured that very few of these indentured labourers ever returned to India. For instance, 'in an environment where a number of races were closely juxtapositioned, Indian diasporics often occupied an in-between space between the colonizer and the territorially-based colonized. They formed a middle stratum between the British and the Black Africans in many parts of Africa' (Raghuram and Sahoo 2008: 8). The inhospitable conditions in the plantations and appalling treatment of Indians by the colonial rulers under the indentured system led to 'very high rate of suicide, a third of which took place in the first year of indenture' (Mahmud 2012: 23).

Emigration to Sri Lanka, Burma and Malaya presents a marked difference in contrast to the African and Caribbean countries. All the emigrants to Sri Lanka and Malaya were from the Southern parts of India and the immigrants were recruited by the headman known as the 'Kangani'. The Indians worked on the tea, coffee and rubber plantations. During the period 1852 and 1937, 1.5 million Indians went to Ceylon, 2 million to Malaya and 2.5 million to Burma. After 1920, the Kangani emigration (totalling around 6 million) gradually gave way to individual or un-recruited, free migration due to fall in demand for Indian labour.

Postcolonial Migration

The labour migration from India were almost came to a halt due to the onset of World Wars. It was only after the end of Second World War that the scenario has changed the whole international migration process by affecting each and every migrant country, and India was not far behind in this process. This period of migration also termed as the post-independence migration. During this period, migration was directed towards the developed countries, and the migrants mostly constituted talented professionals, skilled labourers and entrepreneurs besides the *Anglo Indians*. This post-independence migration, which is also continuing today, was totally different from the earlier migration of indentured, Kangani and other forms of labour migrations. Large-scale migration of Indians took place during this period to the developed countries such as United Kingdom, United States, Canada, Australia and New Zealand. Apart from India, Indians from other parts of the world especially from the former colonies (diasporics) also started coming to these countries. There are two instances: (a) Africanization policies and (b) Ethnic violence in which Indians from former colonies express their interest to immigrate to these new lands.

Indians have migrated to different parts of the world at different periods of time. They migrated to British, French and Dutch colonies during nineteenth and early twentieth centuries as *indentured* and *Kangani* labourers and today they constitute the *Old Diaspora*. They also migrated to industrially developed countries of Europe and North America during the postcolonial era as skilled workers and professionals and constitute the *New Diaspora* (Mishra 2007). Wherever the Indians have migrated and settled, they created their own unique identity, that is, 'Indianness' and today they constitute an invaluable diasporic community having a strong foothold in economy and politics of the respective host societies.

About the Volume

The contributors to this volume all raise important questions about the different issues on Indian diaspora, which is presented under two broad themes: 'contestations and representations'. In doing so, they examine the socio-historical legacies of international migration from India and the trajectories they undergo while resettling in the various diasporic locales. They debate the issues of gender, family, migration, religion, transnationalism, remittances and the representation of diasporic livings in the literary texts.

The volume starts with the essay by Karen Leonard on marriage patterns and practices among second-generation young South Asians in America. She examined how South Asians in America blurred the boundaries between religious and secular practices in their weddings and how marriages even out of religion, caste or national origin are often celebrated according to traditional South Asian religious rituals and customs. Through several case studies she has shown the major changes that have been taken place in the marriage patterns and practices within the South Asian community of late.

Joanna P. Coelho's chapter attempts to articulate the modifications taking place in the concepts of citizenship and nationality in the context of migration with a case study of Goans settled in Swindon, England. She argued that people from the former Portuguese colony in India can exercise the option of becoming citizens of Portugal subject to certain conditions. The Portuguese citizenship gives them passage to work and settle anywhere in Europe as European citizens. There have been a number of Goans who, after acquiring Portuguese citizenship, have settled in various European countries, especially England. The rapidly growing numbers of Goans opting for Portuguese citizenship have implications for not only the migrants and their families, but also the homeland that they leave behind is largely altered by this change. The chapter looks at how a village in North Goa is transformed by this phenomenon. It argues that the Goans who went to Swindon, England, as Portuguese citizens, may have surrendered their Indian Citizenship, but still hold on to their Indian nationality.

Subhadeep Kumar's chapter looks at the modes of global circulation through which the Indian indentured immigration scheme was made possible in the nineteenth century. He focuses on a certain artefact of it – the emigrant ship. The ocean going ship during the industrial revolution is one of the earliest globalized workspace with crews and passengers of a plethora of identities jostling in a constricted space on the high seas. Consequently a number of globalized currents of communication intersected on the shipboard space. Analysing the imperial deliberations on the construction of an officially designated type of ship for the Indian migrants with specific design, rules and regulation, the chapter wants to chart the global discursive processes, which inscribed on the nineteenth century Indian emigrant, while at their passage through Kalapani.

Kishore Kumar Aleti's chapter tries to understand the historical root causes of the contemporary tensions among the three dominant ethnic communities such as Malays (the local) and immigrant communities such as Indians and Chinese in Malaysia. In other words, he tries to understand the hegemonic nature of locals on non-locals related to the public policies of government of Malaysia.

Sridhar Bhagavatula's chapter looks into the changes in the conceptions of sovereignty, citizenship, justice and human rights in the context of transnational migrations and global people-to-people networks and linkages. In order to understand the global changes, in the context of transnational migrations, from a multidisciplinary perspective, he proposes a newer definition of 'transnationality' based on the capabilities approach. He argues that there are three interrelated features of the current phase of 'globalization'. First, the advancements in information and communication technologies led to creation of various platforms that facilitate people-to-people connection through the communications and linkages across the sovereign nation state borders. The social network websites such as Facebook, Twitter, LinkedIn and so on are connecting people across borders, creating groups of the 'like-minded', extreme awareness of occurrences of social 'goods' and 'evils' and understanding different cultural artefacts. Second, the gradual movement of the 'thought process' towards cosmopolitanism, leading to general understanding of 'what is good' and 'what is bad' at a global level. Third, movement across borders is becoming cheaper and hence more number of people are able to travel across nations for various purposes. The immigration policies of the migrant-receiving countries are lesser stringent due to economic and demographic equations. The population-rich countries are speculating better deal for its people, and the population-poor advanced countries are getting access to global labour markets. In fact, the segmentation of labour markets in richer countries is creating increased demand for migrant workers there. The positive trend is that there is an interface between the 'excess' and 'scarcity' at global level. Hence, the three interrelated features take us to the cluster of concepts in transnationalism.

Anindita Shome's chapter, through the study of Amitav Ghosh's *In an Antique Land*, tries to explore the possibilities of medieval era transnationalism. By drawing analogies between the present era transnational trends and the traces of medieval era linkages amongst India, Egypt and Aden (which Ghosh brings out in this text), she studies these linkages as a transnational phenomenon. Trade, languages, culture and personal relationships in host land and homeland and so on are some of the important parameters through which she tries to assert the presence of different kinds of transnational trends existent during the medieval era.

Rakesh Ranjan's chapter focuses on the entrepreneurs who are one of the major catalysts for economic development. The post-liberalization India witnessed a growing diaspora entrepreneurship in different parts of India. Entrepreneurship happens in a complex interplay of political-economic, cultural and psychological factors. Based on the secondary sources (statistics from various sectors and departments at national and international level), he maps out the various patterns of diasporic entrepreneurships in India. He also highlights policy suggestions for harnessing the diaspora entrepreneurship through promotion of entrepreneurial policies that could help in technological transfer as well as knowledge dissemination.

Diksha Jha's chapter examines the analysis of the Indian state's policy vis-à-vis its diaspora. The three categories of diaspora taken for the purpose of analysis are the persons of Indian origin (PIOs) belonging to the older diaspora who migrated in the pre-independence era to African and Caribbean states; the PIOs who are recent migrants belonging to high-skilled and professional class residing in the developed countries such as the United States and United Kingdom and the short-term emigrants who belong to the category of temporary migrant workers going to the Gulf states for temporary employment. The second category, which comprises the very high-skilled, professional class of PIOs residing in the Western states, is the state's model diasporic subject towards whom the state remains most responsive and extends benefits such as the overseas citizenship of India, which may be termed as the Indian version of dual citizenship. The third category of the Indian emigrants who constitute the temporary migrant workers in the Gulf, who are also be termed as short-term emigrants come under the regulatory and protectionist framework of the state. The Government of India believes that this category (which is extremely vulnerable due to its low-skill levels and lesser economic status) needs to be protected and safeguarded against exploitation. However, such practices of regulation and protectionism do no good to make their conditions better, as after reaching the Gulf states, these workers face exploitation on a daily basis and the home state remains under a state of oblivion. Thus, the state strategies towards its different overseas diasporic categories lead to a differential impact on their citizenship statuses. While the high-skilled PIOs residing in the West experience a value addition in their citizenship status through Overseas Citizenship of India, the temporary emigrants in the Gulf (unskilled and semi-skilled migrant workers) experience an evident decline in citizenship in the context of emigration.

Angshuman Kar's chapter focuses on the writings of Abdul Ghani Sheikh's short story 'Two Nations, One Story'. He argues that within diaspora studies one should think of creating a sub-category, 'studies of Indian partition diaspora', for reading stories such as 'Two Nations, One Story', which examine the links between the partition of India and its diasporas scattered in different parts of the subcontinent.

Arnab Kumar Sinha's chapter focuses on the Indo-Canadian diasporic literary writer M. G. Vassanji's novel *The Assassin's Song*. Vassanji's novel is an interesting take on the issue of religious fundamentalism and its impact on diasporic Muslims. It tries to seek to interpret the nexus between religious fundamentalism and diaspora in the wake of events such as 9/11, 7/7 and Gujarat riots. Taking cue from Vassanji's representation of religious fundamentalism in *The Assassin's Song*, he interrogates the problematics of equating religious fundamentalism with Islam across the globe.

Sanjoy Malik's chapter examines how Meena Alexander, one of the most important contemporary Indian American poets, is considered to be the other in spite of her strong sense of belonging and commitment to the country of her adoption. It also seeks to examine how she negotiates her identity in the diaspora space of the United States as a representative of the South Asian immigrants in the post-9/11 period.

Neetu Devi's chapter deals with the experiences of altering self and malleable identity of multiple displaced Indian diaspora and the compound identity attained by this community. Taking the case of Ramabai Espinet's novel *The Swinging Bridge*, Shani Mootoo's novels *Cereus Blooms at Night*, she tries to understand the articulation of religious and cultural identity in the post-modern era. The questions she raises in the chapter are: Do the multiple migrants and converted Indian diaspora feel like an outsider? Do they feel as 'Indian', as a non-convert Indian diasporic would feel? Do they feel that they have been historically exploited by being converted and their historicity of identity and culture has been distorted by the conversion?

Notes

1. According to Judith Brown (2007: 15), it is because of the swift changes in transportation, which was the part of imperial incorporation into the world economy, 'Indians began to move within India and across the seas in far greater numbers and in response to more opportunities … This was particularly significant among higher caste Hindus, for whom travel across the sea had been thought of as ritually polluting' (2007: 18).
2 Hugh Tinker (1977) calls this system as 'a new form of slavery'.

References

Brown, J. 2007. *Global South Asians: Introducing the Modern Diaspora*. Cambridge: Cambridge University Press.

Clarke, C., C. Peach, and S. Vertovec (eds). 1990. *South Asians Overseas: Migration and Ethnicity*. Cambridge: Cambridge University Press.

Devare, H. 2009. Cultural Implications of the Chola Maritime Fabric Trade with Southeast Asia. In H. Kulke, K. Kesavapany and V. Sakhuja (eds), *Nagapattinam to Suvarnadwipa: Reflections on the Chola Naval Expeditions to Southeast Asia*. Singapore: Institute of Southeast Asia Studies, 178–192.

Dubey, A. 2003. *Indian Diaspora: Global Identity*. New Delhi: Kalinga Publications.

Goss, J. and B. Lindquist. 2000. Placing Movers: An Overview of the Asian-Pacific Migration System. *The Contemporary Pacific*, 12(2), 385–414.

Jain, R.K. 1993. *Indian Communities Abroad: Themes and Literature*. New Delhi: Manohar.

Jayaram, N. (ed.). 2004. *The Indian Diaspora: Dynamics of Migration*. New Delhi: Sage Publications.

Mahmud, T. 2012. Cheaper than a Slave: Indenture Labour, Colonialism and Capitalism. *Whittier Law Review*. Available at: http://www.columbia.edu/~lnp3/SSRN-id2155088.pdf (Accessed on 9 August 2016).

Markovits, C. 2000. *The Global World of Indian Merchants 1750–1947: Traders of Sind from Bukhara to Panama*. Cambridge: Cambridge University Press.

Ministry of External Affairs (MEA). 2002. *The High Level Committee Report on Indian Diaspora*. New Delhi: Government of India.

Mishra, V. 2007. *The Literature of the Indian Diaspora: Theorizing the Diasporic Imaginary*. London: Routledge.

Raghuram, P. and Sahoo, A.K. 2008. Thinking 'Indian Diaspora' for Our Times. In P. Raghuram, A.K. Sahoo, B. Maharaj and D. Sangha (eds), *Tracing an Indian Diaspora: Contexts, Memories, Representations*. New Delhi: Sage Publications, 1–20.

Sahoo, A.K. 2006. Issues of Identity in the Indian Diaspora: A Transnational Perspective. *Perspectives on Global Development and Technology*, 5(1–2), 81–98.

Shanmugam, P. 2009. India and Southeast Asia: South Indian Cultural Links with Indonesia. In H. Kulke, K. Kesavapany and V. Sakhuja (eds), *Nagapattinam to Suvarnadwipa: Reflections on the Chola Naval Expeditions to Southeast Asia*. Singapore: Institute of Southeast Asia Studies, 208–226.

Tinker, H. 1977. *A New System of Slavery: The Export of Indian Labour Overseas, 1830–1920*. London: Oxford University Press.

van der Veer, P. (ed.). 1995. *Nation and Migration: The Politics of Space in the South Asian Diaspora*. Philadelphia: University of Pennsylvania Press.

1

Marriage Patterns and Practices Among Young South Asian Americans

Karen Leonard

The marriages of young South Asian American Sikhs, Hindus and Muslims often feature patterns and practices that are different from those of their parents.[1] Drawing the available materials together[2] to put forward a few observations, hypotheses and conclusions, one obvious hypothesis would be that these young people are behaving like other young Americans with respect to courtship and marriage. And, if they are not, are young Hindus, Muslims and Sikhs following similar or different patterns with respect to marriage partners, marital agreements, types of weddings and so forth? Although religious rituals are almost always part of second-generation South Asian weddings, one has the impression that religious meanings and practices have become less important than secular aspects of the wedding ceremonies. A scholar has argued this about Sikh weddings in the United Kingdom (Thandi 2014), that the spiritual significance of marriage and the simple Sikh marriage rituals have been overshadowed by Punjabi,[3] North Indian, Bollywood and even British cultural practices. Thandi saw a trend to 'large fat Punjabi weddings' that celebrated ethnic and cultural heritage, ostentatious displays that ignored or distorted religious teachings. Attributing all this to the brides' desires for status and celebration of ethnic identity, Thandi thought the costly celebrations were achievable because of the brides' rising ages at marriage and successful professional careers.[4] His generalizations seem true for many South Asian second-generation weddings in America too, where the broader cultural patterns, always changing, have major impacts on weddings.

Setting the Context

First, we need to set the context, to delineate the broader cultural patterns of which religion is just one component. In the United States, the marriage rate has been declining (from 90 marriages a year per 1,000 unmarried women in 1950 to 31 in 2011, a 66 per cent decline), but the age at marriage has been rising (it is now 27 for women and 29 for men) and along with that the rate of cohabiting before marriage. Two-thirds of American couples who are getting married are already living together, and the older and more educated a woman is at marriage the more her risk of divorcing decreases, although the divorce rate is rising for the population as a whole. But most Americans marry eventually, and, as a voluntary relationship between two individuals, marriage comes with higher expectations of fairness, fidelity and intimacy than ever (Coontz 2013: 12).[5] Furthermore, marriage and family life increasingly emphasize choice and personal fulfillment.[6]

Analysts discern divergent models of American and British family life. There are some similarities: the proportion of women of working age who have paid jobs in both the United States and the United Kingdom is almost 60 per cent, although there is still a wage gap between the average earnings of full-time male and female employees.[7] There are differences as well. In the United States, there are two models. Education and class are significantly related to marriage: college-educated people marry at higher rates, and, while most mothers under 30 are not married to the fathers of their children, 8 fewer than 10 per cent of births to college-educated women occur outside marriage, while for women with high school or less education the figure is almost 60 per cent.[9] American women are marrying later but cohabiting more: 63 per cent of women aged 35 to 44 have cohabited, 50 per cent of those with college degrees or more and 73 per cent of those without a high school degree.[10] In the United Kingdom, while the marriage rate is declining and the divorce rate increasing as in the United States, analysts discern three distinct models of family life, of university-educated professional classes, native (British) working classes and immigrants.[11] Clearly some immigrants in the United Kingdom also fall in the professional class, probably many Sikhs and Hindus, while Muslims, the majority of them from Pakistan and Bangladesh,[12] may fall in the immigrant category, although British-based researchers must delineate the appropriate context for their studies of second-generation South Asian immigrants.

Finally, trends by religion and race again is different in the United States and the United Kingdom. In the United States, interracial marriages rates are rising, but Asian Americans are recently tending to marry other Asians, including foreign-born partners. An article about this stresses immigrant family values (with groups long settled in the United States, such as Japanese Americans, marrying out more).[13] In the United Kingdom, interracial marriages are rising too, with about 6 per cent of children under five being mixed-race (comparable to the American figure), but Indians, and especially Pakistanis and Bangladeshis, are mixing more slowly there.[14] Mainstream Christianity is declining and secularism is on the rise in both the United States and the United Kingdom, more so in the United Kingdom and especially among the young and well-educated.[15] Interestingly, a survey relating the major religions in the United States to household income showed Hindus second only to Reform Jews, with incomes well above the national average, and the relationship between education and income was very strong (Muslims were below the average and Sikhs were not surveyed).[16]

Keeping these profiles in mind, let us consider second-generation marriages in the diaspora. Decisions are taken on every aspect of a wedding, and it is mattered by whom. Where will it be held? Who will officiate, and in what language or languages? Who pays for the wedding ceremonies? What do the bride and groom wear, and do they have attendants? Is there a pre-wedding shower, a bachelor party or a honeymoon? Are there wedding rings and a wedding cake? Who is invited, to the wedding and/or the reception? What food is served at the reception? Will liquor be served, and will there be a DJ and dancing? Appendix shows the typical schedule of events for traditional 'American', Sikh, Hindu and South Asian Muslim weddings, and further studies could be undertaken using these as models.

Making the Match

In all three South Asian American communities, there has been a strong shift from arranged marriages and from ceremonies and celebrations planned by the parents to other kinds of marriages and various combinations of ceremonies and celebrations, which are planned by the bride and groom rather than by the parents. Looking first at who makes the match, there are now many cases of young South Asian American finding each other on Match.com and other online sites; my impression (or hypothesis) is that a high proportion of marriages across religious and national origin lines features such meetings. A recent study by Aziz Ansari shows general patterns among young Americans, and a study he cites shows that between 2005 and 2012 more than one-third of couples marrying in the United States met through an online dating site (Ansari 2015). But there are few studies of how matches are found and what the patterns are for young South Asian Americans.

Denise al-Johar did an important study of 27 Muslim American marriages in a Texas mosque, marriages she termed arranged, self-initiated and self-achieved.[17] In the first instance, 12 arranged marriages, the parents found spouses of the same national origin and sectarian affiliation, and they tended to marry off their daughters young, even in high school, presumably to avoid movement outside the familiar boundaries of nation and sect. In the second instance, seven self-initiated marriages, the young people were attracted to each other but involved their parents early, seeking and gaining their consent and their help with arrangements (sometimes this took years). These matches were all across national origin lines and also sometimes across sectarian lines, uniting Arab and South Asian, Sunni and Shia. In the third instance, eight self-achieved marriages, the young people crossed national and racial and religious lines, uniting second-generation Muslim immigrants and native white Christian Americans. These self-achieved marriages took place despite parental opposition; usually but not always the non-Muslim spouse converted to Islam sometime after the marriage. Her results were remarkably striking and consistent, and I suggest her terms be used in other studies. However, we need a new category for parent-initiated marriages, one that might be called semi-arranged or assisted,[18] meaning that parents put their children into contact with a pool of potential spouses or with a particular potential spouse. Certainly this type of parent-initiated but youth-decided marriage is becoming more common in both India and abroad than the older type of arranged marriage (Kaur and Palriwala 2014).

I do not know of systematic studies like al-Johar's which is of Hindu or Sikh second-generation marriages in the United States,[19] but I have observed similar patterns. My research on Hyderabadis abroad two decades ago found that sometimes the children went along with a parentally arranged and expensive traditional-style wedding, but if the marriage proved unhappy, most parents accepted a divorce and hoped a better match could be found by their son or daughter.

Marriage ads printed in ethnic newspapers are decreasing, no doubt due to the popularity of Internet services such as Match.com and Shaadi.com, but some people (probably parents or siblings) continue to place such ads, specifying education, profession and citizenship as often as caste or mother tongue.[20] In 1994 listings, the Indian International Marriage Center, located in Orange, California, gave out printed profile lists asking for caste and many were specified (although some put only Hindu or Punjabi Hindu, etc.). Among Sikhs, for example, the following were listed: Arora Sikh, Gursikh, J. Sikh, Jat Gursikh, Jat Sikh, Khatri Sikh, Punjabi Sikh, Punjabi Arora Sikh, Punjabi Khatri Sikh, Ramgarhia Sikh, Saini Sikh, Sikh, Sikh Ramgarhia, Sikh Ahluwalia, Sikh Arora, Sikh Keshavdhari, Tonk Kashmiri Sikh and Turbaned Sikh.[21] Caste within Sikhism is clearly still important, as a recent study of caste and marriage among southern California Sikhs shows. While the study is primarily one of attitudes, it does report that 218 of the 300 interviewees from four *gurdwaras* were married, and 11 per cent of these marriages were intercaste (between Sikhs, all of them). However, when broken down by birth abroad or in the United States, 67 per cent of those born in the United States (and therefore members of at least the second generation) had intercaste marriages, while only 8 per cent of those born abroad had done so (Singh 2014: 397–398).[22]

Interviews with southern California first-generation Sikhs suggest, however, that Sikh youth, both men and women, are marrying Hindus, some white Americans and even a very few Muslims, in perhaps 20 to 30 per cent of second-generation marriages. Other Punjabis and Gujaratis, the largest immigrant groups, provide most of the partners, and parents state that the children born in the United States do not care about caste, within or outside of Sikhism.[23]

About matchmaking among Hindus, we also have little research, but a book by Kavita Ramdya (2010), *Bollywood Weddings*, discusses 20 second-generation Hindu marriages in the New York metropolitan area.[24] She provides only anecdotal evidence about how couples met and about caste or intercaste patterns, although four of the 20 grooms were white Americans. She actually discusses only 13 couples and gives no information about four of these couples; she identifies four grooms as white Americans, four couples as cross-regional within India and one couple of the same caste and regional background.

Wedding Ceremonies and Receptions

Again, we need to set the broader cultural context. In wedding celebrations in the United States, the tradition of the bride's parents paying for all save the rehearsal dinner has been changing rapidly. The bridegroom's parents, as well as stepparents, grandparents, aunts and uncles, and the couples are assuming or sharing the costs. And of course this means 'changes in the dynamics of who gets to call the shots'.[25] This is an important research question and there is hardly any systematic data for South Asian American weddings, although their extravagance in the United States has not gone unnoticed. A 2014 article in *Fortune* compares average American weddings and Indian weddings, the American weddings cost $29,000 with 140 guests and the Indian weddings cost $65,000 with 500 guests.[26] The article really focuses on North Indian Hindu weddings, comments point out and possibly South Indian American weddings differ.[27] Muslim American weddings have also been criticized for their lavishness;[28] a hypothesis might predict that the more religious couples would spend less.

The recent issue of the California-based India journal's *Wedding Magazine* does highlight new patterns in the marriages of

South Asian American millennials, changes that may be in advance of actual practices. Brief articles among the many colourful advertisements for wedding fashions and services, while stating that arranged marriages are 'still in vogue', focus on 'Intercultural Marriages' and 'Interreligious Unions' and even mention same sex marriage. There is a two page article on 'The Millennial "Vivaah"' as a 'modernist and post-modernist interpretation of the traditional Indian vivaah (wedding)', 'a new all American idiom which could be termed as the Millennial Indian American Wedding (MIAW)'. This last article mentions intercultural and interreligious couples, cocktail parties, post-wedding brunches and a variety of venues for weddings and receptions.[29]

Thandi's paper about Sikhs in the United Kingdom suggested that *amritdhari* weddings should be less lavish than those of other Sikhs. Interviews with southern California Sikhs, however, indicate that *amritdhari* family weddings are not less splashy and expensive than those of non-*amritdharis*. Those who have money spend it lavishly on the weddings of their children (but liquor is not served at *amritdhari* receptions). Interviewees say it is not brides driving up expenses but whichever family has more money. One man commented that there may be a trend for clean-shaven young men to grow beards for their weddings (I noticed a preference for clean-shaven grooms in the 1985 *India-West* Sikh matrimonial ads). In the Sikh religious ritual, the Anand Karaj, the granthi reads from the Guru Granth Sahib as the bride's father places the end of the groom's *palla* in the bride's hand and she follows the groom around the Guru Granth four times. Weddings can be held in *gurdwaras* with receptions following elsewhere, then or later, but they can also be held in homes, on the beach or in hotels. The Shiromani Gurdwara Parbandhak Committee in India has forbidden the Guru Granth to be taken to hotels or wedding palaces, where liquor is customarily served, but in the United States sometimes the Guru Granth is taken to hotels for the ceremony. The bride and groom make many decisions about the ceremony and reception, catering to their friends from out of town when setting the one or two day program for the Anand Karaj and the reception, taking into consideration vacation times and national and international flight timings.[30]

Ramdya's book raises the same issues about Hindu marriages in the United States that Thandi raised about Sikh marriages in

Britain, asserting that second-generation South Asian American Hindu weddings are far more cultural than religious.[31] The participants in Ramdya's 20 New York Hindu weddings were middle- to upper-class professionals who were at least college graduates, young people who fit the contemporary profile of American youth of their class in many ways.[32] She writes that these Hindu youth pursued American-style courtships, engaging 'in months and even years of dating, including premarital sex'. She also labels them 'occasional Hindus', secular young people who displayed 'symbolic ethnic capital' during their search for spouses and in the engagement and wedding ceremonies (Ramdya 2010: xvi–xvii, xiv). Her anecdotal evidence about her informants' views is quite convincing: they see 'old India' as characterized by tradition, sobriety and seriousness, 'new India' as Bollywood, and 'the West' as characterized by 'joy, sensuality, and youth', or 'joy, laughter, and play' (Ramdya 2010: xv–xvi).

These young people usually gave their parents major roles in crafting 'traditional' engagement and wedding ceremonies. Most featured is the *kanyadan* or 'gift of a virgin' by the bride's father which takes place under an elaborate *mandap*, a religious canopy or structure, with the bride following the groom seven times around the sacred flame. Engagement ceremonies usually featured a *puja* in a home setting. However, the couples wove together Bollywood and Western customs in their wedding receptions. All 20 Hindu wedding receptions included meat, alcohol, music, dancing and a wedding kiss, and four of the 20 featured the Jewish chair dance, understood to be an American custom (remember they are New Yorkers).[33] At many of the receptions, video shown by friends illustrated the couples' dating histories, histories fully revealed to the parents only on this occasion. Ramdya certainly paints a vivid picture of at least some second-generation Hindu weddings in America.

South Asian young people are blurring the boundaries between religious and secular practices rather than discarding the former for the latter, I would argue. Even marriages out of religion, caste or national origin often are celebrated according to traditional South Asian religious rituals and customs, though the religious and cultural rituals of the other partner may be celebrated as well. Such combined celebrations emphasize ethnic identity and heritage rather than religious commitments. In many cases, participants may be unable to distinguish between religious and cultural aspects of the marriage ceremonies; they are either less knowledgeable about traditional religious rituals or less committed to them.

Contributing to the confusion between religious and cultural aspects of the celebrations is the fact that the young people, the bride and groom, now play major roles in planning the ceremonies, especially the receptions. When parents, members of the first generation, did the planning, they focused primarily on traditional practices and on their own relatives and friends, on their own diasporic communities. One Hyderabadi Muslim father in London told me in 1991, when I speculated that his son's British friends would of course be invited to his son's wedding, that those friends could not be included, there were too many Hyderabadi relatives and friends who had to be invited. But now we see one event, the wedding ritual, being held for the older people and another event, the reception, for the younger friends of the bride and groom: this is one of Ramdya's findings, in fact. And some couples are electing to have even their wedding, not just their reception or honeymoon, abroad in a holiday location, with their own friends as the primary invitees (This can also be a family decision, to hold a 'destination wedding' in a location abroad that may suit more guests based abroad or perhaps reduce costs considerably, for example when held in Mexico). Couples decide who will pay for the wedding, the bride and groom sometimes share expenses themselves to avoid giving the power of whom to invite to a father, stepfather or older brother.

South Asian American brides play very strong roles in planning their weddings. A fine film made by UC Berkeley students about a Goanese Christian wedding in California traces clothing and particularly wedding dress styles for three generations of women, in Goa, Singapore and California.[34] Gender roles in the ceremonies are also changing. I attended a Hindu wedding here in the 1980s which was conducted by a woman priest, and I know of another Hindu wedding where the groom followed the bride as they walked around the fire. And in an American Muslim wedding reported on in my class, the bride and groom were walked down the aisle by their mothers (mentioned below).

Some good examples of wedding plans designed to suit different audiences or invitees surfaced in my class on Muslim American diasporic weddings.[35] All included the religious ritual, the *nikah* or signing of the marriage contract in the presence of an *imam* and at least two witnesses, but other ceremonies reflected more broadly cultural features. When the bride and groom shared a religion but had different cultural or national heritages, the couples crafted their celebrations carefully. In a wedding of a Pakistani Ahmadi Muslim man brought up in Jordan and a Jordanian Shia bride (both spoke Arabic and had met in Jordan), the *nikah* or legal wedding ceremony was held in Jordan, followed by a lavish reception in Istanbul, Turkey, attended primarily by young friends of the couple. The reception featured liquor and dancing, including the *dabka* or traditional Arab folk dance. Finally, a traditional South Asian *valima* was held in Orange County, California, attended almost exclusively by members of the groom's Ahmadi community members. In another case, an Egyptian Sunni groom and a Pakistani Sunni bride worked for four years to win parental approval, achieved when the fathers discovered they were already friends and attended the same mosque. In this Egyptian/Pakistani case, the couple set the *nikah* for 7 pm but invited the Pakistanis for 4 pm and the Egyptians for 5 pm to ensure their guests would be present. This wedding was held in a Heritage Museum rather than a mosque, the bride and groom had their mothers walk them down the aisle, and there were bridesmaids, a ring bearer and a flower girl. After the *nikah*, the bride changed from her Pakistani wedding outfit into a white wedding dress for the reception, where Persian food, a compromise, was served, and guests danced to music provided by a DJ.

Marriages like those above across religious and/or national origin lines were accepted by parents most notably when the daughter was older than the usual age at marriage for the community, I noticed.[36] Sometimes a conversion to Islam was involved when a partner was not Muslim, but this could be quite nominal, undertaken only to accommodate parents or other close relatives.

Other changes in South Asian Muslim marriage practices were quite striking: the *mehr*, traditionally a sum of money set in advance as a gift to the bride and/or as financial security for her in case of a divorce, has become wildly unpredictable. Despite being legally required for an Islamic marriage, sometimes no *mehr* is being required. One parent told me, 'our daughter is professionally qualified, she needn't ask for that'. More often, the bride is asked what she wants and she opts for a sentimental, romantic thing. One young Afghan American bride requested that her fiancée, in Afghanistan, plant 1,000 young trees for her *mehr* (she planned to join him in Afghanistan two years after the *nikah*, after she completes her studies in the United States first). Another South Asian American Muslim bride requested a holiday abroad for her *mehr*, again showing a bride's sentimental choice overriding a religiously mandated financial protection for women.[37]

Another change involves the timing and meaning of the *nikah*, *rukhsati* and *valima*.[38] Young American Muslims are using the *nikah* as an engagement that allows them to meet unchaperoned. They consider the *rukhsati* or *valima*, terms that now seem to be used interchangeably for a reception that is sometimes held a year or more later, to be the real marriage after which they will live together and have sexual intercourse. Although this *nikah*-as-engagement is meant to initiate only dating, I was told, some couples co-reside after the *nikah* but do not tell their parents, and sometimes a couple breaks up rather than proceed to a *rukhsati* or *valima*.

Many changes are reflected in the wedding invitations to second-generation South Asian American weddings, whether lavish traditional cards or trendy modern ones. Recently I got an invitation that directed me to a website showing the Hindu American couple in various foreign holiday locations, obviously traveling together before the wedding, something other couples might be doing but not publicizing. This wedding was in India, to be followed by a reception in San Francisco several months later. And of course I and other friends are being routinely invited to weddings held in India in splendid locations. In a 2014 wedding of a Hindu American groom and a Ukrainian American bride, attendees from outside India were set up on a tour of Rajasthan both before and after the wedding.[39]

Conclusion

I have shown a widening range of partner choices, marriage rituals and celebratory practices among young South Asian

Americans, Sikhs, Hindus and Muslims. Many such changes are occurring in weddings in South Asia too, often involving an America-returned partner. I have proposed some hypotheses, and much research remains to be done. It seems safe to conclude that, in all three South Asian religious communities in the United States considered here, the roles of the bride and groom in planning their weddings are increasingly important and the secular or cultural aspects of the weddings are also increasingly important and come from multiple sources.

This conclusion should be viewed positively, pointing to adaptation and cultural translation at the level of the couples, families, religious or regional diasporic communities, and diasporic communities more broadly defined (as Indian, Pakistani, South Asian and Muslim), reflective of the changing context in America and of the American cohorts of which these young people are members. We see here creative and adaptive acts of broadly cultural, not narrowly religious, translation in a specific contemporary context. Gayatri Spivak, Tony Stewart and Finbarr Flood have theorized about cultural translation in South Asian historical contexts, and I have adopted translation theory to analyse Hyderabad state's cosmopolitan culture, rejecting models of hybridity or synthesis that posits the 'loss of traditional cultures' (Flood 2009; Spivak 2005; Stewart 2001). These changing marriage rituals and celebrations, rather than reflecting weak religious identities, theological ignorance or religious capitulation (Stewart's phrases), show people of different origins, languages and faiths reaching for equivalent terms and practices across what might have been perceived as strong boundaries. The changes reflect the dynamic interaction of actors and ideas in a world they share, that of America's changing demographic profile and popular culture.

Notes

1. A different version of this piece, focusing slightly more on Sikhs, appears as 'South Asian American Millennial Marriages: Sikhs, Hindus and Muslims' in a forthcoming volume edited by Pashaura Singh and Van Dusenbery.
2. I have scattered data from classes I taught at UC Irvine about Muslim American marriages, many involving second-generation South

Asians, and I have been to weddings of the children of South Asian friends here. There are a few good articles, one about 27 young Muslim American marriages in Texas (many participants are South Asian), and another with some data about Sikh marriages in southern California. There is a book about 20 second-generation Hindu marriages in New York.

3. The classic work on Punjabi rituals and practices, see Hershman (1981).
4. He based his paper on eight marriages of young people known to him, two ending in divorce within a year: one was mixed caste (but within Sikhism) and one was an *amritdhari* couple.
5. Stephanie Coontz, 'The Disestablishment of Marriage', *The New York Times*, SR, 23 June 2013, 12. Half of American adults were unmarried in 2012, up from 22 per cent in 1950, and nearly 15 per cent were living alone, up from 4 per cent in 1950; 'Singletons: The Attraction of Solitude', *The Economist*, 25 August 2012, 47.
6. Douglas NeJaime, 'Will Modern Marriage Win?' *Los Angeles Times*, 23 January 2015, A19. No fault divorce, remarriages, adoptions and new reproductive technologies delink parent-child relationships from biology and sexual reproduction, encouraging marriage for both heterosexual and homosexual couples. (The author hopes that the US Supreme Court will endorse a modern rather than an obsolete model of marriage by finding same-sex marriage legal).
7. 'Closing the Gap: Special Report, Women and Work', *The Economist*, 26 November 2011, 3–5.
8. 'Love, Tax and Wedlock', *The Economist*, 17 January 2015. The low wages of unskilled men may make marriage to them less attractive, and women's prospects in the workplace have improved.
9. Jason DeParle, 'Two Classes, Divided by "I Do"', *The New York Times*, National, 15 July 2012, 18.
10. 'In the Season of Marriage, A Question. Why Bother?' *The New York Times*, 26 April 2013, SR 7. Also, a survey of 12, 000 women aged 15 to 44 (taken between 2006 and 2010) showed that 48 per cent of the unmarried women were living with their significant others, and of the married women, only 23 per cent said they had married before living with their husband, down from 39 per cent in 1995; Karen Kaplan, 'More Couples Are Cohabiting', *Los Angeles Times*, 7 April 2013.
11. 'Changing Families: The Post-nuclear Age', *The Economist*, 16 March 2013, 57–58.
12. Bangladeshis are moving up fast however: 'From Brick Lane to the Fast Lane', *The Economist*, 27 October 2007, 65–66; 'Ethnic Minorities: Breaking Out', *The Economist*, 21 February 2015, 55–56.

13. Rachel L. Swarns, 'A Tie That Binds', *The New York Times*, Sunday Styles, 1 April 2012, 2, 10.
14. 'Into the Melting Pot', *The Economist*, 8 February 2014, 55–56.
15. Edward Lucas, 'Christianity at Bay', *The Economist*, 2012, 29.
16. Pew Forum on Religion and Public Life Survey, 2007, with 67 per cent of Reform Jewish households and 65 per cent of Hindu households making more than $75,000 per year (results confirmed in 2010 and 2011 in similar but less comprehensive surveys).
17. Denise Al-Johar, 'Muslim Marriages in America: Reflecting New Identities', *Muslim World*, 95: 4 (October 2005), 557–574. South Asians were prominent participants.
18. Dr Jaswant Singh Sachdev suggests this term, 'Western-born Desi Children: Arranged or Assisted Marriage', *India Journal*, 21 June 2013, A4. Shinder Thandi similarly proposes that 'arranged marriages' needs to be qualified, stating that parent-initiated contacts are, among UK Sikhs, always followed up by meetings and decisions by the prospective groom and bride; he suggests 'assisted marriages' or 'negotiated marriages'.
19. There are two studies of Sikh transnational marriages, one of the marriages of second-generation immigrants in Tanzania and one of second-generation immigrants in Canada, and both feature traditional arranged marriages. Kanwal Mand (2002) focuses on the marriages of two sons from one Jat Sikh household based in Tanzania, with celebrations taking place in Tanzania, Kenya and the Punjab and involving relatives from the United Kingdom as well. Nicola Mooney (2006) shows that Jat Sikh brides from India in Toronto and Vancouver serve to facilitate migration of their relatives using Canada's family unification immigration policy.
20. In a series of clippings from *India West*, April through October 1985, 14 to 25 ads were placed each week, almost always with more grooms than brides being sought. In 2014 and 2015, *India West* and *India Journal* (both published in California) featured only two to six ads each week (although BharatMatrimony.com ran ads in *India Journal* for many issues featuring around 20 ads each time).
21. International Indian Marriage Center lists for males and females for October and November 1994 (1412 E. Chapman Avenue, Orange, AA 92666), 1791 profiles listed in October and 1918 profiles listed in November, with some 100 to 200 more male profiles.
22. I have rounded off Singh's statistics.
23. Inder and Deepi Singh, summer 2014. Jasbir Singh Mann, 31 January 2015. No one seems to have studied whether or not the four *gotra* prohibition has been relaxed or how often marriages are occurring across Malwa-Doaba-Majha regional origin boundaries.

24. The book is disappointing, as no systematic data is presented and the authoress (herself married to an Indian Muslim from Trinidad) often seems naïve. For example, she sometimes refers to herself and her informants as Southeast Asians, and she states that once Hindu children are married their parents 'move onto the next phase in life ... a full commitment to worship ... *vanaprastha*' (p. xvii).
25. Abby Ellin, 'Burden of Paying for Wedding Bells Shifts', *The New York Times*, 4 April 2010, ST 12.
26. Shalene Gupta, 'Big Fat Indian Weddings Get Bigger and Fatter', *Fortune.com*, 8 August 2014. She mentions a Pew Research Center finding that the children of South Asian immigrants have an average income of $88,000, compared to the overall American average of $50,000, but she does not give the source so I cannot be sure this is accurate. She quotes a wedding planner who pegs the average cost at $200,000, with four events requiring 15 to 20 vendors; this compares to an American wedding requiring only four to seven vendors. Thanks to Raghu Cidambi for this reference (viewed January 2015).
27. In India, South Indian weddings do not include *mehndi* and *baraat*, for example, but possibly in America they do.
28. 'Runaway Weddings', *Islamic Horizons*, January/February 2007, 26–36. This quotes Nikki Khan, a California wedding planner of Indian and Pakistani weddings, whose clients spend $60,000 to $80,000 on elaborate celebrations in upscale hotels, compared to average wedding costs of $35,000 for 200 to 250 guests in the LA area and an overall national average of $27,852 (she cites 'The Conde Nast Bridal Group' 2006): 26–27.
29. 'Wedding Magazine', *India Journal* (2015), 20, 24–25, 40–41 and 46–47.
30. Inder and Deepi Singh, summer 2014; Jasbir Singh Mann, 14 and 31 January 2015.
31. Similarly, Philip Lewis (1994) argues that British Muslim youth are navigating between a focus on their religion and a 'Bhangra Beat' culture divorced from a serious Islamic perspective.
32. The brides' parents paid for 19 of these 20 weddings, however, contrary to the national trend in the United States.
33. Three of these four were Hindu couples, one involved a groom who was half-Jewish.
34. *All Dressed in White*, University of California Extension, Center for Media and Independent Learning, University of California, Berkeley.
35. *The New York Times* featured a self-initiated marriage of Pakistani Americans, Shia and Sunni, in a story rich in details: Jill P. Capuzzo, 'In the End, No Matchmaker Need Apply', 8 February 2015, ST 14.

36. Thus two immigrant Muslim California women in their mid to late thirties found an Irish American groom from out of state and a Brazilian immigrant groom, partners who proved acceptable to their respective parents. Family members mingled, combining customary rituals happily at these two weddings.
37. Changing concepts and implementations of *mehr* or *mahr* are commented on in 'Runaway Weddings'. A leading *imam* in Orange County, California, suggested that three-months salary of the groom was sufficient (Dr Muzammil H. Siddiqi, Chair of the Fiqh Council of North America at that time), while one bride, a convert, asked her husband-to-be to quit smoking as her *mahr*: 29. South Asian American Muslims are also taking up the practice of giving *jahaz* or dowry: 31–32.
38. I found *rukhsati* and *valima* being used interchangeably to designate the celebratory dinner traditionally hosted by the bridegroom's family following the *nikah*, but sometimes these are separate, as outlined by Dr Muzammil H. Siddiqi, 'Issues and Questions', *Pakistan Link*, 1 October 2010, P29. *Rukhsati* is the sending off the bride to the groom, allowing the consummation of the marriage, he writes, following the *nikah* or legal marriage, while *valima* is the special feast held to celebrate the marriage and it can occur before or after the *rukhsati*.
39. Thanks to Julia Maher, an attendee, for this information.

References

Ansari, Aziz. 2015. *Modern Romance*. New York: Penguin Press.

Flood, Finbarr B. 2009. *Objects of Translation: Material Culture and Medieval 'Hindu-Muslim' Encounter.* Princeton: Princeton University Press.

Hershman, Paul. 1981. *Punjabi Kinship and Marriage.* Delhi: Hindustan Publishing Corporation.

Kaur, Ravinder and Rajni Palriwala (eds). 2014. *Marrying in South Asia: Shifting Concepts, Changing Practices in a Globalizing World.* Hyderabad: Orient BlackSwan.

Lewis, Philip. 1994. *Islamic Britain, Religion, Politics and Identity among British Muslims: Bradford in the 1990s.* London: I.B. Tauris.

Mand, Kanwal. 2002. Place, Gender and Power in Transnational Sikh Marriages. *Global Networks,* 2(3), 233–248.

Mooney, Nicola. 2006. Aspiration, Reunification and Gender Transformation in Jat Sikh Marriages from India to Canada. *Global Networks,* 6(4), 389–403.

Ramdya, Kavita. 2010. *Bollywood Weddings: Dating, Engagement, and Marriage in Hindu America.* New York: Lexington Books.

Singh, Anantdeep. 2014. Caste and Marriage among the Sikhs of Southern California: Observations from a Statistical Analysis. *Sikh Formations,* 10(3), 393–424.

Spivak, Gayatri Chakravorty. 2005. 'Translating into English'. In Sandra Bermann and Michael Wood (eds), *Nation, Language, and the Ethics of Translation.* Princeton: Princeton University Press, 93–110.

Stewart, Tony K. 2001. In Search of Equivalence: Conceiving Muslim-Hindu Encounter Through Translation Theory. *History of Religions,* 40(3), 260–287.

Thandi, Shinder S. 2014. What Is Sikh in a 'Sikh Wedding'? Ritual, Role of Text and Performance in Diasporic Sikh Wedding Practices. Paper at the 3rd Sikh Studies Conference, University of California, Riverside, 11 May 2014.

Appendix

'American' Wedding Events: Questions for wedding analyses

Proposal/engagement ring
Announcement in paper about the match?
Invitations engagement? How to make it known?
Make or buy dresses
Rent tuxes for pre-wedding events
Bridal shower and pre-wedding obligations
Bachelor party and timing of wedding
Rehearsal/rehearsal dinner and prenuptial contract?
Ceremony site?
Guest list/guest attendance book and performer/language
Photos/videos and other type of service
Seating of guests, bride's/groom's side and music
Mother of bride escorted to seat by best man dressed
Wedding processional/other music roles of father and mother
White wedding dress/other guest list, who attends the wedding
Bridesmaids, maid of honour, sequence of events
Groomsmen, best man and who pays?
Flower girl, possibly ring bearer
Father walks bride down the aisle
Romantic solo song
Wedding rings exchanged
Kiss exchanged
Who pays?
Reception site, guests reception site, guests
Reception line, kiss bride, Dress: changes?
Dinner, drinks: Types of food and drink
Toasts, speeches, dancing: Music and dancing?
Throwing of bouquet, garter, performers/other services used?
Gifts Gifts
Who pays? Who pays?
Announcement in paper after the wedding/reception events?
Honeymoon Honeymoon?
Writing thank you notes, place of residence?
Neo-local residence

Sikh Wedding Events

Rishta: parents meet, set date, perhaps in a home
Kurmai: engagement ceremony, now may be done just before Anand Karaj, as part of wedding ceremony

Mehndi: henna application, women's event, 1 or 2 evenings before wedding

Sangeet: musical event, men and women, perhaps 1 evening before wedding

Baraat: arrival of groom, car/horse/elephant/chariot

Anand Karaj: religious ritual, groom's palla placed in bride's hand by her father, she follows groom around Guru Granth Sahib four times while an *amritdhari* Sikh recites hymns from Guru Granth;

Often done in Gurdwara or home, sometimes in hotel.

Reception: in hotel, other site; possibly langar, in Gurdwara

Hindu Wedding Events

Engagement: often a puja at home

Mehndi: henna application, women's event, 1 or 2 evenings before wedding (just North Indian?)

Sangeet: musical event, men and women, perhaps 1 evening before wedding

Baraat: arrival of groom, car/horse/elephant/chariot (just North Indian?)

Kanyadan: gift of a virgin, by father, religious ritual, under mandap or religious structure; bride follows groom 7 times around sacred fire/flame. Can be done in hotel, home, outside.

Reception: in hotel, other site.

South Asian Muslim Wedding Events*

Engagement ceremony?

Mehndi: henna application, women's event, 1 or 2 evenings before wedding

Baraat: arrival of groom, car/horse/elephant/chariot; not always done

Mehr: payment to bride then or upon divorce, in signed contract, compulsory part of Muslim wedding

Nikah: fathers or walis represent bride and groom, maulvi reads from Quran, may give sermon, proposal and acceptance. Nikahnamah or marriage contract signed by bride and groom and walis and maulvi. Can be in mosque or hotel or home or elsewhere.

Reception: rukhsati/valima, celebratory dinner, bride departs for groom's home. Can be right after nikah or the next night or months or a year or more later.

---

*According to a story from Karachi, Pakistan, the country's Supreme Court had declared mehndi and barat which is a part of Hindu customs must be discarded: I. Hassan, 'Obsession with Hinduism', *The News*, Karachi, 30 November 2004. This does not seem to have had an effect on American Pakistani weddings.

2

Citizenship and Nationality

The Dynamic 'Home' of Goan Catholics in Swindon, England

Joanna P. Coelho

> I *always* [her emphasis] say that I am Ugandan although I carry a British passport. Who you are on the inside is never dictated by what passport you carry.
>
> Abwoli, a Ugandan woman born in Britain (Binaisa 2010)

With its focus on the relationship between the diaspora and the idea of home/homeland, this chapter examines the ubiquitous phenomenon of large-scale migration of Goan Catholics to England that has been taking place in Goa since the last two decades. The substantial migration of Goans to Europe since the early 1990s has altered the nature of both the host and the home societies. Diaspora, by its very definition, takes its *raison d'être* from a sense of belonging to the homeland (Cohen 2007). The socio-cultural baggage that Goan migrants carry with them to the host society underscores the changes that take place in perceptions of nationality and citizenship. The rapidly growing number of Goan Catholic opting for Portuguese Citizenship has not just implications for the migrants and their families but the homeland that they leave behind is also largely altered by this change.

This chapter looks at how Siridao, a village in North Goa, is transformed by this phenomenon of mass migration to Europe. It also examines the idea of home that the Goan Catholic diaspora carries with it. The Goan Catholics who settle in Swindon, England, as Portuguese citizens, may have surrendered their Indian Citizenship, but still hold on to their Indian nationality, more specifically, to their Goanness.

Though a review of various secondary sources, written as well as virtual, and first-hand interviews conducted with villagers in Goa as well as those settled in Swindon, this exploratory chapter posits that the distinction between citizenship and nationality becomes more marked in the case of migrants who acquire the citizenship of the host country but retain the nationality of the home country.

Citizenship and Nationality: An Initial Understanding

Both citizenship and nationality are by-products of the process of building modern nation states. Though concepts of nation, nation state, nationality and citizenship are implicit in modernity and mark transition from fuzzy to enumerated societies, there is no unanimity on what each of these terms imply. In a basic sense, citizenship can be understood as political membership: the possession of citizenship denotes that a person belongs to a particular political authority. It is a contractual relationship between the state and the inhabitants under its jurisdiction. 'Citizenship is a status bestowed on those who are full members of a community. All who possess the status are equal with respect to rights and duties with which the status is endowed' (Marshall 1950: 28–29).

Modern constructs of citizenship have been organized around a fixed relationship between state, territory and the citizen. Citizenship's correspondence with a single nation state is increasingly being called into question by various re-imaginings of identity, belonging and community. The fluid nature of citizenship gets accentuated when we include the diaspora in the ambit of our discourse. The increasingly complex relationships between homeland, host societies and transnationalism give rise to changes in the relationship between nationality and citizenship. It challenges the traditional common tendency to use citizenship and nationality interchangeably. Traditionally, nationalism is the cultural sensibility of sovereignty, the concomitant of the co-ordination of administrative power within the bounded nation state (Giddens 1985: 219).

But immigration has added another dimension to nationality. With immigration, nationality is frequently linked to the concept of membership in a particular ethnic group that may involve more than one geographical location and may cross political boundaries. Nationality and citizenship are analytically separate. David McCrone and Richard Kiely articulate the difference:

> Nationality and citizenship actually belong to different spheres of meaning and activity. The former is in essence a cultural concept which binds people on the basis of shared identity – in Benedict Anderson's (1996) apt phrase as an 'imagined community' – while citizenship is a political concept deriving from people's relationship to the state. In other words, nation-ness and state-ness need not be, and increasingly are not, aligned. (McCrone and Kiely, 2000)

Taking clues from this conception of citizenship and nationality, this chapter posits that the distinction between the two concepts becomes more marked in the case of migrants who acquire the citizenship of the host country but retain the nationality, by which I mean the cultural rootedness of the home country.

A number of theorists of nationalism have tried to identify the social conditions that made this kind of imagining of 'nation' as social group or community possible for large numbers of people at particular historical junctures. Gellner (1983) argued that nationalism, 'national culture' and indeed a sense of 'the nation' were the products of centralized power with the means of generating and effectively delivering standard cultural messages to whole populations. The insistence of the Goans Catholics in Swindon, England, on retaining the nationality of their home state while acquiring Portuguese citizenship can be better understood by examining the socio-historical nuances of migration from Goa.

Migration from Goa

According to the Goa Migration Study (2008), 74 per cent of those who emigrate from Goa are Christian. Given that the size of the Christian population in Goa as per the 2001 Census was 26.7 per cent, this is an extreme concentration. Catholics comprise only a quarter of the state's population, but the emigration rate within the community is 42 per cent for 100 households compared to just 5 per cent among Hindus (Sequeira 2005).

What accounts for such a large-scale migration of Goa Catholics? Such disproportionate numbers begs a deeper analysis. This established migratory pattern of the Goan Catholic can be understood by examining the migratory trends in Goa especially since Portuguese colonial rule.

Since ancient Goan history, migration has influenced the demographic profile as well as culture of Goa. For instance, the Gaud Saraswat Brahmin, who have been the dominant upper-caste community in Goa defining Goa's social, political, cultural as well as economic landscape for centuries, are believed to be migrants from North India. Goa's strategic geographical location made it a centre for trade even before Portuguese colonial rule. Like any other coastal harbour, Goa acquired a form of cosmopolitanism with traders both arriving and leaving from Goa. Goa's political history has also contributed to its demographic heterogeneity. Since recorded history, rulers of the neighbouring kingdoms ruled over Goa. This in turn further facilitated the large-scale in-migration and contact of various cultures in Goa. But the quantum of migration, specifically out migration, though prevalent was limited and sporadic. The scenario changed with the arrival of the Portuguese in Goa in the early sixteenth century.

Migration from Goa during Colonial Times

The first record of migration from Goa started with the arrival of the Portuguese in the sixteenth century. The Portuguese conquered Goa in two phases: the old conquests began in 1510 and lasted until 1543. This period was characterized by extensive religious conversion and Lusitanization. The new conquests were acquired in the eighteenth century. During this phase, the Portuguese abandoned their policies of religious conversions and Lusitanization.

The Portuguese history of maritime discovery and expansion of the fifteenth and seventeenth centuries was facilitated by miracle of Ourique (1139). According to this myth, Jesus Christ appeared to and inspired D. Afonso Henriques, the first Portuguese king to lead his troops to victory against the Moors (Zuquete 2012: 214). This legend, which emerged at the very beginning of the period of discoveries, contributed to the popularization over the subsequent centuries, that the country had a special relationship with the Divine. The Portuguese came to Goa to control the spice trade and to look for Christians. When the fabled Christians were not found, they set about converting the local populace to Christianity. Coercion formed an important tool of this conversion process. A large number of Goans left Goa to escape this Christianization of Goa. The more popular destinations of these Goans were parts of today's Maharashtra such as Bombay, Pune, Dharwad, parts of coastal Karnataka such as Mangalore and areas in Kerala such as Kochi, while some Goans even migrated as far as Karachi in Pakistan.

As the Portuguese equated religion with culture, the Christianization of the populace automatically implied its Lusitanization. The Holy Inquisition was imposed in Goa to ensure the Lusitanization of the new Christians. Various edicts were passed to ensure that the new converts gave up their earlier cultural habits and lifestyle. The punishment for violation was severe and could even include death. A large number of Goan Christians fled to escape the Inquisition. They migrated to the same places that the Goan Hindus had earlier migrated to. But a number of Goans, especially Catholics, also migrated to far off places in Africa, Brazil and the Gulf.

Mass migration from Goa continued in the nineteenth and first half of the twentieth century. Unlike in the early centuries of colonial rule, Goan migration was now largely socio-economic in nature. And this migration was more prominent among the Goan Catholics as compared to the Goan Hindu.

Migration from Goa since Liberation

The Liberation of Goa on 19 December 1961 and its incorporation into the Indian Union did not decrease migration. The demographic profile of Goa underwent significant changes with the in-migration of a large number of Indians to Goa as the underdeveloped former Portuguese colony tried to economically catch up with the rest of India. This period also witnessed out migrations of Goans. A number of Goans, especially the Goan Catholic elite migrated to Portugal in the wake of Liberation, availing themselves Portuguese citizenship.

Goans have also been migrating to the West (Europe, Canada, United States and Brazil) as well as to Australia and New Zealand. Migration to the West is generally a permanent one. A host of socio-economic factors propel this migration – to avail better job opportunities, living conditions and educational facilities.

The oil boom of the Gulf in the mid-1970s encouraged a large number of Goans to go the Gulf for work. One interesting feature of migration to the Gulf was that unlike most other international migrations of Goans, here migration was not dominated by the Catholic community. Also this migration was mainly male migration, as migration to the Gulf was always temporary in nature.

Since the late twentieth century, there has been an exodus of Goans migrating to Europe by availing Portuguese passports. Figures with the passport office in the state indicate 1, 613 Goans between January and December 2014 have surrendered their Indian passports to obtain Portuguese passports. The actual figure is much higher with many Goans in Europe surrendering their Indian passports to the nearest embassy (Monteiro 2015).

Thus since the early nineteenth century, various socio-economic factors encouraged a specific type of migrant to migrate from Goa – the Goan Catholic. This pattern continued even after Liberation with the result that according to The Goa Migration Report 2008, every third Christian home in Goa has an emigrant (Sequeira 2005). The local churches of Goa are deeply concerned about the declining population of Christians in Goa and feel that unless something is done to check the decline, Christian population would vanish from the state altogether (Chatterjee 2005). What is it that makes Goan Catholics more inclined to migration? The Goan Catholic is a product of socio-historical factors that Goa encountered during Portuguese colonialism.

The Social Construction of the Goan Catholic

To say of something that it is socially constructed is to emphasize its dependence on contingent aspects of our social selves (Boghossian n.d.). Social realities – that is, what we regard as real and meaningful – are created through reciprocal, fluid and flexible interactions on a constant basis (Berger and Luckmann

1966). The Goan Catholic has been socially constructed through the interface of Portuguese colonialism in the Goa of the Old Conquest.

While Christianity came to India at almost the same time that it arrived in Europe, it was the Portuguese who brought Christianity to Goa in the sixteenth century. The Papal Bull *Romanus Pontifex* of 1,455 granted Portugal the patronage of the propagation of the Christian faith in Asia. The Bull became the basis of Portugal's claim to colonize lands in the new worlds. The Portuguese colonial policies were characterized by interpenetration and integration (Freyre 1961: 292, cited in Keyes 2011). As they went about integrating the new citizens with the motherland, Catholicism as practised in Portugal became the basis of integration. As the Portuguese saw a close connection between religion and culture, the new converts had to even culturally dissociate with their original culture and take on a lusophone culture and identity.

In order to prevent the new converts from having recourse to what the Portuguese saw as non-Catholic ritual and practices, the Inquisition was instituted in Goa in the sixteenth century. From its introduction in 1560 to its withdrawal in 1812, a concerted effort was made not only to prohibit Hindu sacred rites and worship rituals, but a variety of indigenous cultural practices were also viewed with suspicion and discouraged. The Edict of the Inquisition issued in 1736, in particular, identified various practices that were forbidden by the new converts. Apart from forbidding various Hindu religious rituals and worship patterns, the Edict of 1736 also tried to weed out various indigenous cultural practices of food, dress and entertainment. In short, the Edict of 1736 tried to wipe out all external manifestations of similarity between the Goan Hindu and the Goan Catholic.

As a consequence, not simply in matters of religious faith alone, the Goan Catholic was also socially and culturally different from the Goan Hindu.

Other colonial policies were also instrumental in the construction of the Goan Catholic. Cunha (1944, cited in Desai 2000) argues that the Portuguese state had achieved the alienation of the people from their motherland through various agencies such as the Portuguese system of education, the press which was under the rigid control of the state and the Church which functioned as an arm of the Portuguese state. In his powerful and provocative essay, *The Denationalisation of Goans* (1961) written in 1961, Cunha argues that Goans, especially Goan Catholic elite, were imitative of European culture to such an extent, that they have become denationalized in their own homeland. Yet there is ample evidence to show that there was an unstated gap between principle and practice with respect to the implementation of the Inquisition by the authorities. Robinson (2000) argues that this led to a variety of syncretic interculturalism between Hindus and Catholics in various areas. In areas of individual and collective ritual, one perceives the persistence and vitality of Hindu–Christian cultural interface (Robinson 2000: 289).

Rich cultural syncretism endowed Goans with a more inclusive identity, which facilitated their migration, adaptation and integration into new cultures (Sequeira 2005). According to the Goa Migration Study Report (2008), the destinations of the migrants were determined by economic factors such as opportunities for employment or labour shortage. Ever since the early nineteenth century, there has been a huge demand abroad for staff that could cater to European style of food, drink, music, medicine and dress. This demand was met by Goan Catholics from the Old Conquest. As they were familiar with the Western way of life and religion, they found the transition to Europe smoother than their Hindu counterparts, especially those from the New Conquests. And with the option of availing Portuguese passports now being open to Goans, a rapidly increasing number of Goans, primarily Catholics, are rushing to make their passports and migrate to Europe. As Portugal is now a member of the European Union, having a Portuguese passport now opens doors for Goans, to Europe at large.

Portuguese Citizenship for Goans

Having ruled Goa from 1510 up to 1961, the Portuguese far exceeded the British with respect to the duration of colonization in the subcontinent. But this was not the only criteria that distinguished the two European colonial powers. All through its rule in Goa, the Portuguese recognized the natives as citizens of Portugal with rights equal to that of any Portuguese in Portugal. The rhetoric of equality was firmly established and constantly referred to by Portuguese Indians, whether living in Goa, or as migrants to British India or, indeed, British East Africa where many Goans lived and worked, as bearers of Portuguese citizenship (Ferrão and Fernandes 2013). The natives who were ruled by the British, on the other hand, were designated as subjects. The UK metropole was considered to be superior to the colonial world, and at no point were the colonies regarded as being an integral part of the British state. In contrast, from the nineteenth century onwards, all Portuguese colonies were considered an integral part of the Union, with the word colonies and provinces being used interchangeably. All citizens of the Portuguese nation enjoyed equal status, with no distinction being made between those who live in the metropolis and in the colonies (Horta and White 2009).

India took Goa from Portuguese control in 1961 through military action. Nationalists call this 'Liberation' from the colonial masters. Soon after, by an Act of Parliament Goans were given Indian citizenship. Hindered by an effectively xenophobic understanding of Indian-ness, and its relationship with the countries that surround it, in contrast to many other legal regimes, the Indian state did *not* permit its citizens to hold multiple nationalities (Ferrão and Fernandes 2013). But the Goans were not explicitly asked to surrender their Portuguese citizenship and the ambiguity of the situation remained as both Portugal and India did not discuss the issue of retaining Portuguese citizenship.

Unlike independence from the British for the rest of the Indian subcontinent, liberation from the Portuguese was not a smooth process and for more than a decade, there were hostile relations between Portugal and India. In 1981, a new citizenship law was enacted in Portugal. According to the new law, those born abroad in non-Portuguese-speaking countries whose parent, grandparent or great-grandparent had Portuguese nationality could apply for Portuguese citizenship. It allowed for dual citizenship for those former Portuguese who had to forgo Portuguese citizenship on becoming nationals of another country. This change in the definition of citizen reflected the shifts in Portugal's conception of nationhood and the wish to develop a larger lusophone identity. In the 1980s, official representations became increasingly tied to a conception of the nation as an imagined community of descent which transcended territorial boundaries. Special rights, privileges and the creation of institutional channels for the full participation of Portuguese emigrants and their descendants in Portuguese society attempted to strengthen the economic, cultural and ethnic bonds between Portugal and its communities abroad (Horta and White 2009).

After Portugal joined the European Union in 1986, citizens of Portugal were recognized as being Europeans. This had major implications for migration. Availing Portuguese citizenship became a very attractive prospect for those eligible as it made accessible the larger European labour market. Being a Portuguese citizen helps them bypass stricter European laws against employing 'foreigners' versus local talent. Since the last three decades, thousands of Goans have been taking advantage of this facility and registering themselves as Portuguese citizens. The most preferred destination of Goans acquiring Portuguese passports is England, as the labour market in England has more scope.

A remarkable phenomenon of migration from Goa on Portuguese passport since the 1990s has been the 'Swindon Syndrome'. A number of people have been leaving various villages in Goa, mainly Goa Velha, Siridao, Agaçaim and Santa Cruz and migrating to Swindon. In this chapter, I have focussed on Siridao, one such village that is rapidly losing its people to Swindon. Siridao has had a tradition of sending people to France, and now with the Portuguese passport it sends a large number of villagers to Swindon in England. The arguments are based on my ethnographic fieldwork in Siridao.

The Sending Society of Siridao

Located 10 km away from the capital city of Panjim, Siridao lies along the coast where river Zuari joins Arabian Sea. The village of Siridao comprises two parts: Siridao and Paliyem, divided by National Highway 17. The village has seven wards: four in Siridao and three in Paliyem. Almost all the people residing in Paliyem are Hindu, while the population of Siridao is almost 85 per cent Catholic. There are two Churches in Siridao – one is the Church of Our Lady of the Rosary and the other is the Church of Jesus Nazareth. Most of the villagers have a lot of attachment to the latter church. The land of the entire village is owned by the industrialist family of Dempo. The family also owns the land of the neighbouring three villages as well. Almost 80 per cent of the people in Siridao are fishermen, while there are a few pockets of toddy tappers. The villagers also cultivate crops during the monsoon season. The villagers from Paliyem are cultivators, and today mostly work in various offices.

The Sarpanch of the village recalls that life in the village was difficult. There were approximately fifteen *rampons* (traditional fishing nets) in the village. Most nights would be spent at sea, fishing. The children would also help in this activity. Then in the morning, soon after returning from work, the children had to rush to school. Many dropped out of school. There was also a water problem in village as there was just one well for the entire village. One elderly villager recalls that people from outside the village were reluctant to get their daughters married in the village because of the water problem.

But large-scale migration beginning in the 1990s has brought about a sea change in the village. Today the village wears a deserted look. On a drive through the village, one finds several huge bungalows that are unoccupied and locked. A census of the Catholic population done in the year 2000 indicated a population of 2000. Today the Catholic population in the village is not more than 300.

The Initial Migration from Siridao

Though there is no written record of the history of migration from the village to Europe, from oral accounts I have gathered that during the end of Portuguese colonial rule, seven to eight Goans from Siridao first went to Europe on a tourist visa. They first went to Portugal and then to Spain. As there was not much scope of employment in either of these countries, they then went to France. They preferred France, though they did not know the language, as it was a relatively rich country. So they expected that there would be better chances of getting well-paying jobs in France. But it was not easy to get a visa for France. Hence they swam across a river in Spain and reached France. Once they reached France, they were caught by the French authorities for entering illegally into the country. They claimed to be refugees who had fled from Portuguese harassment. They also took with them a newspaper clipping from Goa to prove the Portuguese harassment of the native Goans in Goa. Some lawyers in France took up their case, as people were aware of Portuguese colonization and atrocities in Goa.

These Goans from Siridao, who settled in Paris, found life very difficult at first. They had a school education only until the eighth standard. They did not know French language and communicated in sign language. After they were accepted as refugees they were then able to take their families to France as well under the Family Reunification Policy.

In the 1980s, as Portugal was part of the Schengen areas, the Goans from Siridao could travel to France on a Schengen visa. In this way even before Goans started going abroad on Portuguese passports, a large number of villagers from Siridao were already in France.

In the 1990s when Goans began availing Portuguese citizenship and moving to Europe, people from Siridao also followed suit. Most of the people acquiring Portuguese passports are from the adjoining villages of Agaçaim, Batim, Goa Velha and Siridao in Tiswadi taluka. People from Bardez and Salcete have also acquired Portuguese passports in good numbers. As indicated earlier, these areas fall under the Old Conquest areas. The people are largely Catholic and find it easier migrating to Europe than their Hindu neighbours.

The Host Society

While in the early phases of migration, France was a preferred destination, after the easy availability of Portuguese citizenship many Goans from Siridao chose to migrate to England. The industrial town of Swindon, near London, became the destination point for many Goans from the various villages in North Goa, though a number of Siridaokars have settled in Reading, Wembley and the surrounding areas as well. The city has one of the highest concentration of Goans anywhere in the world outside Goa (Carvalho 2009).

The Process of Migration

The process of getting a Portuguese passport is fairly simple. Those born in the Antigo Estado da India (Old State of India), that is, in Portuguese ruled India before 18 December 1961, are eligible to get a Portuguese passport, on producing their birth certificate, marriage certificate or any legal document issued during Portuguese rule. There are a number of agencies in Goa that help with this entire process for a substantial fee. The entire process costs two to three lakhs, and it now takes six months to even a year to make a Portuguese passport.

Once they have Portuguese passports, most Goans go to England. Immediately after arriving in England, immigrants get their National Insurance (NI) done. NIs are issued to all non-UK nationals aged 16 or over working, planning to work legally or claiming benefits in the United Kingdom, regardless of how long individuals intend to stay. One migrant to England explains the importance of NI:

> Sometimes, some Indians take you, cash in hand. They don't pay you according to the wages because you don't have NI. And they cheat you. Indian hotels and all, they don't pay you. They ask you to work for long hours. Next you have to have a bank account also. So you can't have your utility bills because you are new there. So NI is a proof for that, so that you can make your bank account.

Job Opportunities

Swindon is home to various companies such as Honda, BMW and Faccenda, one of the largest chicken processing plants in the United Kingdom. The Siridaokars, being not much educated, found unskilled jobs in the various factories, retail outlets, industrial estates, as well as the Royal Mail, hospitals and hotel industry. Most Goans get paid the minimum salary and don't go to work every day. The payment is measured on an hourly basis. While in the beginning it was quite easy to get menial jobs, now Goans face stiff competition from European countries such as Poland who now form the same workforce.

One respondent described working in Swindon, in England, as slavery. As the job as timed on an hourly basis, it also makes things more stressful. Breaks, including lunch breaks, result in a reduction in pay. The nature of work is monotonous and has to be done at great speed without any breaks:

> In the assembly plant, they used to take one hour twenty seconds to assemble a car. Then as more Goans migrated there for jobs, etc. in order to prove themselves and retain their jobs, they began doing the work at a faster pace. Previously you could

> breathe, it was somewhat easy. Now it is very taxing. That target is set.

There are also a few instances of mild racism at the work place encountered by the Goans living in Swindon. While usually these attacks comprise racist taunts by the locals on account of jobs given to immigrants, there have also been complaints of a few department stores and hospitals in Swindon also indulging in racist behaviour.

Housing

The clustering of immigrants in ethnic communities is a characteristic of international migration (Epstein and Gang 2010: 3). The prevailing explanation for immigrant cluster is the existence of beneficial network externalities when previous immigrants provide shelter and work, assistance in obtaining credit and/or generally reduce the stress of relocating to a foreign culture (Grossman 1989). The Siridaokars in Swindon live in a *kudd* – system that was popular among twentieth century Goan migrants to Bombay. Goans migrating to Bombay since the nineteenth century lived in residential village clubs called kudds. This practice is followed in Swindon as well. In this system, one family purchases a large house and then converts it into very small rooms, which are then rented out to fellow villagers at low rents. This same pattern is followed in Swindon. The Siridaokars who settled in Swindon initially invested in houses, which were then converted into small rooms that were rented out to the newly arriving fellow villagers, or at least villagers from the neighbouring villages in Goa. The living conditions are hence cramped.

The parish priest of Siridao informs that the Siridaokars follow the same civic practices that they followed in Goa. So you have people spitting on the road, at times even urinating by the road side, and garbage accumulating on the roads. All these factors have made this area unattractive to the native English person who often leaves the area and settles elsewhere. The vacant houses are then rented out to other Goans. Thus, unwittingly a colony of Goans from neighbouring villages in North Goa develops in many localities of Swindon. A few Goans who visited Swindon remark that localities in there are like migrant slum localities in Goa.

Those villagers who migrated to Swindon in the early twentieth century have managed to buy huge houses, as the salary was much higher at that time. Some of them may keep a few fellow villagers as paying guests.

On entering Swindon, one might think one is entering any village in Goa. A theatre artist from Goa who visits Swindon regularly to stage Konkani plays also adds 'We can even hear neighbours conversing with each other across their front doors loudly in Konkani. I have even heard Goans talking to each other loudly in Konkani in shopping malls'. The aromas of Goan food wafting from the kitchens, and the widespread use of Konkani, the mother tongue of Goans makes Swindon a home away from home for Goans from Siridao.

Retaining Indian Nationality in Europe

For a number of scholars who pioneered the growth of diasporic studies in the 1990s, the idea of 'home' was the *sine qua non* of the concept. The very definition of diaspora implied a real or imagined homeland that the diaspora viewed with nostalgia. Home is perceived as a congregation site of belonging and memory, ideals and affections, space and time, local and global, positive and negative representations of the world. Immigrants usually carry with them their socio-cultural baggage into the diaspora. So while living abroad, they continue with various cultural practices of the home society. Siridaokars too carry their socio-cultural baggage with them to Swindon. Amongst themselves they speak in Konkani. They eat Goan food and there are supermarkets that cater to the Goan palette. If there is a wedding ceremony conducted in Swindon, it is celebrated in strict accordance with Goan customs. The village feasts of Goa are also commemorated with grandeur and fanfare. Various theatre troupes from Goa regularly put up shows in Swindon, which draw a huge attendance. In many ways Swindon is like a mini Goa.

But the Siridao-Swindonians' attachment to Goa goes beyond the socio-cultural baggage. If nationality is an imagined community that binds people on the basis of a shared identity (McCrone and Kiely, 2000), then the Siridaokars in Swindon, though holding European citizenship, retain their Indian nationality in cultural sense. The people of the village who are now settled in Swindon still retain their language, Konkani. In fact, a number of them are fluent only in Konkani. The Swindon authorities aware of this language handicap also have Konkani translations for a number of official documents. There is Konkani mass celebrated once a week in Swindon.

Whatever be their financial status in Swindon, most Siridaokars come to Goa, every year, either for the village feast or for Christmas. They often even borrow money, but they rarely miss an opportunity to make the yearly visit to Goa. Their sense of identity and prestige comes from the approbation and envy of their fellow villagers in Siridao, the recognition that they have 'arrived'.

The parish priest of Siridao informs:

> in the first trip that they make, they buy a big car. That car is never used the whole year; it is only during their vacation that they will drive that car around the village. Next they will go about renovating and building huge houses. While the house is being built, if they are not satisfied with what is built, they will make alterations, and rebuild. They live in the huge houses for only the three weeks of their vacation, and the rest of the year it is unoccupied.

While their huge mansions lie empty in Goa, in Swindon eight to ten people share a house with a single bathroom and toilet. They do not find any irony in living in huge mansions for a three week vacation in Siridao and then living in cramped shared rooms for the rest of the year in Swindon. Their sense of identity, their home, lies here in their village in Goa.

This sense of nationality with India, more specifically with their village, is also prevalent with regard to their marriage celebration and funeral commemoration. In Swindon, around 70 to 80 per cent of the people get married to Goans, mostly to fellow villagers. Most of the matchmaking happens here when they come on vacation. The Sarpanch says that 'they have it in their blood that we should marry a person from the village'. The trend of arranged marriages is also still practiced in Swindon. Many of the Siridaokars living in Swindon still follow the traditional Indian practice of asking for the girl's hand in marriage from her parents, at times without even courting the girl.

Almost all the weddings are celebrated in the village itself. Even if the girl is settled in the United Kingdom and the boy is in

Paris, the marriage is still held here. Even if they get married to a foreigner, the wedding still takes place in the village. No marriage takes place abroad. The Sarpanch explains 'End of the day you want to show what your village is. And whenever there is a wedding, the whole family comes from abroad to attend the wedding. Not just family, friends and well-wishers also come'. Most of the marriages are solemnised during the time of the feast of Jesus Nazareth as during that time a lot of villagers come down from Swindon.

Funerals too are commemorated primarily in the village. Whenever there is a death in the family, whole family will come to Siridao from Swindon and other parts of Europe for the funeral regardless of the expense. Only if there are visa restrictions do they miss the funeral. If someone from Siridao dies in Swindon, the body is brought to Goa for the funeral. Along with the body, the entire family, including relatives, come to Goa for the funeral. This is very expensive. At times, if the family cannot afford the expense, the various Goan Associations contribute money and arrange for the body to be sent to Goa for the funeral. Hence, the sense of home and belonging of the Siridaokars living in Swindon is primarily felt in their village in Goa. The most important milestones of their life are commemorated in their native village. By choosing to marry within the village, though they may have been born and brought up in England, indicates that culturally, they have still retained Indian nationality.

Migration is experienced as a biographical trauma through which migrants lose their sense of home and perceive themselves, at least metaphorically, as homeless. The Siridaokars in Swindon attempt to manage this trauma by recreating their home, that is, Siridao, in Swindon.

Impact of Migration on the Sending Society

Whether the migrants' decision to relocate adversely affects or helps the sending society is highly subjective and situational. In Siridao, the large number of people migrating to Europe, has galvanized almost the entire village to migrate. Fadloullah et al. (2000) stated that the migration culture can become a 'collective psychosis' in which the group becomes almost totally obsessed by the idea of leaving, at any price'. Not only Siridao, but even the neighbouring villages of Agaçaim and Goa Velha are largely empty due to the near exodus of villagers to Europe, via Portuguese citizenship. This has altered the demographic profile of the village. In Siridao, most of the adults and their families are abroad. And of those who are left behind, a large number of them dream and wish to go abroad. The village comprises primarily an elderly population, who are not inclined to move to England, either because of the cold, the loneliness or just because they do not want to leave their village.

This rapid emptying out of the village poses a number of issues for the village. The apparent material prosperity of the migrants has had a demonstration effect on those who are left behind. They are not interested in pursuing their education in Goa, as they are simply waiting to go to Europe. As they are not well-qualified, the job that they get when they go to Europe are usually blue-collar jobs.

Another area which has been affected by the migration of youth to Swindon is the sports. The Sports Secretary of Siridao Sports Club says, ‘In the last ten years, our team has lost at least 75 good football players because so many of them migrated’.

The field of activism has also been adversely affected by current migration trends. For more than a decade now, the village has faced various challenges from the land sharks and real estate agents. Fifteen years ago, the people in the village were once fighting against some illegal constructions in their village. But things got out of hand, wherein they burnt some areas and also attacked the Panchs. There was a case filed against four or five of them. This case has been dragging for 15 years with these people having had to attend court hearings and so on. They cannot go abroad as they do not have police clearance. This case has served as a grim example for others who avoid falling into any trouble so that their chances of going abroad are not hampered. So their attitude is ‘let whatever happens, happen. We will not interfere, as it may disrupt our chances of going abroad’.

The parish priest opines that the religious services have been deeply affected by the migration. He informs that he has already complained to the Church authorities that he cannot do any work in the Parish as the number of people has been reducing drastically. Earlier there were three masses on Sunday, now they will have only one. In Sunday masses, the number of the attendees has come down drastically. He complains:

> I feel that my job here is reduced to only two things: burying the dead and giving certificates that are required to make their passport, either death, birth, baptism etc. People come here to get married. They normally get the bride from here, get married here in Goa, collect the marriage certificate and then process the papers for them to go abroad.

Despite the Priest's subjectivity about the villagers migrating abroad, many villagers feel that the migration has been for the best. The acute poverty that had plagued the village had rendered them helpless and unable to get an education. Now going abroad, their life chances have dramatically improved. The Sarpanch elaborates:

> Life has improved. The atmosphere and relations with neighbours has improved. Financially we were backward, and a lot of quarrels and enmity was there. That is gone, because we understood how to get along with others. With migration you see how others interact and you try to learn.

Of course, he admits that there are problems. One problem that has come about as a consequence of migration is the care and well-being of the elderly. There are around a hundred elderly people in the village. A number of them are living on their own, as their families have settled in Europe. The elderly have not accompanied their children abroad either due to the cold, the language, or simply because they do not want to leave their house and village. Though they do have a support system of friends, and maids taking care of them, they are still away from their families who are settled in Europe. Managing the care and well-being of the elderly thus poses a challenge.

There is also some apprehension in the village regarding the traditional values and upbringing of the children. These stand in direct contrast to the liberal values of the West. Bringing up Goan children in Europe with a different value system remains a challenge. One villager, who just returned from Swindon, says the sensibilities of Europe are different from Goa and India. 'If you are going to England for a job please don't take your family. There are no family values there. They get too much of freedom', he says, echoing a sentiment heard around the world when people leave a traditional society.

Re-examining the 'Denationalization' of Goan Catholics

In the twenty-first century, all modern societies are beginning to live though a time in which nationality and citizenship are in essence problematic. The tendency to view citizenship and nationality as one concept is common. In my view, it is this empirical and conceptual perplexity that makes states reject dual nationality. At present, the issue of dual citizenship is simmering in Goa, with the Panaji Town Police booking two senior police officials, forty-eight lawyers and over five hundred others for illegally having dual citizenship. Issues relating to fuzzy concepts such as nation and nationality need a multi-pronged holistic rational approach rather than one-dimensional evaluative approach. This chapter shows that citizenship and nationality need not be invested in one country only. Both belong to different realms – citizenship to the realm of the political and nationality to the realm of the cultural. The Siridaokars in Swindon show us that both realms can co-exist.

In the early twentieth century, Goan nationalist and freedom fighter Cunha (1961), writing about Goan Catholics complained:

> In the whole of India, no people is so denationalised as Goans. A complete lack of national consciousness, and the most shameful subjection to foreign rulers, either Portuguese or British, render the Goan Christian a stranger in his own land. A servile follower of everything foreign to his country, ... his strange behaviour makes one doubt the purity of his race, which nevertheless in no way differs from that of the neighbouring Indian.

Cunha's prognosis is negated by the experiences of Siridao Goans living in Swindon. Though living in Europe as Portuguese citizens, they hold on firmly to their Goan nationality. Of course, whether the Goans living in Swindon consider themselves 'as Indian as the neighbouring Indian' is debatable. A number of Goans living in Swindon take pains to differentiate themselves from other Indians. But this problematic requires further research.

References

Anderson, B. 1996. *Imagined Communities: Reflections on the Origin and Spread of Nationalism*. London: Verso.

Berger, P.L. and T. Luckmann. 1966. *The Social Construction of Reality: A Treatise in the Sociology of Knowledge*. Garden City, NY: Anchor Books.

Binaisa, Naluwembe. 2011. African Migrants Negotiate 'Home' and 'Belonging' Re-framing Transnationalism through a Diasporic Landscape. Working Papers Paper 41. UK: International Migration Institute (IMI).

Boghossian, Paul A. (n.d.). What is Social Construction? Available at: http://philosophy.fas.nyu.edu/docs/IO/1153/socialconstruction.pdf

Carvalho, Selma. 2009. From Siridao to Swindon. Goan Voice UK: Supplement to Siridao to Swindon. Available at: www.goanvoice.org.uk/supplement/SwindonGoans.htm

Chatterjee, Jacob. 2005. Church Concerned about Declining Population of Christians. Available at: www.christiantoday.co.in/article /church...of.christians.in.goa/193.htm

Cohen, R. 2007. Solid, Ductile and Liquid: Changing Notions of Homeland and Home in Diaspora Studies. Working Paper Number 156. QEH Working Paper Series – QEHWPS156. Available at: www3.qeh.ox.ac.uk/pdf/qehwp/qehwps156.pdf

Cunha, T.B. 1961. *Goa's Freedom Struggle: Selected Writings of T.B. Cunha*. Goa: Dr T.B. Cunha Memorial Committee.

Desai Nishtha, 2000. 'The Denationalisation of Goans: An Insight into the Construction of Cultural Identity' *Lusotopie*. Available at: www.lusotopie.sciencespobordeaux.fr/desai.pdf

Epstein, Gil S. and Gang Ira N. 2010. 'Migration and Culture'. *IZA DP* No. 5123.

Fadloullah, Abdellatif; Abdallah Berrada and Mohamed Khachani. 2000. *Facteurs d'Attraction et de Répulsion des Flux Migratoires Internationaux*. Rapport National: Le Maroc. Rabat: Commission Européenne.

Ferrão Benedito, R. and Fernandes, Jason Keith. 2013. Europeans of an Other Colour: Why the Goans Are Portuguese. Kafila. Available at: http://alice.ces.uc.pt/news/?p=2562.

Freyre, G. 1961. *The Portuguese and the Tropics*. Lisbon.

Gellner, E. 1983. *Nations and Nationalism*. Oxford: Blackwell.

Giddens, Anthony. 1985. *The Nation-State and Violence*. Oxford: Blackwell.

Goa Migration Study. 2008. Scribd. Available at: https://www.scribd.com/doc/85304160/Goa-Migration-Study–2008.

Grossman, J.R. 1989. *Land and Hope: Chicago, Black Southerners, and the Great Migration*. Chicago: University of Chicago Press.

Horta Ana Paula Beja and White Paul. 2009. Post-colonial Migration and Citizenship Regimes: A Comparison of Portugal and the United Kingdom. Revista Migrações, 4, 33–57

Keyes, Mascarenhas Stella. 2011. *Colonialism, Migration and the International Catholic Goan Community*. Goa: Goa, 1556.

Marshall, T.H. 1950. *Citizenship and Social Class, and Other Essays*. Cambridge: Cambridge University Press.

McCrone, David and Kiely Richard. 2000. Nationalism and Citizenship. *Sociology*, 34(1), 19–34.

Monteiro, Lisa Ann. 2015. Herald: 4 Goans give up Indian Passports everyday. Available at: http://www.heraldgoa.in/Review/4-GOANS-GIVE-UP-INDIAN-PASSPORTS-EVERYDAY/83940.html

Robinson, Rowena. 2000. The Construction of Goan Interculturality: A Historical Analysis of the Inquisitorial Edict of 1736 as Preventing and (Promoting) Syncretic Practices. In Charles J. Borges et al. (eds), *Goa and Portugal: History and Development*. New Delhi: Concept Publishers.

Sequeira, Devika. 2005. Christians' Historic Emigration Continues. Available at: www.deccanherald.com

Zuquete, Manuel Paul Christopher et al. (eds). 2012. *Religion and Politics in a Global Society: Comparative Perspectives from the Portuguese-Speaking World*. UK: Lexington Books.

3

Being in Kalapani

The Jahaji Bhai Aboard the Indian Emigrant Ship

Subhadeep Kumar

The nineteenth century witnessed a major thrust in the number of people leaving their ancestral communitarian locale to embark in global journeys of migration and circulation. Millions left Europe for North America, Australia and New Zealand. The long traffic in slavery from Africa across the Atlantic continued for the larger part of the century albeit progressive legislations to eventually halt it. A considerable number of Chinese migrants crossed the Pacific to work in the plantations and railroads of America, laying the foundation of the strong politically formidable Chinese diasporic lobby of twenty-first century. And a million Indian subjects of the British Empire left as indentured labourers for the crown colonies of British Empire. All these significant flows of the age of empire entailed transoceanic passages, often lasting months. Larger and heavier ocean carriers crossed the seas in this era in keeping with the unprecedented increase in the number of people on the move.

Developments in shipping constructions, such as the increased use of iron and eventually steel in place of wood to build stronger and lighter hulls, which increased super cargo space coupled with more sophisticated technologies for meteorological measurements, enabled this spurt in passenger figures to be sustainable in the long run. By the last decades of nineteenth century, steam ships had replaced sail. As a consequence, the age-old dependence on trade winds and currents were cleared, ushering in the era of all-season navigation.

The effects of these changes had not always been salubrious for the passengers as unscrupulous shipping agents and contractors made a rally of it. With increased deck space, more passengers were herded in with little superficial space over journeys lasting months in often inclement weather. The infamous 'coffin ships' (Mangan 1994) that transported famished Irish migrants to Canada and the United States and the convict ships to Australia or Van Diemen's Land bear testimony to the intensity of the migrants' experience.

In that the emigrant ship in the age of empires was perhaps one of the pioneer globalized spaces of modernity. It was positioned in the interstices of the global flows of commodities, capital and people. A globalized workspace is where crews, officers and passengers embodying multitude of languages and ethnicities jostled in cramped surroundings. With inadequate and often rotting provisions, its appalling sanitary conditions led to its characterization as a pathological menace. Its arrival was associated with spectres of dreaded contagious diseases, both corporeal and moral as it provided the perfect image of otherness pouring into the assumed racially homogenous space of the host community, in an era obsessed with 'Race'.

Among these flows the transatlantic passage had hitherto got most attention from scholars. The transportation of slaves from West Africa to the Americas and the Caribbean, with a much longer history spanning over four centuries had attracted the richest body of scholarship. The migration from the British Isles with specific focus on the post famine Irish migrations had brought forth a range of scholastic concerns regarding the dynamics of transportation, migrant subjectivity and reception of migrants in host locales. Same concerns had impressed works on the Australasian routes, both convict and free migrations. These works emphasize the interstices of class, ethnicity and gender in the transformative sites of the voyage not just the shipboard but also the associated maritime infrastructures of inspection depots, quarantine centres and hospitals. It is argued that a host of disciplining impetuses impressed the migrant which had formative effect on the fledgling migrant subjectivities. Migrants had to specifically deal with these factors in their strategies of refashioning identities. The departing emigrants suffering in disease-laden confines of ill-provisioned ships managed by callous and vindictive ship officers were powerful tropes of identitarian assertions for reawakening in sending locations.

Indian Indentured Emigrants in Passage

In case of India, the numbers of indentured labourers who went to other colonial possessions of various European empires are less than European migrations to America and Australasia in the corresponding period and more than the number of Chinese who crossed the Pacific to work in the Americas. Mauritius received 4,66,018 (Benedict 1961) indentured Indians, by far the largest number among all the receiving locations. The British West Indian Colonies of Guyana, Trinidad and Tobago, Jamaica and the other smaller colonial possessions of Britain received 5,34,109 immigrants (Bhana 1991). The French possession in the Indian Ocean, Reunion, received 1,18,000 indentured Indians, and 60,533 indentured Indians were introduced in Fiji between 1879 and 1916. Natal received 1,52,184 indentured immigrants between 1860 and 1911 (Bhana 1991). But in terms of mortality it was significantly higher than the European migrations across the Atlantic and the Australian route.

In 1869, Dr Bakewell, the Health Officer of shipping at Trinidad, exclaimed 'more than 11 times as many immigrants died on board Calcutta ships going to Trinidad than on board English ships going to Australia' (Extracts from report of Dr Bakewell, Bengal Emigration Proceedings).

The initial scheme worked with direct planter involvement in recruitment of Indian labourers. It was found cost worthy to transport the immigrants in cargo ships rather than hiring exclusive emigrant ships such as in the Britain–Australia or Europe–America routes. The indentured Indian emigrants were crowded all together on the inadequately covered tween deck between the gangway and the waste (Report of J.P. Woodcock, in Dickens Committee Enquiry, 1839). Each ship carried 150–200 migrants. Emigration was stopped in 1839 and remained prohibited till 1843 following huge public outcry against these deplorable conditions. Shipboard mortality and testimonies of brutal corporeal punishments of immigrants by crews became a potent symbol of national supinity. Internationally, the anti-slavery activists mobilized public opinion against the traffic; they coined the expression 'new system of slavery' (Tinker 1974), which went on to attain idiomatic resilience in course of the indentureship saga.

The traffic halted later too, like in 1857 and 1865 (from Bombay and Madras) to Mauritius, both triggered by concerns of high disease rate, mortality and fear of spreading contagion in the host locales. Official imperial opinion connected the emergence of contagion in plantation colonies with arrival of Indian immigrant ships.

The 1854 cholera report of the Government of Mauritius put the blame of that year's cholera epidemic in the colony on the arrival of the ship Sultanee with cholera-ridden victims.

In fact, the huge traffic in migrants in nineteenth century was matched by another worldwide flow – of contagious diseases. Large-scale epidemics or pandemics as they were rhetorically put by contemporaries swept across the globe all throughout the century. Known ailments such as plague or malaria attained unprecedented speed in circulation while hitherto unknown diseases in Western medical schema such as cholera and yellow fever were carried from their endemic aetiological locales through the global circuits of circulation, and attained epidemic form when it attacked the cosmopolitan contact zones such as ports, transport nodes and the colonial metropolises. Scholars had suggested links between increased traffic in goods and people with the spurt in epidemics as pathogens were carried from endemic locales to different ecologies where the host population lacked immunity to the new diseases. However, this connection between diseases and migrants as human vectors purportedly circulating unchecked was discursively morphed into diabolic figures of aversion. The spectre of migrant ships arriving in port came to be associated with xenophobic tropes of alien invasion.

The Sultanee left Calcutta on 14 February 1854, with 80 crew members and 375 emigrants. The first case was reported on 25 March 1854, when the ship was on anchor offshore Port Louis harbour (*The Englishman*, 5 January 1857). The ship was put under quarantine at Flat Island off the coast of Mauritius. At that time, the quarantine station was occupied by small pox victims and consequently the immigrants were exposed to a different contagious host. The record state that five persons died in the ship while in quarantine, recorded due to cholera and dysentery. The report notes the rumours that circulated regarding the ship Sultanee. It was widely believed that the captain of the ship broke quarantine restrictions and maintained contact with land. The report is plagued with a number of inconsistencies about the number of people who underwent medical treatment or the number of patients who recovered and only comments that recovery was rapid. Later, a number of these emigrants were infected in estates and 57 of them died. The facts show that no connections can be made between the arrival of Sultanee and the spread of the contagion if it does not disprove the conjecture forwarded. Ultimately however the report concurs with the assumption that the cholera epidemic was brought in Mauritius by the ship Sultanee.

In an another case for instance, in 1896, Durban port authorities kept the ships Courland and Naderi for 23 days in quarantine, just with the suspicion of having plague-ridden migrants on board. The ship was not let off even after quarantine authorities certified absence of plague or any other contagious disease on board. Instead, the belongings of the migrants were fumigated and all contacts with land were severed. The ship was ultimately let out of quarantine following huge pressure from Indian immigrants in Durban. At the time of debarkation at Durban harbour, the Indians were met by a very hostile white South African agitation against letting off the ship from pratique (Memorial by Indians in Natal).

Table 1

Transportation of Indian Indentured Labourers from British India to Mauritius, Natal, West Indies and Fiji

Port of Embarkation	*Period*	*Voyages*	*Mean Length of Voyage*	*Crude Death Rate/month/ 1000*	*Loss Ratio (CDR/Voyage/1 000)*
Calcutta	1850–1872	382	88	19.9	5.8
	1873–1917	876	65	7.1	1.5
Madras	1855–1866	56	62	5.6	1.2

Source: Haines, Shlomowitz (1996).

The Extant Literature on the Passage

Studies on Indian emigrant voyages to the colonies have mostly focused on the embarkation and debarkation part of it. Pioneering work of Saha (1970) and Hugh Tinker (1974) on indentureship had referred obliquely to the purport of the voyage on the migrants, their concern was more with the systematics of the indentureship process and consequently do not engage in a detailed analysis of the passage. Marina Carter in *Voices from the Indenture* (1996) brings forth revealing testimonies of the voyages drawing from epistolary sources, anecdotes and remembrances. The evidences situate the voyage as a formative factor in forming diasporic identity among the voyagers and through subsequent generations. Same force is found in Brij Lal's study focusing on Fiji, *Chalo Jahaji* (2000). However, the book charts the process of 'jahaji' identity formation and deals with the shipboard saga more in its effect post-debarkation. It reiterates the importance of the peculiar space of the emigrant shipboard in this process but desists from a grounded analysis of this space in transit. Scholars such as Shlomowitz, McDonald and Brenan had extensively prodded into the dynamics of transportation through extensive quantifications of mortality and diseases. However, with due acknowledgement to the much-needed quantitative cartography and comparative frame vis-à-vis other migration stream that their work provided, it lacks reflexivity in reading archival sources. The colonial archive such as any other scribal compendia also embodies power. The emigration department files of the British Indian Government, both at central and provincial level, are replete with not so subtle examples of racist stereotyping of the Indian 'coolie' emigrant. The extensive documentation of the 'habits' and ailments of the 'coolies' locked the indentured emigrant in the colonizers' epistemic frame and thus every textual cue, anecdotes or statistics need to be read with grain of salt.

In this chapter, I propose to make a structural analysis of the modalities of power on board the Indian emigrant ships in the era of indentured migration. Existing scholarship stresses on the formative strength of the 'jahaji' identity in the development of diasporic consciousness in the host locales. The jahaji solidarities formed among erstwhile strangers in the highly surveillanced transit space of nineteenth century emigrant ships was a salient part of the migrants' strategies to deal within their new subjectivity in an alien (and often hostile) setting.

The emigrant shipboard became a site of a host of governmental and political concerns with at times divergent and conflicting impetuses that went on to mark the site by very divergent impulses – of disciplining and taking care of population often working simultaneously. Discursively it was variously represented as mother India's unfortunate children or vectors of dangerous diseases. I would chart the construction of the immigrant shipboard chronologically at the intersections of these different discursive endeavours.

Introduction and Premature Truncation of the Scheme

As a legal object, the immigrant ship got continuously amended by these practices throughout the indenture regime. In 1830, when two Colonial Land and Emigration Commissioners were appointed by the GOI, there was little in their writs or capabilities to supervise shipboard provisions. Acts V and XXXII of 1837 widely considered to be the foundations of the Indian indenture emigration led down broad guidelines for supervision of emigrant ships. The acts stipulated inspection of every vessel carrying more than 20 passengers for accommodation, food and general provisions necessary for the said passengers and led a cap of 3 passengers per 5 tons burden of ship and made it mandatory to provide 15 superficial feet, not covered by cargo or provisions for each passenger in the lower deck (Act V of 1837, Parliamentary Papers, Vol. 16, 1841). Every ship with more than 20 emigrants also needed to have a medical surgeon with enough supply of medicine and instruments. The stipulated instruction for doctors on board was to carry a 'chest' of medical supplies. The immigrants had to be provided with five gallons of water and fourteen pounds of rice every week, with additional provisions stacked for situations of emergency.

The inadequacies of the regulations were evident from the outset. Numerous instances were reported of ships loading migrants after sailing far from the port. The stipulations were vague and underestimated. The Dickens Committee instantiated the case of the ship Sofia under the command of captain Rapson to drive home the point of lackadaisical upkeeping of regulations; in 1836 the ship Sofia embarked a huge number of coolies, once the ship had left the port of Calcutta and down river. It was found that two-thirds of all the emigrants in the ship had no police pass, the mandatory embarkation document prior to Act XV 1842 (papers relating to East Indian Labourer's Bill).

The ensuing public outcry against the deplorable treatment of Indian migrants coupled with concerns against resumption of slavery under a new guise led to the promulgation of Act XIV of 1839. It stated, 'no native of India was to be taken out of the country, to work as labourers'. A penalty of ₹ 200 and/or imprisonment of up to 3 months were imposed against violators of the ban.

Indentureship Resumed: Legislations and Concerns of Governmentality

This incident had a salient impact on the period of indentured emigration. When after repeated lobbying by planter pressure groups, the India Office resumed colonial emigration; the ship became a central focus of regulation. Act XV 1842, passed by Lord Ellenborough in the presence of Queen Victoria, considered the prime resumption clause of Colonial Indian Emigration, coupled with Act XXI of 1843, attempted to stipulate provisions, superficial space, medical facilities with the number of personnels and even touched issues considered strictly of maritime concerns such as placing of objects on board, positioning of emigrant dwelling which needed adjustments in design.

However, the issue of indentured transportation was locked in a tug of war between the concerns of well-being and safety of the migrants and the imperative of providing cheap labour to the plantations. The planters, who exercised immense power in the crown colonies which were often dependent on the production of a single cash crop, stressed on the economies of scale in labour transportation. Their special target was the clause of superficial space stipulated to be provided to each migrant on board by Act XV, 1842 (Act XV of 1842, Parliamentary Papers, Vol. 35, 1843). In 1847, the Mauritius government gave in to their demands and decreased the stipulated height between decks (Geoghegan Report). The amendment was approved both by the Government of India and by the colonial emigration commission.

Act IV 1852 supplemented the provisions of the preceding legislations. It created the office of Medical Inspector of Emigrants whose duties were to exercise a sanitary supervision over the various emigration depots, to decide on the eligibility of vessels tendering to transport migrants, to inspect the stores and was supposed to be present at the spot of embarkation, where he was responsible for disallowing emigrants to embark on grounds of inadequate fitness (Carter 1996).

However, the 1850s saw an increase in mortality and sickness on shipboard. In 1856, huge mortality on the Mauritius-bound ships Futtay Mubarak and Hyderee, supplemented by considerable additions in quarantine at Gabriel Island off the coast of Mauritius, led the Government of India to close emigration to Mauritius pending upgradation of quarantine and allied disembarkation facilities. The incident also brought the entire transportation process under renewed supervision by the government. The ghost of 1839 still hung deeply in institutional memory. Various contemporary commentators tried to make sense of the figures; one longstanding focus of blame was of course on the debility of the recruited emigrants. The number of people emigrating also shot up markedly during this period. Some had inferred this to be a result of an influx of refugees and displaced people from the famine stricken districts of United Provinces and Bihar; while mutiny-induced migration was also marked as a factor (Carter 1996).

Following high shipboard mortality in the West Indies route in 1857, the Government of India commissioned an enquiry headed by Mouat, Inspector of Jails and Dispensaries of the Bengal Government. He was considered to be an authority on the health condition of enclosed spaces – the prisons, the barracks and consequently the shipboard. As Clare Anderson (2000) had noted while studying convict transportation of Indians to overseas penal settlements, it is not altogether surprising that the terminologies of overseas convict transportation seeps in and overlaps deliberations on Indian emigrant ships. The indentured emigrant transportation was widely suspected to be a route by which unconvicted rebels of the sepoy mutiny escaped prosecution. The belief gained traction with the unusual increase in the number of intending emigrants in the seasons following the mutiny. However, whether the increase was due to escaping ex-sepoys or due to sudden boom in global sugar production and hence increased demand for labour in the corresponding period is anybody's guess (Anderson 2009).

In fact leaving out the context of the War of 1857, we find the overlap of the indentured 'coolie' emigrant and the Indian convict to be a widespread practice in imperial policy. In Mauritius, where the arrival of the Indian convict predated the Indian indentured immigrants, the former remained a strong frame of reference to observe the Indian labourer. An 1875 Commission of Enquiry into labour conditions in Mauritius reported that earlier convict transportation to the island made the Indian indentured labourer 'not the entire stranger he was in the West Indies and Demerara' (Anderson 2009).

A series of reports followed a similar line, which categorized migrant depots and ships – like other colonial institutions such as jails, penal settlements, asylums and lock-hospitals, as pathological social spaces (Arnold 1993; Anderson 2004). The 1861 emigration committee drew attention to the comparative rates of mortality on ships and in jails (West Bengal State Archives, henceforth WBSA 1861). In 1867, after another season of high death rate on West Indies emigrant ships, the authorities moved to ensure that the space allotted to migrants was the same as that allotted to prisoners in jail (WBSA 1867).

Mouat's appointment to the 1858 commission was thus not anomalous. The staff of Jails and Prison Inspection was looked up as experts in studying Indian dispositions. The carceral aspect of disciplining colonized bodies is presciently hinted by these bureaucratic amicabilities.

Mouat's report absolved the Protector of Emigrants (POE) and the depot personals of laxity in selection and care of migrants. Instead it turned its attention to the absence of sick bays, the high proportion of women and children and recent changes in diet. He objected to the introduction of biscuits and wanted ships carrying grain cargo to have air-tight hatches, privies outside the transom of the ship secured by fore-chains. The drinking water, stocked in the ships, was drawn from the brackish waters of Hooghly River near Calcutta. It was considered by many ship surgeons to be a factor in ill health on ship (WBSA 1860). A plan for installing a distilling apparatus to get drinking water from the ocean and filter it was suggested many times, but nothing came of it till the 1880s.

However, one aspect that Mouat singled out for blame was the newly introduced sleeping platforms for the emigrants. He considered the platforms to be unnecessary and 'liable to harbour vermin' and accumulate dirt and 'obstruct very materially and injuriously the air of the space beneath' (WBSA 1859). The prevailing conceptions of medicine stressed on the connections between air flow and aetiology. Diseases, especially contagious ones, were believed to be produced by miasma that emanate out of the soil and is carried by air. Thus damp, constricted spaces were considered to be more susceptible to harbour disease, which can be made good only by proper arrangement for ventilation. Thus, unobstructed air flow was a prime concern in colonial medical thought; its importance was not lost even when studies with microorganisms proved that pathogen vectors can undergo very complex trajectories for the pathogen to become contagious. The good healthy colonial construction always stressed on unobstructed movement of air. The elaborately constructed ventilators of colonial bungalows in the tropics are a relic of this worldview. The platforms were promptly removed from the 'coolie decks' in the next season but mortality rates increased. Indeed some ship owners and captains pressed for reintroduction of the platforms by regulation willing to bear additional expenses (WBSA 1859). Indeed the reasons forwarded for the reintroduction of platforms also rested on miasmatic conceptions. As the report on the 1860s, mortality rooted for it basing their case on the authority of army medicine, they quoted Dr Henner, who wrote 'it is a fact now well-known that the lower part of atmosphere of an occupied room is invariably the least proper for respiration. About the height of 2 feet, sometimes even 2 1/2 feet the proportion of carbonic acid gas is commonly 8–10 per cent, and close to the floor 20 per cent and even a larger proportion has been observed'.

About the cause of higher mortality in Calcutta ships vis-à-vis Madras ship, Mouat gave in to prevailing orientalist stereotypes of racial fixity, which was widespread and considered perfectly pertinent for a doctor of mid-nineteenth century. He thought the natives of Bengal were more fearful of sea travel than the Madras emigrants. About the overall high rate of mortality in passage, his summation carries a prescient note of scientific fatalism which collapses tropes of race into tropes of vegetation while unproblematically (almost unconsciously) assuming convict transportation as the major premise of his inferential frame.

> All persons who have any knowledge of the natives in India are aware of the extent to which they suffer at first by transplantation from one district to another to so great an extent

... fact is constantly observed with respect to convicts sent to Alipore which immediately joins Bhowanipur for transportation from all parts of Punjab and Bengal Presidency generally ... this is partly due to change in diet ... to a vegetarian race whose physical powers are at all times feeble, compared with the flesh eating families of mankind, their influence are more palpably prejudiced than would a priori be supposed.

So consequently they stay at Calcutta depot for the upcountry emigrant awaiting embarkation, 'although not actually labouring under disease at that time, ... would suffer seriously from any defects of ventilation or cleanliness on board' as opposed to their non-vegetarian counterparts. He did mention the famine in Bihar and Chhotanagpur region in 1856, as a possible reason for the increase in debilitated recruits, but by his arguments it is only a supplement to the overall bleak scenario than a cause in itself.

He does not mention in his report, the unhygienic condition of the location of the depots in Calcutta, which even by the prevailing logic of public health should be considered potent to 'harbour disease and pestilence'. He points to the bad quality of food stuffs provided on board ships, especially rice and flour and called for its improvement by more stringent supervisory regulations. However, with the quantities in the diet scale he expressed satisfaction, except his reservations to the introduction of biscuits. Nor did he undertake a comparative analysis of the 3 diet scales of Calcutta, Madras and Bombay. Saha, in his study on indentured Indian labour in West Indies, had demonstrated that the food rations in the Calcutta ships transporting indentured migrants were significantly lower than in the corresponding ships leaving Madras and Bombay.

The ship surgeons recommended transporting the labourers in ballast in place of the extant practice of transporting them in ships carrying other bulk cargo, especially grain. During the initial days of the regime, the lower deck was filled with grain while the migrants were left in the waste, between the gangway and forecastle (Woodcock's dispatch, Dickens Committee Report). Later, the grain was put in hatches beneath deck, while the lower deck was used to house the migrants. Numerous commentators had objected to the arrangement. It was considered detrimental to the health of the passengers because when the grain rot as it is transported in bulk it causes 'noxious effluvia' which is arose off the hatches. Effluvium was considered to be the prime pathogen carrier in miasmatic conception. Ship surgeons blamed the reasons of contagious outbreaks on board on the effluvia arising out of the hatches, which gained vigour by the abundant breeze on high seas. Their suggestion was to transport migrants in ballast as was the practice in the Britain–Australia route (WBSA, Pro. 54, 1860).

However, the Government of India and the colonial office were reluctant to accede to this suggestion as they claimed it would increase the cost of transportation by at least 40 per cent (WBSA, Pro. 53, 1860). The grain cargo being transported in the immigrant ships they claimed was mostly meant as provisions for the Indian migrants at their locations. They asked for experimental proof of the purported benefits estimated to be accrued by the change in transporting policy. In the end, an experiment was conducted. In December 1858, two ships, 'Northern Light' and 'Catherine Apcar', were dispatched from Calcutta port with emigrants and without cargo. Seventeen people died on board the 'Northern Light' but as she is debutant in the trade, no comparison could be made with her previous voyages. 'Catherine Apcar' lost more number of emigrants than her previous voyages with cargo. As no benefit could be found out of this rare singular experiment, the issue was declared closed for further consideration (WBSA, Pro. 55, 1860).

This episode brings out the fine balance between commercial interests and policy imperatives caused by public opinion that underpinned the logics of imperial governmentality in the colonies. The health of the 'coolie' labourer was crucial. High mortality risked public outcry and increased attention to a traffic widely perceived to be a continuation of slavery. Also, a debilitated labour force incapable of field work was obviously not in anybody's interest. However, the exigency of health was stringently calculated against mercantile costs, in the process the discourse of prophylactic care broadened to become a racialized critique of the 'Asiatic body'; more in need of regimentation than therapy. Indeed regimentation itself was posed as therapy. Hence colonial assumptions regarding the 'contented' coolie shipboard stressed on strict shipboard routine – of work, of washing and exercise and of maintenance of certain demographic distinctions which were seen as vital, of sex, of caste and of race.

Diagram of Ship Carrying Indentured Labourers

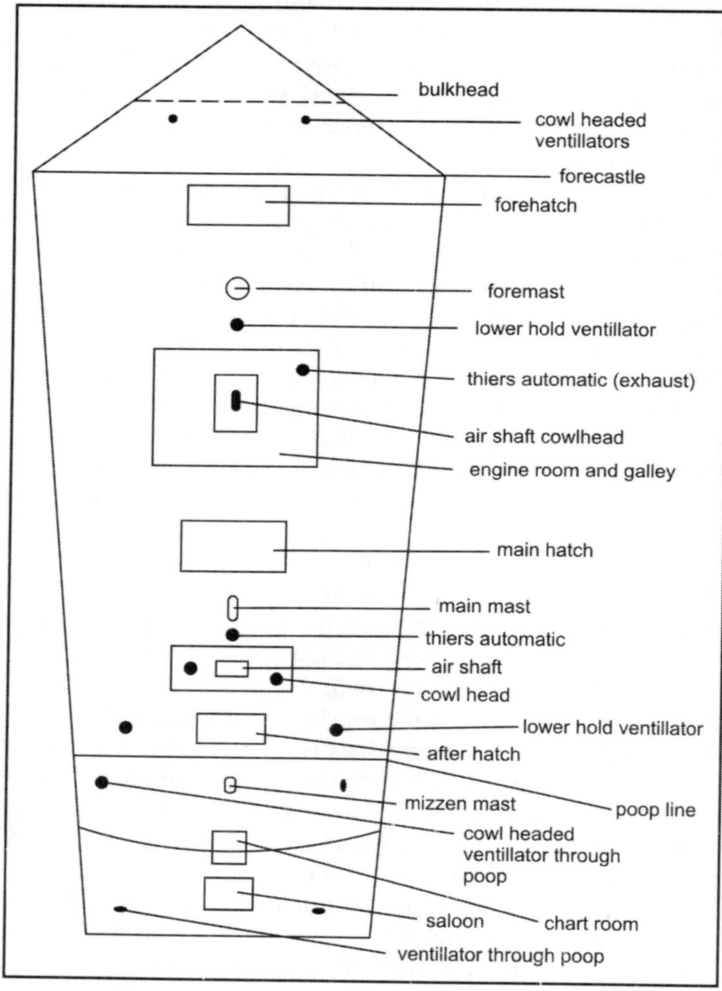

The Women of the 'Asiatic Races' on Shipboard

Marina Carter had pointed out that discussions about the nature of cargo was gradually superseded by the observation that the proportion of women and children had a direct impact on mortality rates (Carter 1996). Contemporary observation held that increase in the proportion of women which often led to corresponding increase in the number of children and infants shot up the disease and mortality rates among the immigrants. On shipboard, the resultant increase in disease purportedly led to outbreaks of contagious diseases. However, since the quota on women came into force recruiters had struggled to meet the quota. Policy practices created a host of adjusting conventions such as carrying over the shortage of women in one ship to other ships sailing in the particular route in the same season. The shortage of a season were at times attempted to be filled up in the next season until the government disallowed the practice.

Official opinion held that immigrants should arrive in colonies before the start of the 'wet season' as it was seen unhealthier in terms of sanitation than the dry season in the miasmatic theory of disease transmission. Wet ecologies were held to effuse more miasma and was thus considered more conducive for spread of disease. Planters thus wanted new indentured recruits to be in plantations before the onset of rainy season so that they get acclimatized and be put to work from the outset (WBSA 1872). When it was seen that arrival of immigrants in the wet season cannot be completely avoided, one proposal put forth was to reduce the stipulated quota of women among the recruited migrants during the wet season. The proposal was mulled by the government on the ground that as it is less than stipulated number of women had been transported since implementation of the quota (WBSA, Pro. 46, 1858).

As Marina Carter had noted that the legislations governing sex ratios were a product of external factors on the migration stream. The anti-slavery activists and missionaries specifically pointed out to the negligible number of women transported in the initial years of the scheme as a telling parallel with slave transportation. It was seen as 'unnatural' and detrimental to the development of a stable filial society for the immigrants in the host locales and may lead to various 'vices' of jealousy, adultery, murder and by extension they hinted at homosexuality (BFASS 1842). In 1843, when Mauritius started re-recruiting, only 13 women were transported per 100 men. A year later when West Indies joined in, the proportion was 21 to 100. This fell to 16 per cent at the end of the decade. Later with legislation, the figure was increased to 30 and later 40 per cent of male recruits (Carter 1996). Lord Russell threatened to put a ban to emigration in

1850s if the disproportion was not addressed. It was pointed out that in the British-Australian route or the British-American route the proportion was four women to every five men (Carter 1996). The issue of sex disproportion was considered more important for far off West Indies than Mauritius as the Secretary of State wrote to the Governor of British Guiana in 1855 (Russell to Wodehouse, 1855, Parliamentary Papers, Vol. 16, 1859). The problem of maintaining a high proportion of women in the emigration stream was pointed out by the Land and Emigration Commissioners' report of 1866 'attended by considerable difficulties, because on the one hand a small proportion of women gives rise to strife and jealousies, ... to require a large proportion leads either to the acceptance of a very inferior class, or to an injurious limitation of the whole number of emigrants'. By the 1860s, legislations required at least one-third or just over 33 per cent of recruits should be women. However greater the numbers migrating, it was more difficult to impose the rules. In situations of deadlock thus the onus was upon the POE to use his discretion. This became a custom as ship captains and depot authorities regularly petitioned the POE of depots being full and ship in anchor waiting for embarkation of emigrants but for the lack of required proportion of women (WBSA, Pro. 11, 1878).

In 1872, when the 40 per cent ratio was implemented, the West Indies managed 37.83 per cent (WBSA, File 75, Pro. 11–12, August 1878). Eventually the rule was relaxed to allow for 25 per cent proportion of women. The rationale of such emphasis was to induce family settlements, which the authorities thought would lead to a chain migration following the filial networks.

It was noticed that when distresses such as famine struck, the number of people emigrating increased and with it the number of women and children. Another concern that bugged the authorities was regarding the 'moral' of the women being recruited. A large proportion of unaccompanied women were noted among the intending recruits, which was promptly read as women of 'loose morals' taking advantage of the indentured emigration scheme to try their luck out of the country (WBSA, Pro. 12, 1878). Recent scholarship on the life history of indentured women had shown that most single women migration was hastened due to domestic quarrels and property disputes especially when they had been widowed and shirked by relations or to escape agricultural debt traps (Carter 1994; Shepherd 2002).

On board the women suffered more than the men. Long deliberations continued about the proper place for housing of the women on ships. It continued till 1872, when it was legislated by an Act – to have the women's accommodation towards the rear of the ship in the coolie deck, with the unmarried women in the far rear, followed by the married women and married men, with the unmarried men taking up the place facing the forecastle. Act XXI of 1843 (Parliamentary Papers, Vol. 30, 1844) directed the employment of two female nurses on board migrant ships with two compounders but few instance of female nurses had been found. Instances of physical and sexual assaults on women, even by ship surgeons themselves, are not unheard of. In rare instances, the doctors or other officers were convicted, in such cases their pay was forfeited and they were disqualified for further employment on board emigrant ships. However, numerous other complaints were summarily dismissed by authorities with the slightest suspicion of moral laxity of the victims.

Maritime commentaries are replete with not so subtle racist observations of the fairer sex on Indian 'coolie' ships. Ship doctors considered them dirty and uncooperative as patients, both in case of themselves and their children. Surgeons' manuals stressed to compel the women to take their offspring to the closets to wash as 'Women of the Asiatic Races' (Mouat's Report) were prone to make the coolie deck dirty (Laing's Handbook), are quarrelsome and interestingly 'vitiate more foul air' in the 'coolie decks' than men (Mouat's Report). One comparatively sympathetic commentator, Mrs Swinton, wife of Captain Swinton, whom she accompanied in one of his voyages carrying Indian migrants to West Indies, commented on the migrant women as 'lacking in feelings of sistership than their counterparts in Europe' (Swinton and Swinton).

As it was observed that the increased number of women led to secular increase in mortality and debility rates on board, it was more convenient to put the blame of diseases on board on the migrants themselves. Thus, the 10 per cent mortality on the West Indian ships in 1865–1866 season was blamed on the migrants rather than the emigration service (Carter 1996). As Dr Bakewell tried to explain the reasons for the exceptional mortality figures in Indian indentured migration, he gave in to the received wisdom of innate racial debilities of tropical 'races' which hinder vigorous acclimatization in alien climatic conditions unlike their European counterparts. The ideas of corporeal racial failings seamlessly give into representations of unhygienic propensities of Asiatic races, against which European medical supervision has little chance to succeed unless the subjects are constantly supervised by European personnel. Discourses of racial somatics thus worked in tandem with discourses of racial predispositions, in which both were conceived as pathological and in need of therapy.

Regulating Care and Order On Board Emigrant Ships

In 1859, Shah Allam, transporting migrants to Mauritius caught fire and only one individual out of 400 passengers and crew survived (Tinker 1974). This incident led to calls for revamping safety measures on shipboard, provisions for lifeboats and fire dousing equipment. Indian migrants generally cooked food on deck for themselves in groups, taking the rations provided by surgeon superintendent. This was a provision reluctantly granted by Act XV, 1842, in view of the caste prejudices of intending emigrants. The wreck of the Shah Allam led to official strictures against cooking on board by migrants. This was just after the sepoy mutiny and the Government of India was itself in a process of large-scale legislative transformation.

In the same year, high mortality on the ship 'Marian Moore', sailing from Calcutta to British Guiana prompted Secretary of State Sir C. Wood to carry out an enquiry (WBSA, Pro. 47–49, May 1860). He called for provisions of increased hospital accommodation for on board Indian migrant ships and provisions for ventilation, referring to the report of Mouat of 1857. He directed to look for some apparatus to induce adequate ventilation in the tween decks 'for dispersing and drawing off the foul air apt to accumulate … on Emigrant Ships'.

All these led to a major structural overhaul of the system in 1860s. The office of a separate immigration agent for each recruiting colony in India was instituted by the Emigration Act, 1860. This made the receiving colonies responsible for the well-being of the migrants once embarkation had happened and the ship is off mooring. A host of established practices in the indentured migration regime was touched by this change. One was, the captain becomes equally answerable to both the Indian and the receiving colony authorities, and moreover, the ship surgeon was now officially employed on behalf of the receiving colony by the immigration agent, though hired in the ports of departure. The law also stated that 'India will be open throughout the year to the agents of all the colonies concerned to do their best for the advancement of the service of which they are employed, with the exception only, of West Indies of the few months in which paramount sanitary considerations render it unfit that coolies should be (shipped)' (Carter 1996).

The changes of 1860 with the general trend in the previous legislations greatly increased the job profile of the ship surgeon. He became the de facto in charge of the migrants on board ships. On land, they were considered the lowest in the imperial medical bureaucracy with often no coveted medical diploma at hand and scarcely a chance to upkeep a good private practice being often in long sea voyages lasting months; they were under constant pressure and suffered from a host of insecurities. A surviving petition of a ship doctor, Dr Nisbet, to the POE in Calcutta, shows that among a host of his concerns, one that particularly erred him was 'now I am liable to be superseded by native doctors' (WBSA, Pro. 11, March 1860). However, offshore the ship surgeon commanded formidable gravity over the few hundred Indian migrants. Apart from dispensing medical care, it was his job to maintain discipline and constabulating over provisions and even infrastructural issues when it came to immigrants' accommodation and maintenance. His job profile hints at the wide scope the institution of medicine had in official conception and the immediate regime on board the immigrant ship became singularly somatic.

As per his professional brief, he was to draw up routines for his putative set of 'patients' and ensure their implementation. His job started with the embarkation of the migrants on the ship. He needed to coordinate and supervise the upcoming recruits over the gangway and in the ship and check each of their tickets issued in the depot, which stated among other things that the intending emigrant is free of contagious ailments, able bodied and thus fit to migrate (Laing's Handbook 1889, WBSA). Patrick Manson, the doyen of tropical medicine and a ship doctor by himself at younger age, noted:

> no one accustomed to work in well-organized shore hospital, with its trained staff can know the difficulties which confront a

> surgeon on an Indian emigrant ship, even in his purely medical work. But in addition to that work he is responsible for discipline, sanitation diet, amusements … . Out of a crowd of ignorant coolies he has to organise nurses, policemen, cooks, cleaners … and to constantly supervise them. His only assistance is from 2 sometime 3 more or less helpful native compounders, who in their turn need constant direction and supervision. (WBSA, Pro. 27–30, B. Nov. 1913)

In later years, a proposal was made to induct the surgeons of Indian emigrant ships in tropical medicine courses. However, the plan was cancelled as a meeting of ship surgeons gave their opinion in 1913, which is as follows:

> The course is highly scientific, involving use of microscope, chemical analysis and such. On board of a coolie ship conditions are unfavorable, we might say antagonistic to accurate scientific work … some idea of the difficulty of pursuing scientific work on these ships can be gained from the fact that owing to noise, vibration etc. it is frequently almost impossible to hear accurately the heart or lung sounds, even in bronchitis or pneumonia … . The diseases from which coolies mostly suffer during the voyage are diarrhea, dysentery, fever, bronchitis, pneumonia, measles, conjunctivitis and such. (WBSA, Pro. 27–30, B. Nov. 1913)

One prescient observation that was made in course of the observation by the ship surgeons, albeit unwittingly is that, tropical medicine does not constitute a separate sub-field of medicine, neither by aetiology nor by disease type. This was in the heydays of tropical medicine that fashioned itself as a 'tool of empire' and would continue to influence global health policies for the tropics for the next 50 years until its methodological edifice lapsed into antiquarian oblivion.

The ship surgeons were paid according to the number of living migrants actually disembarked in destination. So, as veteran ship surgeon James Laing advises to his fellow professionals, 'remember your interest is identical with the coolies', while with the captain it is not so. He insists this to the doctor as a reason for not allowing the captain to interfere in his work from the beginning.

One repeated complaint of the ship surgeons was that at times the emigrants despatched from the depot were already too ill whose conditions only aggravated during the voyage. In these situations, too little too late could be done within the constraints of the shipboard to cure them. Depot authorities did not want to carry out large-scale preventive checks or prophylaxis of diseases, especially diseases that were considered to be contagious. Procedures such as blood or other body fluid sample testing, which were required by norms, were disenchantingly carried out in the depots as they considered such practices create aversion and panic among the intending emigrants and made some of them reluctant to emigrate. The ship surgeons indeed stood with the depot authorities during final checking of recruits before embarkation. One repeated complaint of both the depot and shipboard authorities was that certain old people who visibly looked incapable of undertaking long sea voyage had to be allowed for embarkation as without them none of the other family members or companions would be willing to get on board. It is also noted that these people suffered most on the sea voyages (Swinton).

Indeed the effect of maiden sea voyages on a ship full of maiden voyagers must have taken its toll especially among the old and the infirm. First person accounts and anecdotal remembrances of the diasporic communities had epitomized the trope of the receding shoreline of India seen from the ship as a marker of the moment of traumatic realization of embarking into the 'abyss', into that tentative space where most erstwhile subjectivities becomes unsure while new subjectivities are still in the process of becoming, through the rites de passage of the voyage and thenceforth (Anderson 2000, 2004; Carter 1996; Lal 2000). It was noted, that this was the location where most attempts at ship jumping were tried by the migrants (Swinton; WBSA Pro. 3–6, 1872). Not one instance is available in the entire indentureship history of attempts at rescuing a fallen migrant by life boat reconnaissance. The ship surgeon categorized these instances as suicides. In the surgeon's views, the suicides were often conflated with behavioural traits of panic and depression giving into insanity. Migrants who were seen to be especially quiet and drooping were to be particularly observed by the ship surgeon and compounders. Laing writes, 'I know that many die from nostalgia pure and simple'. As an antidote to these behavioural traits that were perceived to have transmissive effect on the morale of the migrant party, he suggests, 'daily life on board ship should be reduced as much as possible to a regular system'. The new recruits hailed mostly from deeply inland locales that had little information, let alone experience about maritime life. The disciplining endeavours of the ship surgeon were geared towards instilling a maritime conduct on these migrants. Laing is assertive, 'I believe the greatest good of the greatest number ... promiscuously thrown together at sea is attained by some discipline'.

Controlling Bodies, Producing 'Coolies'

The Indian indentured recruitment called for an 'able bodied', 'obedient' and 'industrious' workforce. 'It must no less be admitted that the labourers introduced should be confined to people of suitable habits and constitutions (for which purpose we doubt whether it will not be necessary at least to limit also to races)' (Lord Russell to Emigration Commissioners, Parliamentary Papers, Vol. 33, 1840). For a largely artisanal and agrarian population, it created demand for adapting into a different regime of workplace relation. Especially it worked on a different logic of time management. The shipboard space was a major site of orientation into this new disciplinary regime.

Laing insists that from the first day, the people should be made to go to the scuppers or channels at the side of the ship and wash their plates. As, if this is not insisted upon 'the upper deck will be simply abominable, and if water or other liquid is spilt on, it will lead to constant bickering, (especially among women who will also be found especially among the lower castes) too lazy to take the children to the closets'.

The surgeon superintendent is to select the men to work as topazes while some women of middle age as sick nurse for the women patients. The compounders, translators and bandheries are selected in the depot beforehand. Laing opines that the *bandheries* (cooks for migrants) should be men of high caste so that no disputes occur regarding caste stipulations on board ship. Laing mentions that at times migrants come and tell about their uncomfortability regarding common cooking. He directs the surgeons to explain to the person that this was stipulated by the agreements in the depot and individual cooking on board was not allowed. Laing suggests making arrangements for the man to work in the galley if possible, which would generally take care of his prejudice. As an endnote he adds, 'There are good many pseudo Brahmins too'.

Ships carrying more than 500 migrants had two compounders. Of these, one generally the senior took charge of the dispensary, dispensed and administered medicines to the sick and superintended the preparation and issue of hospital diets and milk to patients in hospital, to the weakly and convalescents and to the nursing women and children on the quarter deck and was supposed to be present at the issue of meals to the immigrants. The duties of the other compounder was to take charge of the galley and superintend upon the bandheries, muster the sirdars each morning upon the deck delegating the days' work, while being in overall charge of the sanitation of the decks and associated entities not directly related to the navigation of the ship.

Every migrant is to rise between 6 am and 7 am and get engaged in their delegated works. The bandheries are to go to the galleys, and the topazes sweep the main deck, flush and disinfect closets under the supervision of the first compounder. Meanwhile, the second compounder goes about collecting the sick to report to the surgeon superintendent. At 7 am, the surgeon superintendent goes out on his round which consists of, apart from checking on the sick, the general cleaning of the decks and cooking. Before 8 AM, once the food is prepared the surgeon superintendent has to taste it and give his opinion about the quality of the cooked food. Breakfast is served between 8 am and 9 am. Then men and women have to exercise every alternate day and the coolie deck need to be cleaned by noon, so that the surgeon superintendent can go down and inspect properly. Then the main deck is to be cleaned second time in a day from poop to forecastle. After which the bandheries and topazes have to wait on the quarter deck for inspection. From sundown to twilight, dinner will take place which will be followed by another round of cleaning and disinfecting the main deck and the closets by the topazes. After 8 pm, migrants were all supposed to be in the coolie deck.

As first person accounts of migrants' resistance is sparse throughout the period of indentureship, more so in case of shipboards, the surgeon's testimonies can be a prized source for critical examination of instances of shipboard resistance.

The belief among the officials connected with the scheme was that the intending emigrants were the 'refuse' of the country. Laing writes, 'There is sometimes a large admixture of those who have been failures in their own country and of bad bargains, whom to say the least, magistrates are not averse to getting out of their districts'. The belief that the indentured emigration scheme was an escape valve for grievous offenders persisted throughout the course of the regime. In 1838, J. Shaw, investigating into indentured labour recruitment, reported his belief that heinous offenders escaped justice through migration. Shaw wrote of one migrant embarked for Mauritius 'who looked like a Thug, and who had never been in the habit ... of passing a single day, as an honest or industrious labourer'. In reality, the man was a religious mendicant. Shaw hinted at the suspicion such men aroused, describing him as 'one of the vagabonds and pests to society called Sunyussees (sannyasi), a most profligate and debauched set of men, than who, are not in existence in Hindoostan' (Dickens Committee 1839). Later it was believed that sepoys escaping conviction were signing in as recruits (Carter 1996). In one report of unrest on board a Demerara-bound ship in 1863, the Immigration Agent General of the said colony opined that the migrants involved appeared to have had 'military training' and had probably belonged to mutinous regiments or participated in civil rebellion (Anderson 2009). He did not elaborate on the reasons of his conjecture. Later too, the connection between the revolt and indentured emigration was referred. Clare Anderson had extensively studied the impress of penal procedures in the governance of indentured labour recruitment and trans-shipment (Anderson 2009).

On board the emigrant ship, most of the disturbances recorded started with the issue of food and at times regarding allegations of mistreatment of coolies by the crew, the surgeon or even by the Sirdars (Laing's Handbook).

The Act VIII, 1873, prohibited the use of corporeal punishment against coolies. Laing is vocal against this new stipulation as he thought it would make management on board the ships extremely difficult. He mentions that none of his fellow ship surgeons were happy with the regulations. He thought that to induce 'moral influence' on the 'coolies', some prior 'examples' need to be set. He draws out some accepted maritime retributive practices such as to put the disturbing elements in irons for some days and later bring him in front of the coolies assembled with his face chalked. He prescribes this act of public shaming as retribution, especially when the 'offender' had tried to organize collective bargaining against the surgeon or some other figure of authority. This he recommends as an educative spectacle to induce moral influence.

He lays down some other accepted modes of maritime retribution such as if two men are fighting they are tied together by a dhoti till their anger subsides. Use of bad language to superiors is punished by making them stand with their tongue out. If it is a woman, she can be put to work to grind grams with curry stone and if somebody is caught stealing he is escorted round the deck by the topazes proclaiming him to be a thief. However, for more serious offences the practice was to isolate the purported offender from the rest of the migrants. Laing cynically comments on the Act XXI of 1884 'the rules contain all that is said about discipline, and, as if further to restrict the power of the Surgeon Superintendent before "moral influence"' can be established, it says 'no emigrant shall for any offence be subjected on board to any reduction of the prescribed quantity of food'. His advice in light of the regulations is, 'If the surgeon superintendent is so unfortunate as to have some of the blackguards on board his ship that I have had to deal with, by all means give him the prescribed quantity but let that daily food be bread and water'. He ends the section with a dose of Galenic observation, '(bread and water) judiciously used (is) a wonderful subduer of malapart spirits'.

Resistance and Solidarity on Board: The Jahaji Bhai and the Spectre of the Return Coolie

One particular figure that Laing cautions against is the reindenturing returned emigrant. His particular advice to surgeons in situations of disturbance is, 'look out for some return coolie as the instigator'. The return coolie had been variously sketched by commentators both in India and in the destination locale as the prefect advertisement of the success of the indentured migration scheme. Sanderson Committee commented on the possibility of using the returned emigrant as the recruiting agent as it was believed more trustworthy for the intending recruits to be recruited by someone who had actually had the experience of indenture and had come back as successful.

However, return coolies were miniscule in number and not everybody who had come back were effusive in their praise of the scheme. Among the time expired emigrants who returned to India most can be categorized as paupers. In fact the testimonials of returned emigrants were later used by the nationalists as exposés of the evils of the system (a report on the emigrants repatriated). Thus, the return coolie became a delicate figure for the authorities whose first-hand knowledge into the machinations of the scheme was potent to disrupt the status quo. On shipboard, his presence was anomalous to the received figure of the 'ignorant Indian coolie' who were perfectly unaware about their destination and mores of maritime life (Dickens Committee, Papers of East India Labourers Bill).

The fear of the informed indentured recruit indicates deep insecurities of the scheme. Insecurity about the legislative apparatus which had been built up purportedly to guarantee the scheme does not slide back into a new system of slavery. On land, insecurity against the development of solidarities among the migrants was guaranteed by punitive laws against collective deliberations and fraternization with other labour groups, notably the blacks, by sundry wage cuts against getting out of plantations even if for complaining against work conditions to the police, and at sea it was treated by anticipatory selective vigilance against the informed emigrant. Ship captains and doctors had long deliberated about the pros and cons of employing Lascar or South Asian crews in emigrant ships. Procuring Lascar crew was cheap, and they were considered adept sailors; however officials preferred to employ European crew if available, the reason being, the Lascars 'speak the same language' as the migrants.

We don't find evidence of fraternal solidarities in the equally coercive regime of overseas penal transportation from India. However, in spite of the carceral control on the bodies of the indentured migrants on the shipboard, the development of jahaji solidarity as an effective tie having enduring resonance post-disembarkation in the host locales indicates the vibrant, almost rebellious spirit of socialization engaged in by the docile Indian migrant. The shipboard spaces were powerful contributors to the impulse of the fledgling diasporas.

References

Anderson, Clare. 2000. *Convicts in the Indian Ocean: Transportation from South Asia to Mauritius, 1815–53.* Wiltshire: Macmillan.

Anderson, Clare. 2004. *Legible Bodies: Race, Criminality and Colonialism in South Asia.* Oxford: Berg.

Anderson, Clare. 2009. Convicts and Coolies: Rethinking Indentured Labour in the Nineteenth Century. *Slavery and Abolition: A Journal of Slave and Post-Slave Studies,* 30(1).

Arnold, David. 1993. *Colonizing the Body: State Medicine and Epidemic Disease in Nineteenth-Century India*. Berkeley: University of California Press.

Benedict, Burton. 1961. *Indians in a Plural Society: A Report on Mauritius.* London: Colonial Research Studies No. 34.

Bhana, Surendra. 1991. *Indentured Indian Emigrants to Natal, 1860–1902: A Study Based on Ships' Lists.* New Delhi: Promila and Co.

Carter, Marina. 1994. *Lakshmi's Legacy: The Testimonies of Indian Women in 19th Century Mauritius.* Mauritius: Editions de L'océan Indien.

Carter, Marina. 1996. *Voices from Indenture: Experiences of Indian Migrants in the British Empire*. London: Leicester University Press.

Lal, Brij. 2000. *ChaloJahaji: On a Journey through Indenture in Fiji.* Australian National University and Fiji Museum.

Saha, Panchanan. 1970. *Emigration of Indian Labour, 1834–1900*. Delhi: People's Publishing House.

Shepherd, Verene. 2002. *Maharani's Misery: Narratives of a Passage from India to the Caribbean*. Kingston, Jamaica: University of the West Indies Press.

Shlomowitz, Haines, Brennan. 1996. Maritime Mortality Revisited. *International Journal of Maritime History,* 8.

Tinker, Hugh. 1974. *A New System of Slavery: Export of Indian Labour Overseas*. London: OUP.

Archival Sources

A report on the Emigrants repatriated to India under the Assisted Emigration Scheme from South Africa, By Bhawani Dayal Sanyasi and Banarsidas Chaturvedi, Calcutta, 15 May 1931.

British and Foreign Anti-Slavery Society. *Emigration from India: The Export of Coolies, and Other L, to Mauritius*. London: T. Ward and co., 1842.

Emigration Proceedings of West Bengal State Archives.

——. Regarding quota of women and ways to make good the shortage, Pro. 46, December 1858.

——. Report on the Mortality of Emigrant Coolies on the Voyage to the West Indies in 1855–1857, General Emigration Proceedings, 1859.

——. Regarding reintroduction of platforms for sleeping of emigrants on board ships – Petition of emigrant ship owners and captains, December 1859.

——. Report on mortality and transporting emigrants in ballast, Proceedings 51–58, March 1860.

——. A.C. Nisbet to the Governor General of India, WBSA, Pro. 11, March 1860.

——. Secretary of state's enquiry regarding mortality on board emigrant ships, Pro. 47–49, May 1860.

——. Regarding drinking on board emigrant ships, Proceedings September, October 1860, January, April, 1861. Also various proceedings in 1864, 1865, 1868, 1882, etc.

——. Report of the committee appointed to enquire into the system under which emigration to the West Indies and Mauritius is conducted, General Emigration Proceedings, August 1861.

——. Numbers in emigrant ships should be the same as limit fixed by Indian jail commission for jails, E. C. Bayley, Secretary to Government of India, to Junior Secretary to Government Bengal, October 1867.

——. Extracts from report of Dr Bakewell, in Murdoch, Esq., to Sir F. Rogers, Pro. 432/21 T.W.C. 16 July 1869.

——. Notice to intending emigrants to Demerara or British Guiana, Pro. 20, April 1872.

——. Regarding suicides on passage and in Mauritius, WBSA Pro. 3–6, 1872.

——. Abuse of recruitment of female emigrants, File 75, Proceeding 11–12, August 1878.

Geoghegan, J. Note on Emigration from India, 1873.

Laing, James. Handbook for Surgeons Superintendent of the Coolie Emigration Service in File 21, Colonial Emigration, 1889. (Laing's Handbook) Patrick Manson's Quote and Extracts of the Surgeon Superintendents' Meeting of 11 June 1913, in Deliberations on the Treatment of Ancylostomiasis, Pro. 27–30, B. Nov. 1913.

Mangan, J. (ed.). 1994. *Robert Whyte's 1847 Famine Ship Diary: The Journey of an Irish Coffin Ship.* Cork: Mercier Press.

Memorial to the Right Honourable Joseph Chamberlain by the British Indians in Natal. LSE Selected Papers.

Papers relating to East Indian Labourer's Bill, India Office, 1839.

Parliamentary Papers, 1840, 1841, 1843, 1844.

Report of the Committee on Emigration from India to the Crown Colonies and Protectorates, 1910. Referred to as Sanderson Committee Report.

Swinton, J. and Swinton, E. *Journal of a Voyage with Coolie Emigrants, from Calcutta to Trinidad, by Captain and Mrs Swinton,* ed. by J. Carlile, originally published in 1859, I accessed the digitized version done by Oxford University.

The Englishman and the Civil and Military Gazette, Calcutta. Indian National Library, Kolkata.

4

Religion and Politics in the Diaspora

The Case of Indians in Malaysia

Kishore Kumar Aleti

Introduction

The Indian diaspora is about 25 million, the third largest diaspora after the Chinese and British diasporas. It has spread to more than 200 countries of the world and more prosperous in many developed and developing countries too (www.moia.com). Even though Indian diaspora is prosperous in many countries, they undergo several problems in few countries. For instance, though Malaysia is considered to be one of the multi-ethnic, multi-cultural and pluralistic countries of the world, there are tensions of living among the immigrant communities such as the Chinese and Indians. According to Means (1978), Malaysia is a multi-ethnic society, but has been affected by persistent communal antipathies and intermittent communal violence. To understand why there are tensions of living in Malaysia among these three communities, it may be required to look at the profiles of the three communities and what happened before and after the independence. So, this study makes an enquiry into the contemporary racial conspiracy among these three communities.

Demography of Malaysia

According to the reports of Department of Statistics of Malaysia (2010), the total population of Malaysia was about 28.3 million. Out of this, 91.8 per cent were Malaysian citizens and 8.2 per cent were non-Malays (see Figure 1; www.statistics.gov.my).

Malaysian citizens consist of various ethnic groups. Based on religion, language and culture, three ethnic communities are formed in Malaysia such as the Malays, Chinese and Indians who have played major role either economically or politically. In other words, the identities such as race, religion and language in Malaysia are divided into major ethnic groups on the basis of race, religion and language (Haque 2003). According to Ahmad (2007), Malays or Bumiputera[1] consists of 65.1 per cent, Chinese 26 per cent, Indians 7.7 per cent and others are 1.2 per cent, while non-Malays are about 5.5 per cent (Ahmad 2007: 142). However, according to the reports of Department of Statistics of Malaysia (2010), the Malays are the largest ethnic community comprising 67. 4 per cent, Chinese about 24.6 per cent and Indians consist of 7.7 per cent, while others were 0.7 per cent and non-Malays are about 8.2 per cent (www.statistics.gov.my). However, according to recent reports of Department of Statistics of Malaysia, which released on 12 March 2015, the total population of Malaysia is about 30. 3 million (www.statistics.gov.my). Islam has been the most widely professed religion in Malaysia with the proportion of 61.3 per cent, Christianity 9.2 per cent, Hinduism 6.3 per cent and Buddhism about 19.8 per cent.

Figure 1
Population of Malaysia

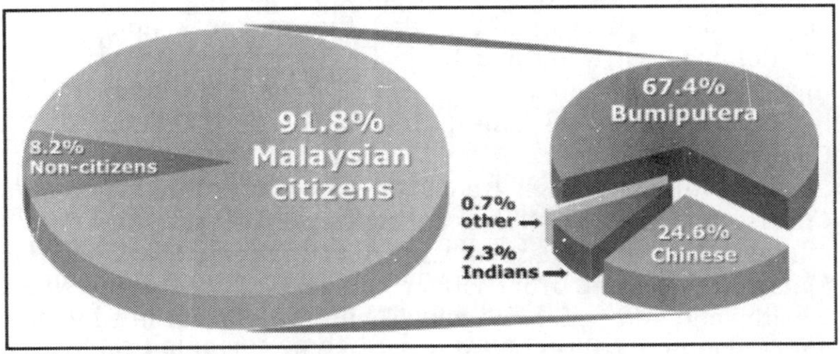

Source: http://charleshector.blogspot.in/2014/03/malaysian-statistics-population.html

The Malays are the locals and the first largest ethnic community in Malaysia. They are also known as the Bumiputera (sons of soil). Majority of Malays are Muslims in Malaysia. Being the sons of soil, majority of Malays predominantly relied on cultivation of rice, which was common for all the village residents, before independence. They lived in small communities, due to which their social contacts were limited to the rural areas and do not have exposure of development that took place in the cities or towns by the British. The Malays were devotees of either Hinduism or Buddhism before the emergence of Islam in the fourteenth and fifteenth centuries in Malacca. Islam in Malaysia started in the early fifteenth century, and largely it was introduced through the ruling elites and the royal courts who took leading role in adopting it (Means 1978: 385). Specific definition about Malays by the constitution of Malaysia developed since independence that the Malays are the followers of Islam, habitually spoke Malaya language and confirms to Malaya customs (Haque 2003). The Malays are the largest ethnic community by and large and more dominant in the country's politics. They speak Malaya language and practice Malaya culture (Ahmad 2007). Being a largest and dominant ethnic community, they got more chances to get power or opportunities in politics, economy and education, which led to development of Malaya community in the post-independence times (www.slideshare.net).

The Chinese are the second largest ethnic community in Malaysia. They are less than one-third of population and they are largely adherents of Buddhism and Taoism, speak Hokkain and are dominant in trade and business. They are concentrated in towns and urban areas, for them it is easy to conduct their business and to access education (Ahmad 2007; Othman 2013). Chinese has 600 years of long association with Malaysia from medieval times through trade and commerce. But majority of Chinese imported to Malaya during the British rule to work on mining mostly and at a small scale in plantations. The Chinese in Malaysia developed from labour category to the businessmen, wealthy and influential category. Their development in education and economy has been dominant compared to other immigrant ethnic groups such as Indians in Malaysia over a period of time (www.slideshare.net). The Chinese mostly embrace a quite diverse mixture of Taoism, Buddhism, ancestor worship and also included a small number of Christianity. However, most of the Chinese in Malaysia are deeply infused with Taoism, Confucianism and animistic beliefs (Ahmad 2007).

Even though Chinese had contacts with Malaysia through trade and commerce, large-scale emigration was taken place during the British rule in Malaya. Chinese in Malaya can be seen in two categories such as entrepreneurs of tin mining and labour in tin mining industry. The British *laissez faire* policy regarding labour and capital created a massive immigration of Chinese population in Malaysia during the last quarter of the nineteenth century and the first quarter of the twentieth century. The Chinese population, for instance, which was 96,000 in 1860 in the Straits Settlements increased to 6,93,000 in 1911 and further in 1913 about 12,85,000, which shows the great volume of Chinese community in Malaysia.

The Chinese enterprisers who were interested in tin as a trading commodity supplied not only capital, but also Chinese immigrant labourers to work in the mines. The Chinese became dominant in tin industry by 1920s and by 1931 they were diversified themselves with a large majority, who had started to get employment in urban petty bourgeois occupation rather than in mining and agriculture (Jain 1989). Chinese over a period of time gave a completion to the European enterprisers in tin industry of Malaysia. In 1929, while European owned mines produced 61 per cent, the Chinese owned 31 per cent. Moreover, the labour-force in mining sector remained predominantly Chinese.

The Indian diaspora or Malaysian Indians in Malaysia are the third largest ethnic community. According to reports of the High Level Committee on Indian Diaspora (HLC 2001), the total population of Malaysia was 2,28,90,000. Of this, 16,00,000 were PIOs and 15,000 were NRIs of Indian ethnic community in Malaysia (www.moia.com). But according to Indiansdiaspora.com (2006), the total population of Malaysia was 2,43,85,858. Indian emigration to Malaysia was predominantly a large-scale emigration since colonial times, even though India had migration relations with Malacca and Southeast Asia way back to the ancient and medieval times. As per the latest reports of the Ministry of Overseas and Indian Affairs (2015), the Indian Diaspora in Malaysia is about 21,50,000. While the PIOs constitute of 20,00,000, the NRIs are about 1,50,000 (www.moia.com).

Historical Background of Indian Diaspora

In the ancient times, India's contacts with Southeast Asia took place through barter system followed by trade. Other reasons to have contacts with Southeast Asia were propagation of religion such as Buddhism and Jainism (Kadekar 2005). Buddhism was a philosophy or way of life which was started by Gautama Buddha – who was the son of an Indian king in the ancient times, who got enlightenment after a rigorous yoga for about 49 days. His ideas were developed as a way of life then developed as philosophy at last. Over a period of time Jainism lost its attraction in people of Southeast Asia due to its extreme hard practices. But Buddhism gradually started to attract a lot of people of Southeast Asian countries and people of China also. Over a period time, Buddhism got faith of all the people of Southeast Asia. Buddhism, which started in the ancient times, continued to be a religion in the Southeast Asian countries up to the emergence of Islam in the Southeast countries such as Malaysia and Thailand in the fourteenth and fifteenth centuries (Means 1978). Certain ritual and ceremonial activates still in Malays are part of Buddhism either by some of the Chinese and Malays. However, Islam has been a dominant religion in Malacca since fifteenth century that was transported through Indian sailors.

India had contacts with Malaysia from ancient times to the medieval times. Historical evidences suggest that India had influenced colonies and kingdoms in Southeast Asia; one of the most remarkable empires was Sri Vijaya Empire in the fifteenth century AD in Indonesia (Wheatley 1961). But before sixteenth century, it was very small in number and limited. In spite of the small scale in volume, India became not only a source for migration but also for the transmission of ideals, new products and technologies (Kaur 2007: 156). Migration of Indians to the Southeast Asia largely took place for trade and commerce. Malacca stood as trade place for Indians and Chinese, which later changed to Malaya, and now it is called Malaysia. Indian business with Southeast Asia led to the predominance of Indian traders in South Asia both for trade and business. The economic activities between India and Southeast Asia either for trade or for exchange of goods and services created a history of manufacturing and sophisticated commerce (www.moia.com). For instance, Gujaratis and Chulia merchants had been trading Indian textile with Southeast Asia in exchange for rice and teak from Burma, pepper, tin and spices from Western Indonesia and Malaysia (Kaur 2007). These economic efforts attracted some of the Indian business communities such as Gujaratis and Chulia merchants in the early years of British period in the Southeast Asian countries. Economic efforts of India with Southeast Asian countries such as Burma, Thailand and Malaysia led to construction of ports on the shores of Bay of Bengal, which later got attraction to develop more with technology. These port cities were developed more with the availability of innovation and technology introduced by British,[2] after they annexed Indian subcontinent and Southeast Asian countries.

Large scale of Indian emigration to Malaya started during the nineteenth and early twentieth centuries. There were three streams of Indian emigration that took place during the British rule in Malaya. The first stream of Indian emigration to Malaya was plantation workers (Kaur 2007). This stream of Indian emigration to Malaya was a large scale consisted of contract labour or plantation workers (indentured or Kangani labour). Even though Indian labour to Malaya in the beginning started under the indentured system,[3] later it shifted to Kangani system, under which millions of Indian labour were transported to work on the plantations. Majority of Indian workers who arrived in Malaya between 1840 and 1910 were recruited under indentured system, estimated to be around 2,50,000 (Jain 1999). While the vast majority of this workforce were of South Indian origin and were largely Hindu, at a small scale few hundreds were from Bengal (Sandhu 1969). According to Jain (1984), between 1865 and 1938, about 11,86,717 Indian immigrants arrived to Malaya under Kangani recruitment. Indian indentured labourers largely consist of adult males aged between 15 and 45 (Arasaratnam 1970). The vast majority were agricultural workers and rural wage earners, who had been disadvantaged or displaced by structural economic changes such as land reforms introduced by the British rule in India. Women and children rarely constituted more than 20 per cent and 10 per cent respectively of this migration flows (Sandhu 1969). The majority of Tamil agricultural labourers who migrated to Malaya belong to the villages of Tanjore and Tinnevelly (Basu 2004). Due to the harsh treatments of Indian indentured labourers under the British rule in Malaya, the indentured system was supposed to be cancelled or replaced with other systems. Indentured system was replaced later by Kangani recruitment which was more flexible and better equipped to meet the immediate requirement of the plantation industry (Belle 2008; Parmer 1960). Unlike indentured migration, recruitment of Kangani labour proved responsive to actual labour demand in Malaya (Jain 1984). A Kangani is a 'field man' or 'coolie of standing', charged with the task of recruiting labour to work on estates; moreover he was supposed to supervise those who he had engaged in work (Belle 2008).

The abolition of slavery in the British, French and Dutch colonies in 1834, 1846 and 1873 respectively led to severe shortage of labour to work in sugar, tea, coffee, cocoa, and rice and rubber plantations, which resulted in search of labour from Indian subcontinent and Mainland China as an alternative source of labour to work in the above-mentioned areas (www.moia.com). Millions of Indian labourers were transported to Malaysia under Kangani and mastery systems. Under Kangani system, between 1840 and 1942, 1.7 million Indian labour were recruited to work in Malaysia (Kaur 2007: 53). By the end of Kangani system in Malaya, around 2 million Indians were transported to Malaysia. Why many Indians were recruited to Malaya as Kangani labourers? The Kangani labour system was immensely profitable to the planters, and huge demand was created for Indians to recruit Kangani labour as indentured system, but it was abolished due to its lapses. Under Kangani system of recruitment, Indians were recruited about 20,000 per annum between 1880 and 1904. Further in the boom state, recruitment of Indians increased from 20,000 per annum to 90,000 between 1911 and 1930 (Jain 1989).

The second stream of Indian emigration to Malaya was auxiliaries, which consisted of both North and South Indians, though North Indians were more in number. The North Indians predominantly consisted of Sikhs, while South Indians were Malayalis and Jaffna Tamils. The North Indians were mainly recruited for the police force and security services, while Malayalis and Jaffna Tamils were recruited in clerical and subordinate civil services occupations (Kaur 2007). The Sikhs initially recruited as policemen in the 'Straits Settlement'[4] in the 1880s, later they were recruited as a paramilitary force, security guard, watchmen and caretakers by the colonial authorities and the private sectors.

The third stream of Indian migration to Malaya comprised merchants or commercial migrants such as Chettiars, a money lending group from South India, and Chilia and Gujaratis from North India. This pattern of Indian emigration to Malaysia was small in number and they were 'free' or 'passage' migrants, which means they travel on their own expenses (www.moia.com). These migrants were widespread and had international trade relations through Southeast Asia. This class of Indian migrants in Malaya is considered to be second major urban Indian group after English-educated Malayalis and Tamils who were recruited as juniors or subordinate administrative staffs, clerical and technical staffs in the colonial administration (Kaur 2007). Prakash C. Jain (1989) divides the entire Indian emigration in Malaysia into two streams such as labour migrants and non-labour migrants. While the labour migrants arrived under the Kangani system to Malaysia, non-labours include professionals and clericals, salesmen, pedlars, petty entrepreneurs, shopkeepers and vendors. Until 1957, the non-labour Indian migrants constituted one-third of the total immigrants into Malaysia (Jain 1989).

According to the Federation of Malaya Census Report (1957) while approximately 4 million Indian labour entered Malaya, 2.8 million left between 1860 and 1957. Around 1.2 million net migrations might be reduced due to diseases, snake bites, exhaustion and malnutrition (Belle 2008: 52). In other sense, between 1886 and 1957, out of a total population of about 42,50,000 gross Indian emigrations to Malaya, nearly 7,50,000 were estimated to have died out of unhygienic conditions, without proper sanitation and so on (Basu 2004: 167). By 1940, Indians were made up to 14 per cent of Malays population, and by the time Malaysia got independence in 1957, the number of Indian diaspora was 8,58,618, of this 62.1 per cent was local born (Brij, V. Lal 2006; Belle 2008: 52). But by 2000, it reduced to 7.7 per cent, which is represented to the total Malaysian population of 21.89 million. Of the total Indian population of Malaysia, approximately nine-tenths of Indians accounted for South Indian origin, while one-tenth were from North Indians (Kaur 2007: 156). In Malaysia, Tamils consist of 80 per cent of Indian community, while remaining are from Andhra Pradesh, Kerala,

West Bengal, Punjab, Sindhi and Gujarat (www.moia.com). But for Lahiri (2008), nearly 85 per cent of Indian Malaysians are Tamils, and 60 per cent of them are the descendants of plantations workers (Lahiri 2008: 4). Majority of Indian community was engaged in rubber and palm plantations, while a small section was involved in services such as police, railway, food business, legal and medical professions. They are settled in Penang state in North Malaysia, Perak in central Malaysia and rest in Kuala Lampur (www.moia.com). Of the total population of Indian origin in Malaysia, 80 per cent are Hindus, 15 per cent are Muslims and rest of them is Christians and Sikhs (Lahiri 2008: 4).

Of the total population of Malaysian Indian community today, around 60 per cent belongs to the descendants of the plantation workers who were recruited under British rule in Malaya. While most of the plantation workers to Malaya were Tamils, very few were others. To better understand the possible development of Indian plantation working class in Malaysia, it may require to compare them with same category of those who were recruited in other countries with same conditions. While studying about Indian workers in Malaysia and Trinidad and Tobago, Ravindra Kumar Jain explored some interesting findings. These findings will help to understand why Indian plantation workers are not developed well compared to plantation workers in Trinidad. While Indians in Malaysia constitute less than 10 per cent, Indian plantation workers in Trinidad comprise half of the total population of Trinidad and Tobago. Most of the Indian workers on plantation were recruited under Kangani system, under which there was no freedom for the workers (Jain 1989: 61). While some of the Indian plantation workers in Trinidad became peasants, in Malaysia Indians became the working class, which hinder the access to get a piece of land, which further gives no chances to cultivate or start a small business. Compared to the plantation workers in Malaysia, there was more number of Indian plantation workers who started their own business in Trinidad and Tobago. On the whole, the socio-economic and political conditions of these two countries also have significant landmarks of development or under-development of the Indian community (Jain 1989).

In Malaysia, Indian community consists of both north and South Indians. From South India, Tamilians are of significant number, while Telugus, Malayalis, North Indians such as Gujaratis and Punjabis constitute very small in number. Representation of Indian presence in Malaysia can be seen in various domains such as socio-cultural spears, economic and political spears. Out of these three, social representation through cultural festivals has been a significant event in the lives of Indian community in Malaysia compared to other domains. Malaysian Indians celebrate broadly regional-based festivals such as the Holi, Deepavali and Navaratri are the major festivals of North India, while Shivaratri and Thaipusam[5] or Thaipukam are the South Indian celebrations. Of the above-mentioned festivals, Deepavali[6] is a national holiday in Malaysia, whereas big Tamil festivals such as Thaipusam is still not a national holiday, even though there has been continues appeal from the Tamil community for the last 30 years (Guan 2001).

Between these two festivals, Thaipusam is an attractive ritual event to attract devotees from all parts of Malaysia. According to Batu Caves temple estimations, there were about 8,00,000 devotees who attended the Thaipusam festival at the temple in the year 1987 (Lee 1999: 318).

Thaipusam is a three-day festival. The first day of this Thaipusam festival starts from the Sri Maha Mariamman[7] temple with a significant event of visesha puja performance. This puja comprises a specific abisekam or ceremonial bathing of the Murugan image with nine items namely water, milk, coconut juice, ghee, honey, ashes, sandalwood, paste, rose water and panchamitram (a fruit dish made from mango, banana, grapes, and oranges).

This ritual event is generally performed by a Brahmin priest who recites the *abisekam mantra* as he washes the images. This abisekam is open to public viewing. After getting ready and have done some ritual proceedings of the Murugan image at Sri Maha Mariamman temple, it starts its journey to Batu Caves temple by chariot in the early morning. This journey covers all the shops of Indian merchants in the capital city of Malaysia. On the way to Batu Caves, the chariot that carries the image of Murugan stops at many shops, which are decorated with banana leaves on the two sides of shop doors. This is to signify that the shops are owned by Hindus who wish to receive blessings by the sight of the image of Murugan (darsan).

Day two starts from the Batu Caves, where many penitents gather at the Batu Caves River to wash themselves in preparation for *kavati* carrying. Kavati carrying is the primary or significant event of this festival.

Carrying *kavati* is performed by both the males and female penitents. While male penitents wear only waist cloth in the three colours such as white, yellow and red, female penitents are dressed in ethnic wears such as sarees and Punjabi suits. While middle-aged women appear with sarees, young women and girls dressed in Punjabi suits. Most of young female devotes wear yellow colour Punjabi suits, while middle aged and more aged female devotes wear sarees. These sarees can be in three colours mainly red, yellow and saffron. Sometimes women come wearing green colour sarees too. But green sarees are very less compared to other three colours. Most of the female penitents and devotees bring milk in steel vessels to the god Murugan.

At least ten types of *kavati* are observed in the processing of penitents to the shrine such as *Pal kavati,* the most common one which offers milk, while *Vel kavati* which is a short needle in the shape of a lance pierced through the penitents tongue. These two are frequently practiced by women and boys. Others are *Puspam kavati* which will be in the shape of temple tower and is carried to offer to Ganesha. *Cantanam kavati* is made of sandalwood paste in the shape of a gopuram. Some kavatis are also carried by hand that includes *Agni kavati* or pot of fire placed on top of veppilai leaves, *Pannir kavati* or pots of jasmine fragranced water. *Agri kavati* is habitually carried as an offering for Sakti karumpu kavati is carried by married couples whose wish for a child has been granted (Lee 1999).

Before independence of Malaysia, the Malaysian Indian community was about 14 per cent of the total population of Malaysia, but after independence, it gradually started to reduce the number of Indians in Malaysia due to various reasons (Kaur 2007: 156). There are various reasons for decline of Indian community in Malaysia. All those problems can be discussed at various levels. Most of the problems for the non-Malays such as Indian and Chinese are created by the Malaysian government's preferential policies only, which are designed for the development of the Malays while ignoring the immigrant communities Indian and Chinese.

Problems of Indian Community in Malaysia

The Indian diaspora, which started to immigrate to Malaysia since British rule in Malaysia, reached to two million populations by the 1950s. But after independence due to Malaysian government's policies towards public, there were many problems either to live happily or to receive the fruits of development of modern Malaysia. Policies for the development of Malaysia after independence became more on ethnic based, which led to unhappiness of immigrant communities such as Indians and Chinese. While compared to the Chinese, Indians are more vulnerable. They are the third largest ethnic community and are at the bottom of development. It is observed that many of the reasons of conflict that happen in Malaysia represent a complex nature of various dimensions of ethnicity that include race, religion and language (Haque 2003).

The basic foundations of the development of Malays in Malaysia can be seen at two phases: one is through constitution of Malaysia, which provided special provisions, and the other is New Economic Policy (NEP), which provided Malaya special rights or gave more priority to Malays than the other ethnic communities in Malaysia. The preferential policies either by constitution or NEP led to get many benefits for Malays in politics, administration, business, education and on religion too (Haque 2003: 248).

Malaysia's Preferential Policies in Business

Since independence Malaysian Government gave priority to Malays in development of business activities. It adopted Malaya preferential policy in business, by framing certain quotas of proportion of business and trade licenses for Malays (Government of Malaysia 1977). These special provisions resulted Malays to get licenses in business and gave autonomy on sectors such as construction, mining, transport timber industry and so on (Crouch 2001). These preferential policies continued after 1970s under the NEP. According to the first Outline Perspective Plan (1971–1990), Malays ownership and their participation in industry and commercial activities are scheduled to be 30 per cent by 1990s. Similar agenda was continued in the second and third perspective plans to develop the Malays commercial and industrial sectors (Haque 2003). Further to strengthen the Malays, the government introduced the Industrial Coordination Act of 1975, under which any non-Malay firms with capital and reserves funds worth more than M$2,50,000 and more than 25 employers must provide at least 30 per cent of Bumiputera equity ownership or participation to get business licenses approved or renewed (Lee 2000). On the whole, this kind of ethnic-based policies not only led to Malays as dominant ethnic community on various sectors of economy, but also strengthened the ideas of Bumiputera, which is primarily aimed to rectify the historical exclusion of Malays from business sectors (Haque 2003).

Preferential Policies in Education

Malaysian government or authority practiced discriminatory practices in education too. The Education Act of 1971 recommended that all the Chinese secondary schools should convert to English secondary schools, out of force or pressure 54 out of 71 Chinese secondary schools were converted to English secondary schools, while 17 opted to be independent (PGRM 2001). Further it tried to change into Malaya schools – during the 1970s and 1980s the government gradually cautioned those Chinese schools to either convert to Malaya schools to become a part of national education system or remain as private schools. The schools that are not converted to Malaya schools will not get any benefits from government. On the whole, the Malaysian National System of Education divided four major education streams such as Malays, Chinese, Tamils and English with Malaya as the medium of instruction (Means 1986). All these policies of government of Malaysia remind that how government played a significant role in reinforcing the special rights or preferential policies for the majority of Malays in the domain of education and language (Haque 2003).

Ethnic preferential policies in education and employment have been made a considerable progress to Malaya in Malaysia. Public universities mostly admit Malays and very few the non-Malays, due to which there was a crux of complaints that many Chinese and Indian students were unable to continue their education in universities after their high school (Othman 2013). As a result, many students of families of lower income level are moving to job market with their preliminary educational qualifications. For instance, the enrolment of students in the University of Malaya between 1964 and 1970 was increased from

21 to 40 per cent to Malays, while it reduced from 60 to 49 per cent for Chinese and 19 to 11 per cent for Indians (Mah 1985. 258). Similarly between 1970 and 1985, the proportion of Malaya students increased from 40 to 63 per cent on the whole, while it was reduced from 49 to 30 per cent for Chinese and 15 to 11 for Indians. On the whole, by 1991, the total enrolment for Malays increased to 72.7 per cent while dropped to 27.3 per cent for non-Malays that include both Chinese and Indians (Haque 2003: 252).

Preferential Policies in Religious Matters

Malaysian government made preferential policies in the domain of religion that affect the cultural practices of the ethnic communities in Malaysia. In Malaysia, Malays are the largest ethnic community, and 100 per cent are followers of Islam. Article 11 of the constitution of Malaysia provides freedom for all religious practices by various groups. But the same constitution through its Article 3(1) clearly defined that Islam as the official religion of the country. However, it does not prescribe that Islamic state and other ethnic communities such as Buddhist, Christian, Hindus and Sikh communities are free to practice their respective religions (Haque 2003). The government in Malaysia has been accused for its active involvement in pursuing the Islamization process through various Islamic programs, institutions and provisions. For instance, the followers of Islam in general enjoy certain preferential treatment in religious matters compared to others. Islam in Malaysia encourages others to convert to Islam, but it discourages the Muslim to convert to other religions. If any Malaya Muslim converts to other religion or if any individual preaches any religion among the Muslim areas, such people may have to face certain consequences (Haque 2003).

Other efforts of government in Malaysia for the development of Muslims are establishment of Islamic Bank and International Islamic University, expansion of Sharia courts and religious schools and allocation of space for building of mosques compared to the worship places for other religions (Haque 2003). All these avenues are made for the expansion of Islam and to strengthen Muslims in Malaysia. However, with the more preferences of government in preservation of Islam, the two identities such as Islam and Malays have increasingly became intertwined (Derichs 1999). Moreover in the religious aspects of Malays and non-Malays, the government has shown a significant role in favour for the religious and cultural belief of Malays (Haque 2003).

Two prominent controversial issues of Indian community in Malaysia are Shamala and Moorthy cases. While the first was in 2003 and other one was in 2005, where in the first case husband of Shamala Sathiyaseelan gained custody of his two children and had converted to Islam without informing his Hindu wife. In the second case, Moorthy Mariam whose body was buried with Muslim rites by the Kuala Lumpur religious authority despite his wife's claim that her husband was a practicing Hindu until his death (Lahiri 2008). Both of these issues were brought for justice, but did not receive expected justice from the authority of Malaysia. On the whole, the preferential policies of Malaysian government not only aimed to provide benefits to Malays from religious aspects but also created problems to other ethnic communities such as Indians and Chinese and Christians and others who are not Muslim or not converted to Islam.

At first, the Malaysian government tried to highlight that the causes for the latent ethnic hostilities that took place in Malaysia as a product of relative economic deprivation of the indigenous Malays while compared with immigrant communities such as the Chinese, Indians and others, who tend to dominate the modern sectors of the economy (Means 1978). The answer for this statement can be seen from Anbalakan. According to Anbalakan (2003), there may be some truth in that argument, but to understand the riot was due to frustration of economically deprived Malays is not at all reasonable. Moreover he also rejected the other statement that Malay government completely neglected to take measure to overcome the economic backwardness of the Malaya community, which led for the racial riot. He also pointed out that Malay's complain about backwardness of Malaya are not new, which was there in the pre-independence and post-independence.

Economically and socially, the Indians were no better than the Malays, and since independence, none of the government's economic plans addressed the economic backwardness of Indians in Malaysia (Anbalakan 2003). For instance, when the estates were fragmented and sold in 1950s, Indian labour lost their jobs, but government did not come up with any plan to help them. Similarly between 1956 and 1967, around 3,24,931 acres of estates were fragmented and sold out, which led to 28,363 labour lost their jobs, majority of whom were Indians (Anbalakan 2003). The displaced Indians were unable to find alternative jobs as they did not possess any other necessary skills. As a result, the unemployment rate among the Indians in 1967 was about 12.3 per cent, which was highest for that time (Anbalakan 2003).

Conclusion

The concept of racial tensions among the ethnic communities in Malaysia brings about two sides of opinions. On the one hand, a group of scholars point out that Malaysia is a multi-ethnic, multi-religious and multi-cultural country, where plurality is maintained and opportunities are created for the development of Malays irrespective of races. But this has become an ambiguous notion for the immigrant communities of Chinese and Indians, who experienced the preferential policies and discriminatory practices of Malaya where priority is always given to Malays only in development. Unless there is a proper policy for ethnic minorities such as the Indian community, it may lose its identity by less participations in all the avenues of development to survive. When there is problem for the survival, it should be rectified by proper measures, unless it reduces its identity and form from the existing position to less in representation. To eradicate such ethnic conflicts, identification of person based on one's culture, language and race have to be eliminated.

Religious and ethnic tolerance is required to maintain, without which the common relationship between Malaysians and non-Malaysians will complicate the effect in building a harmonious life in Malaysia. To annihilate ethnic conflict in Malaysia, non-communal attitude and universal values are needed to be cultivated in the minds of Malays towards the non-Malays or other ethnic communities and religions. Moreover that attitude has to transform from the older generations to younger generations, because they become instruments for either conflict or peace that happens in Malaysia due to the socio-economic and political consequences. Unless there is change in the attitude of Malaysia towards the Indians, the profile of Indian community will not change from its problematic position to the prosperous position.

Notes

1. Refer to the most of Malays and indigenous of East Malaysians (www.architecture.com).
2. The establishment of a British port in Penang in 1786 encouraged the migration of Indian labour to Malaya. For the requirement of British, about twenty-five artificers were landed to Penang in 1787. Since 1790s, there was a small-scale migration from Tamil Nadu to Malaya. However, about 1,000 were immigrated to Malaya, as shopkeepers and coolies. Most of them were sojourners who after earning a few dollars usually return back to their homes (Basu 2004).
3. Indentured was a contract by which the emigrant was bound to work for a given employer for three to five years, performing the tasks assigned to him for a specified wage. At the end of the contract, the immigrant was free to re-indenture or to work elsewhere in the colony, after ten years he was entitled to a subsidized return passage (Jain 1989).
4. The 'Straits Settlements' was a British colony which comprises Singapore, Penang and Malacca.
5. Thaipusam is currently a regional holiday in the states of Johor, Negri, Sembilan, Perak, Penang and Selangor (Guan 2001). Thaipusam is a Hindu celebration of devotion, which happens on the full moon in the Tamil month of Thai. It's nothing but giving thanks to Muruga, the son of Shiva.
6. Deepavali or Diwali has got national holiday position in Malaysia when Malaysian Indian Congress (MIC) was with North Indian leadership. In South India, it is known as Deepavalim while it is known as Diwali in North India.
7. The construction of this Hindu temple in Malaysia began in 1874. This was founded by the Tamil immigrants who arrived in Malaya as contract labourers to build the railways and roads or work in the rubber plantation (www.kuala-lumpur.ws). But this was opened to the public 1920 onwards (www.wonderfulmalaysia.com). Significant renovation was taken place in 1968 with the construction of temple tower, which is about 75 feet tall.

References

A paper presented at the International Seminar on Poverty and Sustainable Development, 22–23 November 2001 organied by Université MonParis, France. (Fully funded by UNESCO) Sandhu, Kernial Singh. 1969. *Indians in Malaya: Some Aspects of their*

Immigration and Settlement (1786-1957). London: Cambridge University Press.

Ahmad, Z. 2007. Multiculturalism and Religio-Ethnic Plurality: The Malaysian Experience. *Culture and Religion*, 8(2), 139–153.

Anbalakan, K. 2003. The New Economic Policy and Further Marginalization of the Indians. *Kajian Malaysia,* XXI (1–2), 379–398.

Arasaratnam. S. 1970. *Indian in Malaysia and Singapore*. London: Oxford University Press.

Basu, R. 2004. Search for Pastures: Tamil Migration to Malayan Plantations in the 19th and Early 20th Centuries. In Ghosh, L. and Chatterjee, R. (eds), *Indian Diaspora in Asia Pacific Region: Culture, People, and Interaction*. Jaipur: Rawat Publications.

Belle, C.V. 2008. Forgotten Malaysians? Indians and Malaysian Society. In Raguram, P. et al. (eds), *Tracing an Indian Diaspora: Contexts, Memories and Representations:* Rawat Publications.

Derichs, C. 1999. Nation Building in Malaysia under Conditions of Globalization.

Guan, Yeoh Seng. 2001, 'Producing locality: Space, Houses and Public Culture in a Hindu Festival in Malaysia', *Contributions to Indian Sociology,* 35(1), 33–64.

Government of Malaysia. 1977. *The Federal Constitution*. Kuala Lumpur, Malaysia. Government Printer.

Haque, M.S. 2003. The Role of the State in Managing Ethnic Tensions in Malaysia: A Critical Discourse. *American Behavioral Scientist*, 47(3), 240–266.

High Level Committee on Indian Diaspora (HLC). 2001. The High Level Committee on Indian Diaspora. New Delhi: Ministry of External Affairs.

Jain, P.C. 1989. *Racial Discrimination against Overseas Indians: A Class Analysis*. Concept Publishing Company.

Jain, R.K. 1984. South India Indentured Labour in Malaya 1840–1920: Asylum, Stability and Innovation. In K. Saunders (ed.), *Indentured labour in the British Empire* 1834–1920. London: Croom Helm, 158–182.

Jain, R.K. 1989. Race Relations, Ethnicity, Class and Culture: A Comparison of Indians in Trinidad and Malaysia. *Sociological bulletin*, 38(1).

Jain, R.K. 1999. Culture and Economy: Tamils on the plantation frontier in Malaysia revisited 1998–1999.

Kadekar, L.K. 2005. *Global Indian Diaspora: An Overview*, Research Monograph.

Kaur, Amarjit. 2007. Malaysia. In Brij V. Lal, Peter Reeves and Rajesh Rai (eds), *The Encyclopedia of Indian Diaspora*. New Delhi: Oxford University Press, 156–167.

Lal, Brij. V. 2006. *Encyclopedia of Indian Diaspora*. Delhi: Oxford University Press.

Lahiri, D. 2008. Malaysian Indian Community: Victim of Bumiputera Policy. www.orfonline.org, February 2008.

Lee, H.A. 1999. The Barisan Nasional: Paternalism and Patriotism.

Lee, H.G. 2000. *Ethnic Relations in Peninsular Malaysia: The Cultural and Economic Dimensions*. Singapore: Institute of Southeast Asian Studies.

Mah, H.L. 1985. Affirmative action, ethnicity and integration: the case of Malaysia. *Ethnic and Racial Studies,* 8(2), 250–276.

Means, P.G. 1978. Public Policy towards Religion in Malaysia. *Pacific Affairs,* 51(3), 384–405.

Ministry of Indian Overseas Affairs (MOIA). 2015. http://www.moia.gov.in /services.aspx?mainid=17

Othman, N. 2013. Three Cultures and a Variety of Religions: The Quest for Malaysian Identity. *Journal of Post-colonial Cultures and Societies,* 4(3), 114–131.

Parmer, J. Norman. 1960. *Colonial Labor Policy and Administration: A History of Labor in the Rubber Plantation Industry in Malaya 1910–1941.* New York: J.J. Augustin Inc.

Parti Gerakan Rakyat Malaysia. (PGRM). 2001. Dong Jiao Zong vs. the Government on Chinese Education: The Historical Background. Retrieved from www. gerakan.org.my/Current/vs002.html.

Wheatley, P. 1961. The Golden Chersonese. *Transaction and Papers* (Institute of British Geographers), No. 21, 1995, 61–78.

5

Transnationality

Enabling Individual Capabilities, Amplifying Diasporic Linkages and Redefining Policy

Sridhar Bhagavatula

Introduction

It's been more than two decades that privatization, liberalization and globalization[1] got transformed to reality, impacting the human relations – positive[2] as well as negative.[3] The earlier phases of globalization(s) were different in terms of approach, magnitude and reach.

I would like to point out at least three interrelated features of the current phase of 'globalization'. First, the advancements in information and communication technologies led to creation of various platforms, which facilitate people-to-people connection through the communications and linkages across the sovereign nation state borders. The social network websites such as Facebook, Twitter, LinkedIn and so on are connecting people across borders, creating groups of the 'like-minded', creating extreme awareness of occurrences of social 'goods' and 'evils' and understanding different cultural artefacts. Second, the gradual movement of the 'thought process' towards cosmopolitanism, leading to general understanding of 'what is good' and 'what is bad' at a global level. Currently there are number of international instruments that are binding on the sovereign nation states. The mixing of cultures are becoming popular and the education curriculums pertain to enhancing global knowledge systems and global production requirements. Third, movement across borders is becoming cheaper and is helping more number of people to travel across nations for various purposes.[4] The immigration policies of the migrant-receiving countries are lesser stringent due to economic and demographic equations. We have reached to that stage of globalization where the voluntary migrations are the order of the day and the sovereign nations are not considering it as a negative trend. On the contrary, many of the countries are facilitating such movements. The population-rich countries are speculating better deal for its people and the population-poor advanced countries are getting access to global labour markets. In fact, the segmentation of labour markets in richer countries is creating increased demand for migrant workers there. The positive trend is that there is an interface between the 'excess' and 'scarcity' at global level! All the above three interrelated features take us to the cluster of concepts in transnationalism.

The challenge here is whether the external populations in labour-receiving countries are seen as persons who possess, what John Rawls calls, 'social primary goods' covering – liberty and opportunity, income and wealth, and the basis of self-respect.[5] But, if we make an analysis of the migration policies of the population-receiving countries, it can be said that the external populations are viewed, at least initially, as 'production assistants'[6] vis-à-vis 'socio-economic contributors'[7] to their growth and development. However, I would argue that the migration policies of the host countries must focus on persons' capabilities to retain an alien citizenship and must not focus only on the basic economic functioning of a person.

Over a period of time, the number of people settling in the destination countries and have not returned to their home countries were on rise, enabling the destination countries to rethink their perception of external populations as significant 'socio-economic contributors' vis-à-vis 'production assistants'. This would give the immigrants required space in the local socio-political conceptions of equality and justice.

More importantly, the home countries, whose nationals have extensive presence in various host countries, are taking steps to strengthen their diasporic links. It is perceived that greater transnational linkages by the diaspora would enhance greater resources to the home country, adding to the strengths of the 'source' economy.

A larger role for the skilled and highly skilled immigrants is perceived in the current global labour market. Taking Indian emigration as an example, Khadria (2007) points out that within a short span of time (1990–2000), there has been a shift in the perception about the highly educated or skilled professional; 'from persons supposedly "draining" India of its knowledge wealth and human resources, to now being seen as "angels", that is, perfect transnational "global citizens".' This shift in the perception of professional migrants leaving India (for that matter most of the 'developing sending countries'), however, has taken place in phases – from the 'brain drain' of the 1960s and 1970s to the 'brain bank' of the 1980s and 1990s, and subsequently to the idea of 'brain gain' in the twenty-first century. The perceived benefits to the 'developing sending countries' that supposedly derive from the migration of its people may be classified as stereotypes that involve: the return migration of workers with enhanced skills from the developed host countries to their home countries, remittances and the transfer of technology (Khadria 1999).

These global trends, processes and migratory patterns have its impact on the socio-political concepts. In the scenario of greater people to people interactions and transnational linkages, the socio-political concepts of sovereignty, citizenship, justice and human rights have undergone major changes and are been redefined in the global context, which is broadly discussed in the 'transnationalism' literature.

In this chapter, I will provide a detailed analysis of the changing conceptions of sovereignty, citizenship, justice and human rights, which indeed are four pillars of cosmopolitanism. In order to capture the changes into an all encompassing multidisciplinary framework, this chapter would propose a newer definition of 'transnationality', which is based on the capabilities approach.

Cosmopolitanism

The idea of progress was central to many enlightenment theorists. Marquis de Condorcet, one of the enlightenment philosophers, opined that the emancipation of individual from ascribed roles and identities is required for the individual to progress (Kymlicka 2001: 203). Individuals should be free to judge for themselves in the light of their own reasoning and experience, which traditional beliefs and customary practices prescribe and are worth maintaining (Kymlicka 2001: 203). Condorcet thought that this phenomenon, which we call cosmopolitan, would be the natural and inevitable outcome of this emancipation of the individual.

It was Immanuel Kant, who systematically dealt with the issue and theorized it as cosmopolitanism, as early as in the late eighteenth century, and even the modern theorists of globalization, borrow concepts on international law and international relations. Kant attacked the Westphalian order in which 'each state sees its own majesty ... precisely in which "the glory of its ruler consists in his power to order thousands of people to immolate themselves for a cause which does not truly concern them, while he need not himself incur any danger whatsoever"' (Kant 1991: 103). He criticized this model as one in which either there was no notion of international law or international law was interpreted merely as a right to go to war, which was in effect no law at all (Fine 2007).

In order to confront the violence and lawlessness that characterized relations between states, Kant reconstructed the cosmopolitan ideal in congruence with the moral norm within the framework of enlightenment thought (Schlereth 1997). He turned it into a new form of social contract at the interstate level that placed a political demand on sovereigns to renounce their 'savage and lawless freedom' and submit themselves to public coercive laws (Fine 2007). He constructed cosmopolitanism as an international political order designed to establish 'lawful external relations among states' and a 'universal civic society'. These terms referred to the establishment and consolidation of international laws to guarantee the sovereignty of nation states prohibit interference in the internal affairs of other states and create peaceful relations among states. It also referred to what Kant called cosmopolitan right in the proper sense of the term, which he identified with the 'right of hospitality' belonging to strangers in a foreign land (Kant 1991: 47, 172). Kant envisioned an institutional framework for cosmopolitanism where a Federation of Nations, based on mutual cooperation and voluntary consent among a plurality of independent states (Kant 1991: 105, 114). Kant wrote the cosmopolitan condition as a rational necessity linking nations together on the grounds that in the modern age 'a violation of rights in one part of the world is felt everywhere' (Kant 1991: 107–108). The writings of Condorsant and Kant in the late eighteenth century continued to have their impact on the current research in internationalization, globalization and new cosmopolitanism. In fact, since 1989, cosmopolitanism, within the social sciences, has evolved into interdisciplinary movement with its own distinctive research agenda.[8]

Robert Fine (2007) identifies three shared commitments, which are gravitating towards new cosmopolitanism research in the social sciences. These include the following (Fine 2007: 2):

- *Conceptual*: The overcoming of national presuppositions and prejudices within the social scientific disciplines themselves and the reconstruction in this light of the core concepts we employ;
- *Societal*: The recognition that humanity has entered an era of mutual interdependence on a world scale and the conviction that this worldly existence is not adequately understood within the terms of conventional social sciences; and
- *Normative*: The development of normative theories of world citizenship, global justice and cosmopolitan democracy

In the politico-philosophical discourse, there has been a consistent appraisal of the idea of cosmopolitanism, as we have seen in the earlier descriptions of Kant and others. In the recent 'Neo-Kantian' discourses, probably led by Habermas, define the cosmopolitan as one whose politics is 'based upon reason rather than patriotism or group sentiment' and is 'truly universal' rather than 'communitarian' (Nussbaum 1997).

Habermas strive for the reconciliation of cosmopolitan values, laws and institutions with the re-affirmation of national and transnational identity in the form of 'constitutional patriotism' (2001: 74–76).[9] He maintains that the challenges posed by the catastrophes of the twentieth century and the forces of globalization have given new impetus to Kant's idea of a cosmopolitan condition. He talks about constitutional patriotism as the particular type of national consciousness most appropriate to nation states seeking to inspire rational loyalty on the part of their citizens (Habermas 2001: 64). The constitution serves here as a bridge between the universal and the particular. On the one hand, constitutional patriotism refers to a shared attachment towards universalistic principles implicit in the idea of constitutional democracy. On the other hand, popular attachment to the idea of a constitution entails the sense of attachment citizens feel towards the particular ways in which abstract principles are interpreted and applied through national institutions (Michelman 2001: 265).[10]

In this short journey from Kant to Habermas, we have seen how the conceptions and perceptions on cosmopolitanism grew over a period of time. I would put myself into a school of thought who thinks that due to the increasing people to people contacts through various means, thanks to revolutions in communication and information technology, the cosmopolitanism is here to stay and get strengthened.

We will now look into four socio-political concepts, which are impacted by cosmopolitanism, sovereignty, citizenship, justice and human rights.

Sovereignty

Sovereignty is a central concept in political theory, political philosophy, modern history, international relations and international law. Indeed it predicts the separation of these disciplines (Jacobsen 2008). However, it's meaning and effect is unstable and is contested within and between those disciplines, especially since Cold War. Most theories of sovereignty operate at the level of states and nations. The common definition of sovereignty is 'the capacity to determine conduct within the territory of a polity without external legal constraints'.

In the late twentieth century, discussions about sovereignty reappear with demands for national self-determination and the challenges of regional integration and transnationalism.

There is a need to see, in the present global processes and international practices, how adequate are the territorial configuration of sovereignty.[11] Countries consider migration to be in a 'non-negotiable sovereign territory' (Khadria 2009). However, it is to be noted that the operation of sovereignty in international law separates the territory of one state from another. The prevailing concept of the international legal system is that territorial boundaries establish statehood and that territorial boundaries are the basis for state sovereignty (McCorquodale 2001). As a matter of fact, the territorial demarcation is the basis for membership in international organizations and for participation in the international state system.[12] Khadria (2009) opines that the multilateral discussions in which policy makers of the developed countries and the developing countries can influence each other's decisions is through an equitable adversary analysis of the dynamic conflict of interest with regard to migration issues. This can ensure optimal, balanced and equitable 'intertransnationalization' between the developed and the developing countries (Khadria 2009: 119).

However, the transnational challenges to territorial sovereignty have produced sites of contestation, such as global cities, international courts, transnational financial and intergovernmental networks, and transnational civic spaces, though it continues to define the lives of the people through its binding (or influential) agenda, and where territoriality is not the issue! Taking note of the literature in the political science and sociological disciplines on the important issue of sovereignty and globalization, the present study would like to argue that the focus should not be on the content and degree of sovereignty that states possess but on the form that it assumes in a globalized economy.

A useful approach to this issue can be found in Carl Schmitt's work, where he distinguishes the elements of the constitutional state and its political essence, identified in terms of the political identity of the people, which he argues has priority over the liberal components of the constitution. Here the political essence is the ethical and cultural identity of the people. Schmitt suggests that the antinomy between the sovereign power and the heterogeneous society is appropriate to a model where the governmental powers are centralized and concentrated within the state apparatus [Schmitt 1996 (1932)] a suggestion whose essence is taken but not the method!

It is argued that as the law and the territorial state in the present set-up of any democratic structure is divorced, powers of governance are increasingly fragmented and diffused within the market and the civil society. This is an instrumentalist argument, which holds great relevance in the present globalized context. This brings us to the governance model of sovereignty vis-à-vis the governmental model of sovereignty.

Sovereignty becomes fragmented and distributed across a range of institutions. One of the important manifestations of these developments may be found in the tremendous growth of private international authority. For example, the international standard associations are now having a major impact on the rules and procedures of corporations and states; there is a rapid growth of arbitration impending on the traditional legal domain of the state, and in increasing the importance of trade associations (Cutler et al. 1999). Private authority in international systems is only one aspect of these developments. Equally important is the role played by domestic regulatory agencies such as independent central banks that operate relatively autonomously from the structures of political accountability. The very growth of these aspects of the global economy has reinforced the rise of modes of institutional self-regulation (Cutler et al. 1999). However, the underlining fact remains that sovereign states have the ultimate authority, in a sense that Foucault and Schmitt mentioned, to check the growth of these relatively autonomous institutions.

An equally important aspect of the transformation of the form of sovereignty is the blurring of the division between the domestic and the international. We have seen that much of the literature on globalization takes what could be termed as external perspective on sovereignty, since it focuses on the external constraints of state action. Susan Strange (1996), a political economist, elaborated on the growth of powerful non-state actors in the global system like the financial markets, which are constraining the ability of the states to effectively intervene in the larger areas of economic life. However, as observed earlier, the rule-based WTO's Doha Round is still an issue to be resolved and does not show any signs of successful negotiations.

It is also observed that such analysis suffers from a zero-sum conception of sovereignty, which neglects the degree to which sovereignty is being transformed from within the state rather than from external sources (Jayasurya 2006). In other words, it is an externally driven sovereignty. Jayasurya points out that as against the externally driven model of globalization, the main source of change is to be found in changes to the internal structure of firms, markets and the state. Increasingly the emergent global economy requires regulations of areas previously considered part of domestic domain. This in turn means examining the way state structures operate at the interstices of the domestic and international arena (Jayasurya 2006). For example, the move to globally standardize the accounting practices leading many countries to transform their local accounting practices to International Financial Reporting Standards (IFRS); changes in the securities regulations to tune it with the international financial markets; besides others. But this legal harmonization can be achieved by institutionalized structures of cooperation between domestic and international agencies. Moreover, the regulatory cooperation implicit in the harmonization of law reflects the fact that the imperatives of a global economic order cannot be easily subsumed under the traditional notions of international law. This is because such regulatory cooperation requires the removal of the very boundaries between the international and the domestic that have been so central to the practice and theory of international law and international relations (Jayasurya 2006).

The analysis on sovereignty in the global context brings us to an understanding that, as Calhoun (2008) noted, as a result of globalization the nation state has not lost its significance, but it is equally clear that the nature of modern political theory has changed somewhat irrevocably.

The above description on sovereignty clearly indicates that the sovereignty of a nation is not coming on the way for an individual's display of capabilities at the global level.

Citizenship

The sovereign states, as they exist today, have different conceptions of what it means to be a 'member' of them and what the responsibilities and privileges of membership involve, some of which are community based and some of which are individual based (Hampton 1998: 217).[13] Hampton argues that some policies are more defensible on moral grounds than others and reject most of the membership policies driven by a strong sense of nationalist identity. She then argues that individualist membership policies are necessary for the defence of multicultural policies in liberal states, which would mean that she is not in favour of nationalist conception of political membership (Hampton 1998: 217). It is observed that the individualist notion of membership fits in tune with the larger cosmopolitan scheme but at the same time we cannot negate the concerns raised by the 'nationalist' conception of membership.

Citizenship is seen as one of the most important membership right that every individual in the world must possess. Citizenship can be described as participation in or membership of a community (Barbalet 1998).[14] The modern conception of citizenship as merely a status held under the authority of a state has been contested and broadened to include various political and social struggles of recognition and redistribution as instances of claim making, and hence by extension, of citizenship (Isin and Turner 2002). As a result, Isin and Turner observes that the struggles based upon identity and difference (whether sexual, racial, ethnic, diasporic, ecological, technological or cosmopolitan) have found new ways of articulating their claims as claims to citizenship understood not simply as a legal status but as political and social recognition and economic redistribution (Isin and Turner 2002: 2).

The notion that there could be a 'citizen of the world' has long been part of the utopian imaginary of the citizenship traditions (Isin and Turner 2002: 8). It was implicit in Augustine's idea of the City of God within which the legacy of Roman global society would be perfected. It was part of Kant's vision of a 'perpetual peace' in which the enlightenment dream of a world free from irrational prejudice could be realized (Isin and Turner 2002: 8–9). Isin and Turner talked about the classical idea of virtue, from where the cosmopolitan idealism developed. He says, the tradition in the modern period has attempted to distinguish between love of country (Patriotism) and respect for the state (nationalism). 'We have lost this tradition, failing typically to recognize any distinction between patriotic and nationalist commitments' (Isin and Turner 2002: 8).

There are at least two important aspects of citizenship, when we look it in the global context – first, its prescriptions for the cosmopolitan structure; and second, the transnational characteristics of citizenship. We do have certain cosmopolitan structures activated, but they too are subject to the umbrella of multiple citizenship policies. On the other hand, we are in an age where multitasking and multiple allegiances, though not easy, is becoming a norm and the individuals and the sovereign states are amending their approaches accordingly.

The Cosmopolitan Prescriptions on Citizenship

One of the important developments is the delinking of 'territory', 'nationality' and 'citizenship'. One manifestation of de-territorialized memberships is the increasing number of states permitting, and even promoting, dual or multiple citizenships (Baubock 2007a, 2007b; Jones-Correa 2001). Whereas a century ago most states viewed dual citizenship as bigamy, increasing numbers of states allow legal attachments to multiple countries, sometimes because of international conventions, at other times because of domestic policy or emigrant mobilization (Spiro 2007).

Dual citizenship[15] was viewed with hostility as long as the countries were at war and divided. It is only when 'peace' is restored, in general, and economic globalization expanded, dual citizenship was considered as a policy option. The Hague Convention of 1930 began with an oft-quoted preamble that prescribes: 'Every person should have a nationality and should have one nationality only' (League of Nations 1930: 89). Alexander Aleinikoff pointed out that the Council of Europe, a decade after the European Convention on Human Rights (which endorsed, more or less, multiple nationality), proceeded to adopt a 1963 Convention designed to reduce the incidence of multiple nationality (United Nations 1963: 221).[16] Many of the National Laws, though, formally did not oppose dual citizenship, but was asked to surrender all other allegiances for taking up the citizenship of a new country through naturalization.[17]

The world has become progressively more interconnected through new technologies that greatly facilitate communications, travel and commerce and through political changes that are increasingly receptive to cross-border trade and investment. More and more people, at all levels of the economic and social ladder, now live, for a time at least, outside their countries of origin. Cross cultural marriages have proliferated, and the offspring in such cases obtain parents' nationalities *jus sanguinis.*[18] Even among couples of the same nationality, more births occur outside the national territory. If the country of birth observes the *jus soli*[19] rule transmission of citizenship, the child then typically gains multiple nationalities (Aleinikoff and Klusmeyer 2002: 23).

Aleinikoff observed that the major countries of immigration have generally favoured strong *jus soli* rules, while most countries of emigration adopt *jus sanguinis* regimes – despite their nominal opposition to dual nationality. In this setting, he says, dual nationality inevitably proliferates as the global economy and cheaper transportation results in more family migration. Moreover, a growing literature is not content with merely advocating tolerance of dual nationality, many writers strongly support its expansion as a means of fostering global peace, enhancing international trade, spreading democratic values and observing human rights.

Facilitating Multiple Allegiances

Legal regimes often formally require the loss or renunciation of all other nationalities at the time of naturalization. In the 1960s, the code of the major democracies generally contained such a restriction. There were exceptions[20] earlier, but in recent decades, the exceptions came to be applied with increasing liberality, for example, Germany and The Netherlands (Koslowski 1998: 734, 744).[21] Statutes of many countries accept dual nationality on the part of naturalizing immigrants, notably including other countries with significant levels of immigration, such as Australia,[22] Canada[23] and France.

A similar shift in attitude towards naturalization can be discerned on the part of countries of recent emigration. Traditionally, many tended to regard their nationals who took up full citizenship elsewhere as virtual traitors who could not be allowed to retain their original nationality. But since 1990s, many key emigration countries enacted laws to facilitate retention of the original nationality despite naturalization elsewhere, for example, El Salvador in 1983, Dominican Republic in 1994, and Mexico in 1998 (Jones-Correa 2002). Hence, a trend is on the cards where naturalization increasingly leaves the naturalized member as dual national – a status, which Aleinikoff and Klusmeyer points out, that is tolerated or even encouraged by one or both of the states involved, but several key states have not made these changes, and in others the continuation of a renunciation requirement, even if often waived or treated as ineffective, sends a confusing signal to those considering naturalization (Aleinikoff and Klusmeyer 2002: 26–27).

Different countries have different considerations of the provisions of dual citizenship. For example, countries more used to emigration than immigration can target their own emigrants abroad, but not extend dual citizenship to immigrants who live in their own borders, as in the case of Poland (Faist et al. 2007) and also India for that matter. Conversely, some traditional immigration countries show limited enthusiasm for dual citizenship, worried about the trade-off between political autonomy and transnational citizenship (Baubock 2007a: 81). In the United States, Supreme Court decisions and state department directives permit multiple citizenship, yet the oath that all would-be citizens must swear still contains a promise to renounce prior allegiances (Spiro 1997).

In the European Union, the dual citizenship of non-EU nationals has been a central sticking point in debates of German citizenship reform, with those concerned about multiple memberships arguing that dual citizenship may prevent immigrant integration (Faist et al. 2007). In Sweden, however, dual citizenship, adopted in 2001, was seen as a human rights issue (Sp'ang 2007). The contrast between Germany and Sweden demonstrates that arguments against dual citizenship attempt to make 'citizenship conditional on the assumption of certain duties by immigrants, whereas arguments in favour of dual citizenship emphasize individual rights' (Gerdes and Faist 2007: 138).

Importantly, all versions of multiple citizenships continue to see a political unit, one with some ability to make political decisions and exercise enforcement, as the source of rights and membership status. In sum, both post-national and cosmopolitan citizenship link legal status to persons rather than territory, raising questions about how to secure rights that are overwhelmingly guaranteed by states. Transnational and dual citizenship extend people's ability to participate in and belong to multiple, territorially based political units. All these treatments of citizenship question the link between citizenship and a single nation state. However, the dimensions of citizenship – status, rights, participation and belonging – remain the salient axes in evaluating notions of equality (Bloemraad et al. 2008).

Aleinikoff and Klusmeyer put forward some of the arguments favouring recognition of dual citizenship. There are good reasons for states to adopt a tolerant stance towards dual citizenship as a matter in its own right. Some of the reasons explained are as follows (Aleinikoff and Klusmeyer 2002: 36–37):

- *Reflecting Deeply Felt Affiliations, Connections, and Loyalties:* In our increasingly interconnected world, many people live outside the country of their birth or are born in nations different from where their parents were born. Many regard links with both these countries (through family, property, business ties, culture and religion) as important, vital, worthy of nurture and perhaps even foundational to their identities. In wishing to deepen their ties with one of the countries, they neither wish to nor see the need of casting off completely their links to the other country. A commitment to respecting pluralist differences, whether cultural, political or social, is fundamental to modern democratic principles. This respect applies to those same differences expressed by nationality.

- *Promoting Naturalization and Integration:* Lengthy lawful residence outside the country of one's nationality has grown increasingly common. States experiencing this phenomenon have come to appreciate the importance of promoting the civic, political and social integration of long-term residents. Accepting dual nationality on the part of citizens who naturalize can contribute towards improved integration and a healthier level of identification with the country of residence.
- *Facilitating Free Movement Between States:* Some long-term residents in a host country would feel that if naturalization can take place only by denouncing other allegiances, they could not then move freely back and forth between the two states with which they have links because they would become subjects to the varying qualifications for admission of noncitizens in the country of their birth. Today both business connections and family needs may dictate frequent migration and the continuation of close ties despite long distances. The assurance of admission that dual citizenship can afford is therefore more significant.

Going a step ahead, many scholars also talked about 'global citizenship'. One important work, which needs to be considered, is the concept of 'flexible citizenship', which is developed by Aihwa Ong. She points out that as the globalization process produces multiple diasporas, we can expect very complex relationships between homeland and host societies that will make the traditional idea of national citizenship increasingly problematic (Ong 1999). The increasing rates of labour migration and the growth of dual citizenship arrangements indicate that citizenship itself will become differentiated to accommodate these new status positions and identities (Ong 1999).

From the above analysis, it is observed that dual citizenship (theoretically 'multiple') can breed itself only in a world of peaceful co-existence and that the legal and constitutional changes must take this into consideration. It is also recognized that the developmental aspects of the underdeveloped and developing countries, on the one hand, and the need for working populations in most of the developed countries, on the other, bring us to study more seriously the greater need for linkages. Hence, it is suggested that the states should explicitly repeal legal provisions that restrict any form of dual citizenship. In this case, the Indian Government's initiative of 'Overseas Citizenship of India' is unique, which is able to attract large number of people among Indian Diaspora, without renouncing their country of citizenship.

We have seen that over a period of time, citizenship has delinked with territoriality and we now have good number of legislative measures in both immigrant receiving countries and countries of emigrating populations, facilitating access to their multiple involvements across the borders.

In order to fit into the framework of transnationality, the chapter proposes that, first, if dual citizenship is not allowed, the source countries must make appropriate provisions for enabling their diasporas to participate in the socio-economic engagements of the respective source countries; and second, the host countries must allow the long-standing immigrants to have access to local conceptions of equality and liberty. Such provisions would not impact the sovereignty of independent democratic nations.

Justice

The principal grounds for migratory movements are economic, and that border-crossing movements must be viewed in the context of world economic interdependence. The contemporary Kantian cosmopolitans treat international movement, whether they are those of refugees, asylees or immigrants, within the framework of global distributive justice (Benhabib 2004). In general, distributive justice is achieved when entitlements to economic goods are allocated to people as they ought to be. Throughout most of the history of political philosophy, the attempt to specify the principles of distributive justice so conceived has been pitched at the domestic level: As the cosmopolitan tendencies increased due to globalization of communication and economic activity, the idea that the demands of distributive justice should be pitched primarily at the global level, at the level of mankind as a whole, started gaining momentum. For those following this track, it would seem natural that whatever conception of justice was deemed plausible for the distribution of resources between members of a particular society should also provide a suitable characterization of global distributive justice (see Beitz 1979: part III, for some early philosophical formulations).

Any analysis on contemporary justice will not be fruitful without referring to John Rawls Theory of Justice (*read, distributive justice*). The framework of political and social analysis initiated by John Rawls's classic contributions has had a profound impact on contemporary understanding of the nature of justice. In the Rawlsian framework, fairness for a group of people involves arriving at rules and guiding principles of social organization that pay similar attention to everyone's interests, concerns and liberties. In working out how this may be understood, the Rawlsian device of the 'original position' has proved useful. In the hypothetical original position, which is an imagined state of primordial equality, individuals are seen as arriving at rules and guiding principles through a cooperative exercise in which they do not yet know exactly who they are going to be.

Rawlsian analysis proceeds from the original position to the identification of particular principles of justice. These principles include the priority of liberty (the first principle) giving precedence to maximal liberty for each person subject to similar liberty for all. The 'second principle' deals with other matters, including equity and efficiency in the distribution of opportunities, and includes the 'difference principle', which involves the allocation criterion of holding of primary goods (or general-purpose resources) of the different individuals, giving priority to the worst-off people in each conglomeration (Sen 1999a).

The Rawlsian thesis is one of the widely accepted theses and considered as one of the most important works of the twentieth century with far-reaching implications in the twenty-first century.

However, there has been important criticism, especially with regard to its applicability in a cosmopolitan situation. It is argued that Rawlsian conception of distributive justice is state centric and cannot do justice either sociologically or normatively to questions raised by international migration (Benhabib 2004; Pogge 1989; Sen 1999b).

By not granting conditions of entry and exit into the political community, a central role in a liberal-democratic justice, Rawls assumed that the state-centric model of territorially delimited nations, with fairly closed and well-guarded borders, would continue to govern our thinking in these matters (Benhabib 2004: 74). Benhabib (2004) opines that in the Rawlsian scheme, viewing the political society as a 'complete and closed social system' is incompatible with other premises of Rawlsian liberalism. It is observed that the Rawlsian theories do not apply to international migration and global justice (Benhabib 2004; Sen 1999b), as he argued for limiting immigration. Rawls argues that unless a definite agent is given responsibility for maintaining an asset and bears losses for not doing so, Rawls reasons, a people's territory cannot be preserved in perpetuity for others (Rawls 1999: 39). That is, he is pointing for the need for some kind of boundaries. It is to be noted that Rawls is arguing against radically open borders.

Benhabib opines that there is sufficient empirical evidence, however, that open and porous borders which enable the free movement of peoples, goods and services across state boundaries are highly beneficial to the functioning of free-market economies (Benhabib 2004: 88). In a special survey on immigration by *The Economist*, which refers to a magisterial study of the economic impacts of immigration by America's National Research Council in 1997, found that the first-generation immigrants imposed an averaged net fiscal cost of $3,000 at present discounted value, but the second generation yielded a $80,000 fiscal gain (*The Economist* 2002: 12–13).

There is a general consensus that the Rawlsian application must be extended to a global civil society, where peoples organized as states would be the major players, but by no means the only players. Hence a cosmopolitan perspective, taking leads from the Kantian view, that 'if the actions of one can affect the actions of another',[24] then we have an obligation to regulate our actions under a common law of freedom, which respects our equality as moral agents (*The Economist* 2002: 12–13).[25] Thus, it can be argued that social justice is a global public good and once provided by one country, it benefits everyone everywhere through its contribution to world peace and stability (Kapstein 1999).

Amartya Sen (2009) also talked extensively about justice, especially in the global context, and deviating from his *guru* John Rawls. Sen, in his book, *The Idea of Justice*, comes up with a distinctive approach to justice, which is substantially different from the earlier approaches. Justice, for Sen, is about comparative assessment rather than construction of ideally just provisions. Sen contrasts two ways of thinking about justice: 'transcendental institutionalism', which encompasses the bulk of contemporary political philosophy and 'realization-focused comparison', which characterizes his own approach. To bring out this contrast, Sen invokes an old distinction from Sanskrit literature on ethics and jurisprudence. In classical Sanskrit, he writes that the word 'justice' has two forms: '*niti*', which refers to organizational propriety and behavioural correctness, and '*nyaya*', which stands for a comprehensive concept of realized justice. While Rawls and others are focused on *niti*, Sen draws our attention to *nyaya*. Sen's central thesis is that justice is about real-world choices to improve human lives. Sen's approach to justice seems to direct us to practice comparative assessments rather than abstract philosophizing and is rather reminiscent of Marx's famous eleventh thesis on Feuerbach, 'the philosophers have only interpreted the world; the point is to change it'. What motivates the common perception of injustice, he observes, is not that the world falls short of being completely just, but that there exist manifest and remediable injustices which we want to eliminate (Sen 2009).

Sen, elsewhere, argues that the conception of global justice must be based on, what he calls, 'plural affiliation' and where he recognizes the fact that we all have multiple identities, and each of these identities can yield concerns and demands that can significantly supplement, or seriously compete with, other concerns and demands arising from other identities.

From the above analysis of 'justice', we could see that it has travelled across the borders impacting the lives of 'others' and constantly modifying the local conceptions of justice, mainly due to the irrevocable socio-economic contributions of naturalized and immigrant populations. In the context of cosmopolitanism, 'justice' is evolving to the extent of facilitating people to people linkages and demonstration of skills across the borders.

However, cosmopolitan justice seeks to have institutions and instruments at the global level to suggest a direction on 'quality of life' and also to deal with any disputes in this process. In this regard, we are currently having International Court of Justice and international arbitration mechanisms in place. As a step ahead, the framework of transnationality proposes that in addition to the institutional processes of justice at international level, it is also important to constantly modify and update the domestic judicial systems within the respective democracies, keeping in view the international developments of socio-political relations.

Human Rights

When we look into the trends towards global justice, there has been a constant growth of 'Universal Human Rights'. Will Kymlicka describes that history has enough examples of various oppressive policies towards the minorities (or as opposed to the dominant group). Some minorities were physically eliminated, either by mass expulsion or by genocide. Other minorities were coercively assimilated, forced to adopt the language, religion and customs of the majority. In yet other cases, minorities were treated as resident aliens, subjected to physical segregation and economic discrimination, and denied political rights. Various efforts have been made historically to protect cultural minorities and to regulate the potential conflicts between majority and minority cultures, mainly through bilateral treaties.[26] This treaty system was extended, and given a more multilateral basis, under the League of Nations. However, at a larger level, this was not the solution, as the minority cultures exceeded the number of countries, and moreover, the equations between the countries were not always based on 'cooperation'.

It is in this context that the idea of Universal Human Rights came into being. Human rights are conditions that enable the exercise of personal autonomy; first and foremost as a moral being you have fundamental rights to justification (Forst 1999). Your freedom can be restricted only through reciprocally and generally justifiable norms, which equally apply to all. In the sphere of morality, generality means universality, and universality refers to what would be valid for all human beings considered as beings equally entitled to respect and concern (Benhabib 2004).

The human rights movement took an important turn after the World War II with the 1948 Universal Declaration of Human Rights, which forbids arbitrary denaturalization (a move for which Hannah Arendt fought for!). It meant that considering loss of citizenship as a loss of nationality is a violation of human rights.[27] Benhabib argues that the entitlements to all civil rights – including rights to association, property and contract – and eventually to political rights, must itself be considered as human right (Benhabib 2004: 140).

It is important to note that the United Nations deleted all references to the rights of ethnic and national minorities in its Universal Declaration of Human Rights.[28] There has been a general consensus from various quarters of the world regarding the basic values, which the Declaration proposes: these include respect for human life and dignity, equality of rights, respect for personal integrity and inviolability, recognition of basic human worth and protection of fundamental human interests. These general values in turn entail and are realized by such measures as the prohibition of torture, genocide and slavery, freedom of association, liberty of conscience, equality before law, fair trial, popular accountability of political power, protection of privacy and respect for the integrity of familial and other intimate relationships (Parekh 2000: 134).[29]

Brian Barry (2005) argued:

> 'the Universal Declaration of Human Rights has implications – and very important ones – for the international community as a whole, not just for individual states. If government's simply do not have the means of supplying everyone with such things as adequate nutrition and housing, pure drinking water, sanitation and a generally healthy environment, education, and medical care, then the wealthy countries, individually or in any combination, have an obligation to ensure that, by one means or another, the resources are forthcoming. (Barry 2005: 28)

The removal of global poverty and other economic and social deprivations has thus come to centre stage in the global engagement with human rights.[30] Deen Chatterjee had argued that the global recognition of endemic poverty and systemic inequity as serious human rights concerns has put pressure on individual countries for internal democratic reforms and made vivid the need for more just and effective international institutional directives (Chatterjee 2008: 2).

However, the UN Declaration is not free of defects. It is observed that the rights specified in UN Declaration do not correspond with 'duties'. Such a correspondence would exist only when a right is institutionalized (Sen 1999b: 382).

Bhikhu Parekh (2000) observes that the Universal Declaration retains a distinctly liberal bias and includes rights which, though admirable, cannot claim universal validity. It takes a statist view of human rights and emasculates their universalist and critical thrust. The rights are deemed to have the obligation to be respected and to realize them. Like Sen, Parekh talks about 'duty'. 'Since there are good reasons to respect the autonomy of the state, human rights are its primary but not exclusive responsibility. If a state is unable to secure the conditions of their effective exercise for lack of resources, civil wars or other reasons, outsiders have a duty to render it such help as it needs and that they can afford. Universal human rights imply universal human obligations including a duty to create a global regime of justice (Parekh 2000: 134).

At a practical level, the concept of cosmopolitan idealism came in the shape of the Universal Declaration of Human Rights and few other important international legal provisions. All this came at a time when there were unprecedented international movements.[31] Challenges posed by these international migrations to the international community call for a comprehensive understanding of the normative framework and the legal content of the freedom of movement.

Yasemin Soysal (1994), in her book, the *Limits of Citizenship*, argued that a new and more universal concept of citizenship has unfolded in the postwar era, one whose organizing and legitimating principles are based on universal personhood rather than national belonging (p. 1). The language of human rights is becoming increasingly central to the government of world affairs, as respect for the person challenges the idea that states are sovereign in relation to their citizens and that other states or international bodies have no right to interfere in this primary relationship (Soysal 1994: 1). The growing importance of human rights, however, means that the benefits of citizenship are becoming less important. Soysal further points out that the significance of citizenship has been reduced to the point where 'noncitizens' rights do not differ significantly from those of citizens (Soysal 1994: 119). As such, social membership is increasingly post-national and based upon personhood rather than citizenship (Soysal 1994: 44).

There has been a growing importance of human rights in world politics. It is observed that the freedom of movement across borders as a right cannot be found in international human rights instruments. The general concept of freedom of movement finds its normative expression through the right to leave any country and to return to one's own country. This latter right is embodied in numerous multilateral instruments relating to human rights both at the universal and at the regional level (Chetail 2003: 47).

The Universal Declaration of Human Rights (United Nations 1948) recognizes the right to freedom of movement across boundaries: a right to emigrate – that is, to leave a country – but not a right to immigrate – a right to enter the country (Article 13). Article 14 anchors the right to enjoy asylum under certain circumstances, while Article 1 of the Declaration proclaims that everyone has 'the right to a nationality'. The second half of Article 15 stipulates that 'no one shall be arbitrarily deprived of his nationality nor denied the right to change his nationality' (www.unhchr.ch/udhr/lang.eng.htm).[32] Benhabib (2004) points out that the Universal Declaration is silent on states' obligations to grant entry to immigrants, to uphold the right of asylum and to permit citizenship to alien residents and denizens.

The 1990 International Convention on the Protection of the Rights of All Migrant Workers and Members of Their Families endorses the right to leave and return within their own fields of application.

Chetail (2003) brings to notice two declarations addressing the issues of the right to leave and return: The Declaration on the Right to Leave and the Right to Return adopted by a colloquium held in Uppsala, Sweden, in 1972 and the Strasbourg Declaration on the Right to Leave and Return adopted by a 1986 meeting of Experts.[33] Although UN did not use these directly, but it used them in the provisions set forth in the different UN instruments (Chetail 2003: 52).[34]

As we have seen that the right to leave any country and to return to one's own country is expressly guaranteed in a series of regional and universal multilateral treaties ratified by the great majority of the international community. Hence, we could confirm that the right exists in international law. However, it must be noted that there is no duty upon the state to admit the foreigners, which leaves loopholes in the system. States are increasingly reluctant to enter into new legal obligations restricting their sovereign rights to decide on the admission of foreigners. It follows from the general international law on principle of sovereignty that a state has the right to determine who can enter and reside on its territory. B.S. Chimni (2003) points out that the 'reception of "aliens" is a matter of discretion, and every state is, by reason of its territorial supremacy, competent to exclude aliens from the whole or any part, of its territory'. However, this right, Chimni observes, is subject to a state observing its international legal obligations.

As the HRC had pointed out in the General Comment No. 15, 'in certain circumstances an alien may enjoy the protection of the Covenant [i.e. International Covenant on Civil and Political Rights 1966 (ICCPR)] even in relation to entry or residence, for example, when considerations of non-discrimination, prohibition of inhuman treatment and respect for family life arise'.

The International Refugee Law also places certain constraints on state action. Article 33(1) of the 1951 Convention on the Status of Refugees provides, for instance, that no person can be returned, for any reason whatsoever, to the frontiers of territories where her life or freedom is in danger. The convention principle of non-refoulement is a part of customary international law and therefore to be observed by states that are not party to the 1951 Convention. The principle is also contained in human rights instruments such as Article 3 of the 1984 Convention against Torture (Chimni 2003: 256).

The regulation of migration movements must occur through cooperation among all the states concerned. The contemporary challenge of the legal regulation of migration calls for a large and comprehensive approach through a more intensive cooperation between the state of immigration and the states of emigration (Chetail 2003: 59).

The effort to regulate the movement of workers and to provide protection for this vulnerable category has many gaps. Bilateral agreements between sending and receiving countries providing for orderly migration are less widespread than in the past. An integrated system such as the European Union has extensive provisions concerning workers from within the Union, but lacks provisions concerning workers from outside the Union. ILO migrant worker conventions have not been widely ratified. The major UN convention on migrant labour is also faced with ratificatory problems. The human rights conventions, such as the European Convention on Human Rights and the International Covenants, have not been widely applied to migrant workers.

At the same time, it is a known fact to all the respective sovereign states that international migration facilitates economic development and it provides millions of workers the opportunity to better their economic situation by working abroad, particularly skilled workers whose services are desired in developed countries. However, the international response remains fairly inadequate, especially so in the case of not so highly skilled migrations.

The Global Commission on International Migration in its final report of 2005 described international responsibility for managing migration as 'diffuse', in the sense that responsibility is fragmented horizontally among different UN agencies and organizations, each managing one particular aspect of migration, such as refugee protection (UNHCR), the rights of migrants (UNHCHR) and labour standards (ILO) (GCIM 2005: 63). Panizzon points out that an important body of soft law is emerging for managing economic migration, but what is missing are global institutions for implementing and enforcing the principles for actions and recommendations suggested by the related international bodies such as Global Commission on International Migration, International Agenda for Migration Management (IAMM) and also the UN High Level Dialogue on Migration and Development (2010: 3). What unites these soft law initiatives is the attempt to consolidate national and regional best practices on recruiting, admitting, integrating and readmitting migrant workers. Yet, none of these short-lived efforts have paved the way for a new international organization managing all aspects of migration, nor for that matter have they succeeded in formulating an international obligation to liberalize temporary labour migration (Panizzon 2010: 4).

From the above analysis, one could see that there is a huge scope for the bodies such as UN to grow towards greater integration of the world and especially delve upon the equations with regard to international migration and citizenship.

The global instruments for economic cooperation are an important trend towards cosmopolitanism. I think that the progress towards cosmopolitanism, among various disciplines must go hand in hand, keeping two parameters in the priority – the 'ethical connect' and the 'internal adjustments'. In the rapidly changing global societies, we are in the midst of a significant political realignment where cosmopolitanism is likely to play a leading part in the construction and reconstruction of *our collective* imaginations (Stevenson 2002). When we talk about collective imaginations, there is a need to address the issue of 'group identity', which I argue is beyond cosmopolitanism.

Multiculturalism

The trend towards cosmopolitanism takes care of the individual identity, vis-à-vis group identity or more specifically protection, preservation and promotion of cultural identity. The issue, at the larger level, was dealt by many theorists under the paradigm of 'multiculturalism', which includes group representation and rights, the rights and status of immigrants, the recognition of minority nations and the status of new social movements. It is pointed out that all modern states face the problems of multiculturalism even if they are far from endorsing multiculturalism as a policy agenda or official ideology (Kelly 2002: 1).

Charles Taylor (1992), in a significant work, seeks to link what he calls the 'struggle for recognition' with the politics of multiculturalism. Taylor starts from the view that both personal and collective identities are shaped by the intersubjective processes of recognition and misrecognition. That is images of the self are mirrored back by intimate relations and social institutions informing our individual and collective identities. The struggle for recognition is a dialogic process that is negotiated with intimate and distant others. These processes, for Taylor, encompass basic human needs that depend upon the recognition of the uniqueness of our identities and notions of equal respect. The problem comes however in reconciling the universal demand for equal dignity, while our differences are also respected.

Will Kymlicka, with a series of publications on the subject, laid emphasis on the need for accommodating the minority rights in the multicultural framework. However, Kymlicka was more concerned about the National Minorities, whose characteristics he defines as territorially concentrated, institutionally complete, common language and culture, a distinct cultural unit and a strong sense of collective identity (Kymlicka 1995). In this scheme of understanding, immigrants do not come into picture. Kymlicka opines that immigrants are ethnic and not national minorities because they are neither territorially concentrated nor institutionally complete and moreover their culture is now cut-off from its national moorings and cannot be reproduced in the new environment (Kymlicka 1995).

In this context, he further argues that immigrants can claim poly-ethnic rights: Right to not be discriminated against; exempt from laws that unjustly disadvantage them and maintaining their language, besides few other similar provisions. Unlike the national minorities, they cannot claim national rights to self-government and cultural autonomy. At a generalized theoretical level, Kymlicka argues that 'poly-ethnicity is dealt with by integrating ethnic minorities into the national culture'.

Kymlicka's vote for accommodation with assimilation, as far as immigrants are concerned is something that does not go with the larger idea of cosmopolitan multiculturalism. However, Kymlicka's later impressions[35] opine that the older models of assimilationist and homogenizing nation states are increasingly being contested and often displaced, by newer 'multicultural' models of the state and of citizenship. But increasingly this shift has an international dimension to it. International intergovernmental organizations are encouraging, and sometimes pressuring, states to adopt a more multicultural approach. He says, 'we are witnessing the increasing "internationalization" of state–minority relations, and the global diffusion of multiculturalism as a new framework for reforming those relations' (Kymlicka 2007: 17).

In fact, the international legislative mechanisms are recommending in favour of cultural identity but not at the cost of 'individual identity' and the rights associated with it. The

UNESCO Universal Declaration on Cultural Diversity states that 'No one may invoke cultural diversity to infringe upon human rights guaranteed by international law, nor to limit their scope' (Article 4). The UN's Declaration on minority rights states that any rights or duties recognized in the Declaration 'shall not prejudice the enjoyment of all persons of universally recognized human rights and fundamental freedoms' [Article 8 (2)]. The International Labour Organization's convention on the rights of indigenous peoples says that the right of indigenous people to maintain their cultural practices should be respected 'where these are not incompatible with fundamental rights defined by the national legal system and internationally recognized human rights' [Article 8 (2)]. The Council of Europe's Framework Convention on the rights of national minorities says that the convention must be interpreted in a way that complies with the European Convention on Human Rights (Article 23). In fact, every international declaration and convention on these issues makes the same point – the rights of minorities and indigenous peoples are an inseparable part of a larger human rights framework and operate within its limits.

Though the multicultural policies have come up in a big way and institutionalized in some of the countries with diversified populations, such as Canada and Australia, it is to be noted that the process is proving to be one of the toughest.

Bhikhu Parekh (2000) also makes an important observation that the politics of culture is integrally tied up with the politics of power because culture in itself is an institutionalized power and is deeply involved with other systems of power. Cultural self-esteem cannot be developed and sustained in a vacuum and requires appropriate changes in all the major areas of life. No multicultural society can be stable and vibrant unless it ensures that its constituent communities receive both just recognition and a just share of economic and political power. It requires a robust form of social, economic and political democracy to underpin its commitment to multiculturalism (Parekh 2000: 343).

When we look into the cosmopolitan critique of multiculturalism, it is contended that the multicultural argument for the preservation of cultures is premised on a problematic view of culture and of the individual's relationship to culture. Cultures are not distinct, self-contained wholes, they have long interacted and influenced one another through war, imperialism, trade and migration. As Jeremy Waldron argues:

> We live in a world formed by technology and trade; by economic, religious, and political imperialism and their offspring; by mass migration and the dispersion of cultural influences. In this context, to immerse oneself in the traditional practices of, say, an aboriginal culture might be a fascinating anthropological experiment, but it involves an artificial dislocation from what actually is going on in the world. (Waldron 1992: 100)

To aim at preserving or protecting a culture runs the risk of privileging one allegedly pure version of that culture, thereby crippling its ability to adapt to changes in circumstances (Waldron 1992: 110; see also Benhabib 2002 and Scheffler 2007).

In the year 2010, Angela Merkel, the German Chancellor, declared that multiculturalism (*multikulti*) is a failure in Germany. Nicolas Sarkozy, the French counterpart defended her argument and pointed out that multiculturalism is also a failure in France. David Cameron, the British Prime Minister, also expressed his fears of a bleak future for multiculturalism in the United Kingdom.

The cosmopolitan understanding of multiculturalism is based on 'tolerance'. Cosmopolitans would say that in order to enjoy the fruits of globalization, there is a need to tolerate each other especially in the context of culture and migration. However, what is important is to give equal opportunities to display his/her multiple capabilities and that the 'culture' should not be a limiting factor. Going a step ahead, the framework of transnationality enables people to people contacts across the borders, especially through economic linkages and social networks for mutual benefits.

So far we have seen an analysis of the changing paradigms in the concepts of sovereignty, citizenship, justice and human rights taking us closer to the cosmopolitan principals. However, there is a mismatch between cosmopolitanism and multiculturalism, as the former does not accommodate 'group identities' and is purely based on 'individual'. There is a need to go beyond and look for a framework that enables the 'individual' to perform and at the same time take into cognisance the existence and performance through 'groups'. It is here I would talk about 'transnationalism', which has grown as one of the important multidisciplinary concept that exclusively deals with various aspects of cross-border migrations especially the one that maintains its connections with the 'origin' countries.

Transnationalism

Anthony Richmond, as early as 1969, developed a concept 'transilience'. The term originally referred to the exchanges of skilled and highly qualified migrants between advanced societies and as such they were referred to as 'transilients'. The term is now used more broadly by Richmond (1994: 31; cf. Wong 1997: 330) and others to apply to a wide range of movers whose permanence in one locale is neither expected nor necessary. Richmond points out that the transilients do not necessarily acculturate or integrate into the receiving society, but rather they maintain close ties with family and friends; are aware of changing economic, political and social conditions in their former country and elsewhere; and have high rates of re-migration and return (Richmond 1994: 51; cf. Wong 1997: 330). The current literature on transnational migration owes a lot to this concept of transilience, which originally referred to skilled migrations.

Migration scholarship has undergone a sea change in the past two decades. David Held opines that the improved transportation, technology and telecommunications facilitated (and not caused) globalization, which has entailed the increasing extent, intensity, velocity and impact of global interconnectedness across a broad range of human domains (Held et al. 1999). Most scholars now recognize that many contemporary migrants and their predecessors maintained a variety of ties to their home countries while they became incorporated into the countries where they settled. Migration has never been a one-way process of assimilation into a melting pot or a multicultural salad bowl but one in which migrants, to varying degrees, are simultaneously embedded in the multiple sites and layers of the transnational social fields in which they live (Levitt and Jaworsky 2007: 130). More and more aspects of social life take place across borders, even as the political and cultural salience of nation state boundaries remains clear (Levitt and Jaworsky 2007).

There has been a series of literature in the transnational studies from various disciplines, many of which has come up in the first decade of the present century; and a short understanding of those will be useful for the present study. Before that the study would briefly look into the definitional aspect of transnationalism. Transnationalism is defined by Steven Vertovec as 'multiple ties and interactions linking people or institutions across the borders of nation-state' (1999: 447). The present study would take this as an operational definition, but with two modifications: First, replace the word 'or' to 'and', as in the present age we find movement both at the individual and institutional levels, involving both the 'state' and 'non state' actors, simultaneously; and second the word 'nation-state', though generally used and accepted, would be politically incorrect as political theory gives the 'nationality' status to any ethnic community with distinct language, culture and a strong sense of 'separate' identity, whereas presently most of the states are multi-ethnic! Hence, a 'nation state' would necessarily mean a country with single ethnic identity (like Korea!), which is not the case here. Based on this observation, the study would revise the definition of transnationalism as 'a phenomenon which facilitates multiple ties and interactions linking people and institutions to their counterparts across the borders of independent sovereign states'.

The phenomenon of transnationalism is seen as being analysed from all the social sciences discipline. The present section is divided into four subsections, which would discuss the transnational transformation process in the disciplines of economics, politics, social and cultural. The idea is not only to understand the transformation process at the transnational level but also to make note of the available scholarship in the field.

Economic Transnationalism

As early as since 1970s, there has been an emergence of a global system which was brought about by the worldwide expansion of technology and industrialization, some scholars call this 'Techno-Industrial Oligopoly Capitalism' (Amin 1972; cf. Villamil 1979: 68), in its new phase of transnational organization (Villamil 1979). The highly dynamic technological innovation process, which lies at the heart of the expansion of techno-industrial oligopoly capitalism, gradually disseminated to the developing countries and created a greater need for interdependence (Villamil 1979). In this context, some scholars see transnational migration as a by-product of this late capitalism, which renders large industrialized countries dependent on cheap labour and small, non-industrialized countries dependent on the remittances workers send home (Itzigsohn 2000; Portes 2003). Remittances have been of great importance to the current transnational order. According to the World Bank, the money migrants send home has doubled in the past decade ($232 billion in 2005 alone, with $167 billion to developing countries) (World Bank 2006). Remittance flows to developing countries are estimated to total $351 billion in 2011, an increase of 8 per cent over the previous year (World Bank 2011).[36] In at least 36 countries, including Albania, Bosnia and Herzegovina, Croatia, El Salvador, Haiti, Samoa, Yemen and Jordan, remittances exceed private and official capital inflows and are the primary source of foreign currency, rendering these countries so dependent on remittances that their economies might collapse if they declined (Hussain 2005; World Bank 2006).

Political Transnationalism

Migrants' political transnational practices include a variety of activities such as electoral participation (either as voters or as candidates), membership in political associations, parties or campaigns in two different countries, lobbying the authorities of one country to influence its policies towards another and nation building itself. In Europe, the ways in which Turks and Kurds in various settings are transforming the functions of sending states, from politics to corporate marketing, have been the subject of considerable research and theory (Ostergaard-Nielsen 2003).

The domain of immigrant politics refers to those political activities undertaken by a community to improve its social status in the host country, including attempts to improve access to services, fight discrimination or heighten the groups' recognition and rights; it sometimes involves homeland resources. For example, the Turkish Government has intervened actively on behalf of its nationals in Germany (Ostergaard-Nielsen 2003). Not all immigrant politics is transnational, although aspects of it may become so over time. Some groups organize across borders by building alliances with supporters in other receiving states who help lobby regional or international institutions, for example,

Kurdish migrants pressuring the Council of Europe or Eritrean rebels who organized a referendum for independence (Kastoryano 2000).

Peggy Levitt points out that there is another set of transnational political activities, which are recorded, called as 'trans-local' politics and differs from the above as it does not always involve host or home country governments at the outset. It includes the activities migrants undertake to support specific localities in the home country. The many Caribbean and Latin American hometown associations that finance development projects in their homelands fit under this rubric. These primarily economic actions are transnational but they become political when the state intervenes to support or control them (Levitt 2007). States generally support such efforts because they promote development. Simultaneity characterizes the political realm, not only through these domains of action but also through political membership and its attendant rights and responsibilities. Although political borders are increasingly permeable, they do not challenge territorial jurisdiction; at the same time, there is a growing overlap in political identities and legal statuses (Baubock 2003).

Yet another important aspect of transnational political transformation is the issue of dual nationality. Dual nationality needs not always be seen as a subject tied to 'immigrants' as it could be claimed through birth, marriage, claiming ancestral lineage or through naturalization (Vertovec 2009). Spiro points out that earlier there was distaste for dual nationality, but particularly since the post-Cold War that distaste is disappearing and we are moving towards a more universal acceptance of dual nationality (2002: 19–20).

When we look into the empirical aspects, Irene Bloemraad (2004) note only details a rapid rise in dual nationality claims in Canada between 1981 and 1996, but also notes differences among dual citizens surrounding characteristics such as income, birthplace and province of residence. Thomas Faist (2001) provides a description of the rise in dual nationality claims in Germany, which is traditionally not tolerant on dual nationality issues. One-third of all naturalizations from the 1970s to 1990s resulted in multiple nationalities.

As a matter of fact, there is a huge presence of undocumented migrants in the world. Saskia Sassen describes them as 'unauthorized yet recognized' migrants, who have no formal status or rights but who practice the duties associated with citizenship, such as raising a family, schooling children or holding a job. In contrast, she also talks about the presence of migrants who are 'authorized yet unrecognized'. Migrant citizens may have full legal status but are not recognized as political subjects because of factors such as discrimination and cultural stereotyping (Sassen 1999: 85–87).

Social and Cultural Transnationalism

Transnational migration scholarship has also identified striking changes in social life, documenting transformations in kinship and family structure and how these inform constructions of class, gender and race. Peggy Levitt observes that a transnational moral economy of kin involves putting family first, such as strategies for collective mobility or marrying into the right kinship network and accumulating social capital in the host society. The boundaries of family and kinship also change over the life course. In many households, living transnationally across generations becomes the norm. But whether individuals ultimately forge or maintain some kind of transnational connection at some point in their lives depends on the extent to which they are reared in a transnational space (Levitt 2007).

It was observed that transnational strategies were adopted over several generations, depending on individuals' changing needs and desires throughout the life cycle. Research has focused on living arrangements, finances and generational reproduction in the everyday lives of transnational families (Pries 2004). Recently, however, scholars have begun looking more closely at the experiences of parents, children and the elderly, and at how they are gendered. Steven Vertovec talked about affordable communication and travel, which became an important part of transnational practices (Vertovec 2004, 2009). Presently the modes and apparatuses, such as Internet and mobile phones, respectively, also increased.

Sociologists point out that the class and race are also constituted in transnational social fields (Gardner and Grillo 2002; Mahler and Pessar 2006; Willis 2000; cf. Levitt 2007). The impetus to participate across borders and the ability to do so varies by both class and race. The differentiated nature of labour migration affects more than just economic outcomes; it translates into differences in migrants' access to informal but crucial knowledge and networks for success in the mainstream. In contrast, middle-class and professional migrants have sufficient social and cultural capital that they can selectively assimilate elements of where they come from and where they settle (Levitt 2007).

With regard to cultural transnationalism, Peggy Levitt talks about two important debates: first the one that concerns the extent to which globalization creates a juggernaut of Westernized culture that reaches even the most remote corners of the world; and second, a parallel debate involves the age-old structure versus agency question, which, at its extremes, sees a massive culture industry influencing powerless consumers versus a view of postcolonial subjects liberated by the expressive potential of culture (Levitt 2007). Here, we focus on the different cultural mixes created when people from different places come into real or imagined contact with each other. Music is one of the important cultural artefacts, which the migrants get associated with and maintain a sense of belonging to their homeland. For example, *bandas* are an integral part of everyday life in many indigenous Mexican communities, accompanying rites of passage and reinforcing alliances and networks of reciprocity and obligation between villages (Levitt 2007: 141). We often see a great demand for the Indian Classical, Hindustani and Carnatic music, which is mostly demanded by the first-generation Indians. It is viewed that the second- and later-generation Indians (or for that matter any diasporic community of later generations) associate with the host country's cultural artefacts.

In the existing literature on transnationalism, we could see that the limitations in the conceptions of 'cosmopolitanism' and 'multiculturalism' are taken care of by facilitating the 'individual' and the 'group' identity(ies). However, I think there is a need for an all encompassing framework that would record the global transformations and suggest a system that would facilitate not only the 'flow' conceptions of transnationalism but also its 'stock' attributes. In this regard, I propose 'transnationality framework', which is essentially based on the capabilities approach.

Capability Approach

When we analyse at an individual level, it is widely believed that the 'Man is a social animal' ... adding to that '*the society is globalizing*'. The transition towards a globally linked world system characteristic of the current era has transformed the functional unit of the social system from the individual towards a more globally conceptualized form.[37] These rapidly evolving realities place increasing demands on the exercise of personal and collective agency to shape personal destinies and the national life of societies.[38]

Subsequently, with access to global information and developments in communication technology, person's thought process is widening and going global. Such an environment would add more items into a person's capabilities, multiplying his/her functioning and increasing his access to intervention beyond borders.

Philosophers such as Aristotle, Adam Smith, Karl Marx and more recently Martha Nussbaum and Amartya Sen dealt with this subject and talked about the importance of giving space to realize person's multiple capabilities. The freedom to achieve well-being is to be understood in terms of people's capabilities, that is, their real opportunities to do and be what they have reason to value.[39] This is analysed extensively in the capabilities approach by Amartya Sen and Martha Nussbaum.

This chapter suggests that the proposed definition of transnationality is based on the capability approach. We will now briefly understand the capability approach in the context of transnationality.

The capability approach purports that freedom to achieve well-being is a matter of what people are able to do and to be, and thus the kind of life they are effectively able to lead. The capability approach is generally conceived as a flexible and multipurpose framework, rather than a precise theory of well-being (Sen 1992: 48).

The capability approach recognizes human diversity to a great extent. Its criticism of other normative approaches is often fuelled by, and based on, the claim that the full human diversity among people is insufficiently acknowledged in many normative theories, such as theories of distributive justice.[40]

The capability approach thus takes account of human diversity in at least two ways. First, there is a focus on the plurality of functioning and capabilities as important evaluative spaces. By including a wide range of dimensions in the conceptualization of well-being and well-being outcomes, the approach broadens the so-called 'informational basis' of assessments, and thereby includes some dimensions that may be particularly important for some groups but less so for others (Robeyns 2003).[41]

Second, human diversity is stressed in the capability approach by the explicit focus on personal and socio-environmental conversion factors that make possible the conversion of commodities and other resources into functioning, and on the social, institutional and environmental context that affects the conversion factors and the capability set directly. Each individual has a unique profile of conversion factors, some of which are body related, others are shared with all people from her community, and still others are shared with people with the same social characteristics (e.g. same gender or class or race characteristics) (Robeyns 2003).

According to Sen, the various kinds of resources we have should never be misunderstood as goals in their own right. Rather, they are needed to achieve certain functioning. The latter can be broadly defined as 'the various things, a person may value doing or being' (Sen 1999b: 75). The number of potential functioning is unlimited ranging from very basic ones, such as being sufficiently nourished or having access to adequate housing, to complex ones, such as having self-respect or being able to participate in society. The specific characteristic – and to large extent the attractiveness – of this approach is constituted by the way how Sen distinguishes his ideas from notions of justice as equality of resources (as material resources, primary goods, opportunities, etc.) as well as from notions of justice as equality of outcomes (Pfister 2012: 242). When you talk of 'resources' it is essentially 'national' but when we talk of 'outcomes', it is essentially transnational. The capabilities approach gives due diligence to 'universality' as it provides enough space for human diversity and democratic negotiations.

Through the capabilities approach framework, and considering the changes in the concepts of sovereignty, citizenship, justice and human rights, as discussed earlier, I would now propose a new definition of 'transnationality', which would accommodate not only the 'flow conceptions' but also 'stock attributes' of transnationalism.

Defining Transnationality

The word transnationality was so far used in a limited extent for anthropological studies on globalization[42] and also to some extent in the management studies especially dealing with transnational corporations.[43] In the socio-political context, it is Thomas Faist (2013: 2), who used the term to mean 'the degree of connectivity between migrants and non-migrants across national borders'.

Any case, there is no general agreement on one definition on transnationality. This chapter observes a larger scope for the term and accordingly proposes the following definition:

> Transnationality is a multi-disciplinary framework which strives to optimize individual capabilities by creating an enabling environment for sustainable socio-economic global linkages, operating under the universal cosmopolitan principles of individual rights, equal opportunities and global justice through territorial institutions and non-territorial prescriptions, without disturbing the sovereign structures of the independent nations.

Transnationality: A Step Ahead

So far we have seen a descriptive analysis of facilitating people to people interaction across the borders and the accommodative aspects of the concepts of sovereignty, citizenship, justice and human rights. We have also seen that the capabilities approach can be a good platform for the optimal utilization of individual's multiple functioning, which is epistemological to transnationality.

Transnationality supports individual's capabilities of multiple functionalities (freedom to choose) on a non-territorial basis and also with non-intervention by the sovereign state(s).

Based on the discussions and analysis given in this chapter, 10 points can be mentioned as a summary, which are essentially the features of transnationality.

Transnationality

- Gives due importance to the existing conception of territorial definition of the sovereign states

- Recognizes societies as multicultural and countries as multi-ethnic
- Argues in favour of full membership in more than one sovereign state
- Encourages dialogical pedagogy, which must prepare human beings for multiple roles
- Calls for standardization of the governing principles by taking required inputs from the existing cosmopolitan structures.
- Gives due recognition to the importance of duties and responsibilities of the citizens and not just focus on 'rights'
- Facilitates individual freedom to achieve his perceived conception of 'good life'
- Facilitates moral commitments among human beings and encourages equal treatment towards the fellow human being
- Facilitates optimal utilization of technological advancements in the social and political domains respectively
- Institutionalizes transnational linkages at various levels

These features of transnationality would ensure greater transnational involvement of people, especially the knowledgeable ones, who has more probable functioning in their capabilities basket.

Acknowledgements

My special thanks to Dr Ajaya Sahoo, Director, Centre for Studies in Indian Diaspora, University of Hyderabad, for providing me an opportunity to share my thoughts on the subject. I also thank Professor Binod Khadria, Professor of Economics at Zakir Husain Centre for Educational Studies, School of Social Sciences, Jawaharlal Nehru University, for his valuable inputs and guidance. However, any gaps in this chapter would remain with the author.

Notes

1. The concept of globalization is complex. David Held (1999: 16) defined it as 'Globalization may be thought of as a process (or set of processes) which embodies a transformation in the spatial organization of social relations and transactions – assessed in terms of their

extensity, intensity, velocity and impact – generating transcontinental or inter-regional flows and networks of activity, interaction, and the exercise of power'.

2. It has increased the sphere of applicable knowledge to a great extent, changing the thought process.
3. Also, having negative impact because of the increasing cases of international terror networks and cybercrimes which impact the human ethics.
4. Cross-border migrations is not a phenomenon of the current phase of globalization (1990s current), rather it is associated with growth of civilizations. There are different phases of international migration patterns – migrations as slaves, migrations as indentured labour, migrations in search of economic opportunities, labour imports and skilled migrations. However, it is important to note that the pressures for international migrations are considerable and appear to be mounting in the fluctuating immigration laws. This is not surprising in a world where income disparities and population imbalances between countries are vast, while the spread of education combined with the revolution in transport has led to a significant increase in the mobility of labour (Nayyar 2002).
5. John Rawls, one of the most influential contemporary political philosophers, talked extensively about justice. In his general conception of justice, he considered the concepts such as liberty and opportunity, income and wealth, and the basis of self-respect as social primary goods (Kymlicka 1990: 52).
6. The immigration policies of most of the population receiving host countries are designed to address their labour scarcities and hence they tend to consider the receiving populations as 'assistants'.
7. However, over a period of time the assistants tend to become managers and their entrepreneurial capabilities make them 'economic contributors'.
8. For example, see Archibugi 2004; Archibugi et al. 1998; Beck and Sznaider 2006; Cheah and Robbins 1998; Held and McGrew 2002; Vertovec and Cohen 2003.
9. Fine (2007) observes that Habermas concept of constitutional patriotism is based on the German experiences with nationalism. Germany appears as an exemplary nation in the sense that it has 'learnt' from history of the dangers of a non-rational sense of political belonging and has adopted 'a post national self-understanding of the political community' (Habermas 1998: 119). In Germany, national identity can be rebuilt only through a sense of joint responsibility among Germans to keep alive the memory of those murdered by German hands, a responsibility which carries over into next generations.

Habermas points out that constitutional patriotism finds a special home in Germany for the German condition highlights the essential lesson of twentieth-century history – that nationalism is no longer defensible as an ethical ideal (1998: 119).

10. In bit of a deviation, cosmopolitanism was a potential source of hope for Jacques Derrida, where in his essay, 'On Cosmopolitanism', he proposed an open city for immigrants where they would be protected from persecution, intimidation or exile. The idea of the open city had been marginalized by the rise of the nation state, and Derrida wanted to recover it as a potential solution to the problem of European immigration. This 'confessional' cosmopolitanism differed from Kant's 'triumphant' one in that Kant's cosmopolitanism was dependent upon the sovereignty of the state, where all values became politicized and ultimately subordinated to the state's ends. By contrast, Derrida recovered the notion of a 'confessional' cosmopolitanism where unconditional hospitality should be offered to all immigrants, while, at the same time, recognizing that some limitation on the rights of residence had to be in place (Trepanier 2012).
11. The traditional notions of sovereignty still carry enormous symbolic weight and practical consequences, precisely at this historical moment when states' ability to assert sovereign authority is weakening.
12. In the political science literature, this is termed as 'external sovereignty'. This underlines the Westphalian model of international political life, in which external actors are excluded from 'domestic authority structures'.
13. Anthony Giddens calls this as the 'duality of structure'. For Giddens, the individual and the community cannot accurately be understood as opposed and antagonistic ideas. Indeed they are mutually dependent. Through exercising rights and obligations, individuals reproduce the necessary conditions for citizenship (Giddens 1984: 25). For further analysis and commentary on these lines, see Faulks (2003).
14. The *Encyclopedia of Britannica* defines citizenship as 'a relationship between an individual and a state in which an individual owes allegiance to that state and is in turn entitled to its protection'.
15. In theory, it should be 'multiple citizenship', but 'dual citizenship' is widely used when we understand the concept empirically. The words 'multiple nationality' or 'dual nationality' is also used by many scholars interchangeably.
16. The Council of Europe, sources of 1963 convention explicitly designed to limit the incidence of multiple citizenship, adopted several protocols that greatly softened the restrictive message, and in 1997 it accepted a new European Convention on Nationality that

readily accepts dual nationality and attempts in modest but important ways to regulate it (Council of Europe 1993, 1997). This convention entered into force with three parties (Austria, Moldova and Slovakia) in 2000. Presently 29 countries signed the convention and 20 of them ratified. The United Kingdom did not sign this convention, and France is yet to ratify. None of the non-member states of the Council of Europe signed the convention. This is the status as on 16 June 2012.

17. Some countries such as Austria, Cyprus Saint Kitts grant citizenship by monetary investments in their country! Much of the developed countries such as the United States, the United Kingdom, Australia and Switzerland have no restrictions on holding dual nationality, whereas countries such as Singapore, Austria, India and Saudi Arabia do not 'recognize' or 'restrict' dual citizenships, leading to automatic loss of citizenship upon acquiring others. However, 39 countries allow dual citizenship with some limitations; and around 50 countries do not allow. India has come up with 'Overseas Indian Citizenship', which, I think is as good as 'dual citizenship', in all practical purposes.
18. *Jus sanguinis* is a social policy by which citizenship is not determined by place of birth but by having one or both parent who are citizens of the nation. It is a Latin word for meaning 'right of the soil'. The countries that have *jus sanguinis* policy for citizenship are Bulgaria, Croatia, Estonia, Finland, Germany, Greece, Hungary, India, Ireland, Israel, Italy, Kiribati, Liberia, Poland, Rwanda, Serbia, Slovakia, South Korea, Spain, Turkey and Ukraine.
19. *Jus soli* is a right by which nationality or citizenship can be recognized to any individual born in the territory of the related state, irrespective of his/her original roots. The independence of the English colonies in America, and the French Revolution, laid the foundations for *jus soli*. With the social and economic development of the nineteenth and twentieth centuries, and the massive migrations to the Americas and Western Europe, *jus soli* was established in a greater and greater number of countries. The countries that follow *jus soli* citizenship are Antigua and Barbuda, Argentina, Barbados, Belize, Bolivia, Brazil, Cambodia, Canada, Chile, Colombia, Costa Rica, Dominica, Ecuador, El Salvador, Fiji, Grenada, Guatemala, Guyana, Honduras, Jamaica, Lesotho, Mexico, Nicaragua, Pakistan, Panama, Paraguay, Peru, Saint Kitts and Nevis, Saint Lucia, Saint Vincent and the Grenadines, Trinidad and Tobago, Tuvalu, the United States, Uruguay and Venezuela. Some countries that followed *jus sanguinis* modified their citizenship policies with the provisions of *jus soli*. Some of them are Australia, Dominican Republic, France, Germany, New Zealand, Ireland, South Africa and the United Kingdom. As a matter of fact, most of the countries are presently using a combination of both *jus soli* and *jus sanguinis* (Wikipedia.com, accessed on 15 June 2012).

20. For example, when a country of initial nationality makes it difficult or prohibitively costly to secure release from its citizenship.
21. The United States, for example, retains by statute its formal requirement, as part of the naturalization oath, that new citizens renounce all prior allegiances. But the US Department of State now treats this provision as essentially unenforceable, sometimes advising prospective new citizens not to worry about plans to continue exercising the rights and privileges of the original nationality. This stance is rationalized by a judgment that the renunciatory language in the US naturalization oath would not be regarded by most other countries as effectively terminating their nationality.
22. Australia, in 1986, deleted the requirement that naturalizing citizens renounce their former nationality (Zappala and Castles 2000: 46–47).
23. The 1947 Canadian Citizenship Act contained no renunciation requirement. Canada continued this policy in the comprehensive revision that resulted in the 1977 Citizenship Act. A step further, it eliminated a provision that had decreed loss of Canadian citizenship for its nationals who naturalize elsewhere. For more see Galloway (2000).
24. Kepstein (1999), observes that instability and war bred in one country had shattered international peace. He says 'The Bolshhevik revolution in 1917 and interwar Germany demonstrated that economic deprivation anywhere could lead to political conflict everywhere' (Kepstein 1999: 113).
25. Rawls argues that justice requires citizens to aim for a national economic order that satisfies the difference principle, that is, that allows social and economic inequalities to arise only in so far as they tend to optimize the lowest socio-economic position (Rawls, 1999: 11, 12, 17). For more debate on Rawls and his applications at the global level, see Sen (1999a) and Thomas Pogge (2001).
26. For example, Germany agreed on according certain rights and privileges to ethnic Poles residing within its borders, so long as Poland provided reciprocal rights to ethnic Germans in Poland.
27. The language of Article 15 of the Universal Declaration of Human Rights (1948) reads, 'No one shall be arbitrarily deprived of his nationality nor denied the right to change his nationality'. This permits sovereign states some latitude in determining what would be 'non-arbitrary' denaturalization (For more commentary see Benhabib 2004).
28. The new philosophy expressed through the Universal Declaration of Human Rights ensured that attention was focused on the issue of universal rights and human dignity; as Musgrave notes, 'a proposal to

include a provision protecting minorities in the Declaration was expressly rejected by the General Assembly, which concluded that it would be too difficult to formulate a provision applicable to all the minorities' (1997: 129) and, at a multilateral level, 'there was clearly a reluctance in the early post war period to grant special rights to minorities' (1997: 133). For more commentary see Laden and Owen (2007).

29. This is quite a radical departure from the confined limits of the American Declaration of 1776 or the French affirmations of 1789. It was observed that even President Abraham Lincoln had not initially demanded political and social rights for the slaves – only some minimal rights, concerning life, liberty and fruits of labour (Sen 2009: 380).
30. The works of Thomas Pogge, and his collaborators, have opened up many areas of policy analysis broadly based on the idea of human rights and the demand of justice. See Thomas Pogge [2002 (2008)].
31. Some scholars consider that the control over migration remains one of the last bastions of the truly sovereign state.
32. The first reference to migration in a declaration of human rights is found in the Argentine Constitution. It is also found in other constitutions: Bolivia, 1938 (Art. 6); Brazil, 1937 (Art. 151) (subject to quota system of 2 per cent) and 1946 (in a far more liberal way); Cuba, 1940 (Art. 12 and 14); Chile, 1925 (Art. 10); Ecuador, 1906 (Art. 26 and 28) (as related to freedom of movement and equality of rights); Guatemala, 1879 (Art. 19); Honduras, 1936 (Art. 67); Mexico, 1917 (Art. 11); Panama, 1941 (Art. 40); Paraguay, 1940 (Art. 9); Peru, 1933 (Art. 67); Uruguay, 1934, subsequently amended (Art. 36) and Venezuela, 1936 (Art. 100). The texts of these constitutions can be seen in Rives (1952). For more analysis on legal instruments in migration, see Aleinikoff and Chetail (2003).
33. For the text and a commentary of the Strasbourg Declaration, see Hofmann (1987).
34. Chetail (2003) also discusses on the regional instruments relating to the right to leave and to return. For example, Protocol No. 4 of the European Convention for the Protection of Human Rights and Fundamental Freedoms adopted in 1963; 1961 European Social Charter and the 1977 European Convention on Legal Status of Migrant Workers; The Final Act of the Conference on Security and Cooperation in Europe, 1975; 1948 American Declaration of the Rights and Duties of Men; 1969 American Convention on Human Rights; 1981 African Charter on Human and Peoples' Rights and Arab Charter on Human Rights, besides others.

35. Especially with reference to his later book *Multicultural Odyssey*, published in 2007.
36. The top recipients of officially recorded remittances in 2011 were India ($58 billion), China ($57 billion), Mexico ($24 billion) and the Philippines ($23 billion). Other large recipients included Pakistan, Bangladesh, Nigeria, Vietnam, Egypt and Lebanon. However, as a share of GDP, remittances were larger in smaller and lower income countries; top recipients relative to GDP were Tajikistan, Lesotho, Nepal, Samoa and Tonga. Remittances sent home by migrants to developing countries are three times the size of official development assistance and represent a lifeline for the poor. Despite the current global economic weakness, remittance flows are expected to continue growing, with global remittances expected to exceed $593 billion by 2014, of which $441 billion will flow to developing countries. For more on this, see World Bank (2011).
37. The challenge of social change for psychology: see Sampson, Edward E. June 1989. Globalization and Psychology's Theory of the Person, *American Psychologist*, Vol. 44(6): 914–921.
38. Bandura, Albert. February 2001. The Changing Face of Psychology at the Dawning of a Globalization Era. *Canadian Psychology/Psychologie canadienne*, Vol. 42(1): 12–24.
39. The approach has been developed in a variety of more specific normative theories, such as (partial) theories of social justice or accounts of development ethics. It has also led to a new and highly interdisciplinary literature in the social sciences resulting in new statistics and social indicators and to a new policy paradigm, which is mainly used in development studies, 'human development approach'.
40. This also explains why the capability approach is often favourably regarded by feminist philosophers, or philosophers concerned with care and disability issues, since one of their main complaints about mainstream moral and political philosophy has precisely been the relative invisibility of the fate of those people whose lives did not correspond to that of an able-bodied, non-dependent, caregiving-free individual who belongs to the dominant ethnic, racial and religious group. People of colour, marginalized people, the disabled and many women do not fit that picture.
41. For example, in standard outcome assessments, women as a group virtually always end up being worse off than men. But if the selection of outcome dimensions is also shifted to include the quality and quantity of social relations and support, and being able to engage in hands-on care, then the normative assessment of gender inequality becomes less univocal and requires much further argument and normative defence, including being explicit about how to aggregate different dimensions.

42. Anthropologists such as Barbara Kirshenblatt-Gimblett (1994), Arjun Appadurai (1991) and Steven Vertovec and Robin Cohen (1999), besides others.
43. Transnationality index is brought out by UNCTAD.

References

Aleinikoff, T.A. and Chetail, V. (eds). 2003. *Migration and International Legal Norms*. The Hague: TMC Asser Press.

Aleinikoff, T.A. and Klusmeyer, D. 2002. *Citizenship Politics for an Age of Migration*. Washington DC: Carnegie Endowment for International Peace and Migration Policy Institute.

Amin, S. 1972. '*Accumulation on a World Scale*', Monthly Review Press, New York.

Appadurai, A. 1991. 'Global Ethnoscapes: Notes and Queries, Recapturing Anthropology – Working in the Present'. Chapter 10, Santa Fe: School of American Research Press, 191–140, references.

Archibugi, D. 2004. *Cosmopolitics*. London: Verso.

Archibugi, D., Held, D. and Kohler, M. (eds). 1998. *Re-imagining Political Community: Studies in Cosmopolitan Democracy*. Cambridge: Polity Press.

Barbalet, J.M. 1988. *Citizenship*. Milton Keynes, England: Oxford University Press.

Barry, B. 2005. *Why Social Justice Matters*. London: Polity Press.

Baubock, R. 2003, 'Towards a Political Theory of Migrant Integration', 37 (3); *International Migration Review*, 700–23

Baubock, R. 2007a. The Trade–Off between Transnational Citizenship and Political Autonomy. In Faist, T. and Kivisto, P. (eds), *Dual Citizenship in Global Perspective*. London: Palgrave Macmillan, 69–91.

Baubock, R. 2007b. The Rights of Others and the Boundaries of Democracy. *European Journal of Political Theory*, 6, 398–405.

Beck, U. and Sznaider, N. (eds). 2006. *British Journal of sociology*, 51(1). Special Issue on Cosmopolitan Sociology.

Beitz, C. 1979. *Political Theory and International Relations*. Princeton: Princeton University Press. Revised edition 1999.

Benhabib, S. 2002. *The Claims of Culture: Equality and Diversity in the Global Era*. Princeton: Princeton University Press.

Benhabib, S. 2004. *The Rights of Others: Aliens, Residents, and Citizens*. Cambridge: Cambridge University Press.

Bloemraad, I., Korteweg, A. and Yurdakul, G. 2008. Citizenship and Immigration: Multiculturalism, Assimilation and Challenges to the Nation State. *Annual Review of Sociology*, 34, 153–179.

Bloemrraad, I. (2004), 'Who Claims Dual Citizenship? The Limits of Postnationalism, the possibilities of transnationalism, and the persistence of traditional citizenship', 38 (2); *International Migration Review*, 389-426.

Calhoun, C. 2008. Cosmopolitanism and Nationalism. *Nations and Nationalism*, 14(3), 427–448.

Chatterjee, D. 2008. *Democracy in a Global World: Human Rights and Political Participation in the 21st Century*. London: Rowman and Littlefield.

Cheah, P. and Robbins, B. (eds). 1998. *Cosmopolitics: Thinking and Feeling Beyond the Nation*. Minneapolis: University of Minnesota Press.

Cheltenham Waldron, J. 1992. Superseding Historic Injustice. *Ethics,* 103(1), 4–28.

Chetail, V. 2003. Freedom of Movement and Transnational Migrations: A Human Rights Perspective. In Aleinikoff, T.A. and Chetail, V. (eds), *Migration and International Legal Norms*. The Hague: TMC Asser Press.

Chimni, B.S. 2003. Development and Migration. Chapter 5, In Aleinikoff, T. A. and Chetail, V. (eds.), *Migration and International Legal Norms*. The Hague: TMC Asser Press.

Council of Europe. 1993. 'Second Protocol Amending the Convention on the Reduction of Cases of Multiple Nationality and Military Obligations in Cases of Multiple Nationality'. 2 February, CETS No. 149.

Council of Europe. 1997. 'European Convention on Nationality', 24 November, CETS No.166 Available at: http://conventions.coe.int/Treaty/Commun/QueVoulezVous.asp?NT=166&CL=ENG (accessed on 16 June 2012).

Cutler, A.C., Haufler, V., and Porter, T. 1999. Private Authority and Global Governance. In Cutler, C., Haufler, V., and Porter, T. (eds), *Private Authority in International Affairs*. New York: State University of New York Press.

Faist, T. (2001), 'Dual Citizenship as Overlapping Membership', *Working Paper*, 3/01, Willy Brandt Series, School of International Migration and Ethnic Relations, Malmo

Faist, T., Gerdes, J. and Rieple, B. 2007. 'We Are All "Republican" Now': The Politics of Dual Citizenship in Germany'. In Faist, T. (ed.), *Dual Citizenship in Europe: From Nationhood to Societal Integration*. Aldershot: Ashgate, 45–76.

Faist, Thomas; Margit Fauser and Eveline Reisenauer. 2013. '*Transnational Migration*', Cambridge, UK: Polity Press

Faulks, K. 2003. *Citizenship*. London: Routledge.

Fine, R. 2007. 'Cosmopolitanism'. Oxon: Routledge.

Forst, R. 1999. 'The Basic Right to Justification: Towards a Constructivist Conception of Human Rights'. *Constellations*, 6, 35–60.

Galloway, D. 2000. The Dilemmas of Canadian Citizenship Law. In Aleinikoff, T.A. and Douglas Klusmeyer, D. (eds), *From Migrants to Citizens: Membership in a Changing World.* Washington, DC: Carnegie Endowment for International Peace.

Gardner, K. and Grillo, R. 2002. 'Transnational Households and Ritual: An Overview', 2; *Global Networks,* 179–90

GCIM. 2005. Report of the Global Commission for International Migration. UN/POP/MIG-FCM/2005/09, Fourth Coordination Meeting on International Migration, Population Division, Dept. of Economic and Social Affairs, United Nations, October.

Gerdes, J. and Faist, T. 2007. Varying Views on Democracy, Rights and Duties, and Membership: The Politics of Dual Citizenship in European Immigration States. In, Faist, T. and Kivisto, P. (eds), *Dual Citizenship in Global Perspective*. London: Palgrave Macmillan, 137–160.

Giddens, A. 1984. *The Constitution of Society*. Cambridge: Polity Press.

Habermas, J. 1998. *Inclusion of the Other: Studies in Political Theory*. Cambridge: Polity Press.

Habermas, J. 2001. *The Post-national Constellations: Political Essays* (ed. Max Pensky). Cambridge: Polity Press.

Hampton, J. 1998. *Political Philosophy*. New Delhi: Oxford University Press.

Held, D. 1999. The Transformation of Political Community: Rethinking Democracy in the Context of Globalization. In Shapiro, I. and Cordon, C.H. (eds), *Democracy's Edges*. Cambridge: Cambridge University Press, 84–111.

Held, D. and McGrew, A. (eds.). 2002. *Governing Globalization*. Oxford: Polity Press.

Held, D., McGrew, A., Goldblatt, D. and Perraton, J. (1999) Global Transformations: Politics, Economics and Culture. Cambridge: Polity Press.

Hofmann, R. 1987. The Right to Leave and to Return to One's Own Country: The Strasbourg Declaration on the Right to Leave and to Return: Results of the Meeting of Experts Held on Strasbourg in November 1986. *Human Rights Law Journal*, 8, 478–484.

Hussain, M. (2005), *'Measuring Migrant Remittances: From the Perspective of the European Commission',* Presented at World Bank Int. Tech. Meet. Meas. Migr. Remit., Jan. 24–25, Washington, DC.

Isin, Engin F. and Turner, Bryan S. 2002. Citizenship studies: An introduction. In: Isin, Engin F. and Turner, Bryan S. (eds) Handbook of citizenship studies. London, UK: Sage, 1–10.

Itzigsohn J. (2000), 'Immigration and the boundaries of citizenship: the institutions of immigrants' political transnationalism'. 34: *International Migration Review,* 1126–54.

Jacobsen, T.S. and Ramesh C.T. (eds). 2008. *Re-envisioning Sovereignty*. Oxon: Ashgate Publishing.

Jayasurya, K. 2006. *Statecraft, Welfare and the Politics of Inclusion*. Hampshire, UK: Palgrave Macmillan.

Jones-Correa, M. 2001. Under Two Flags: Dual Nationality in Latin America and Its Consequences for Naturalization in the United States. *International Migration Review*, 35(4), 997–1029.

Kant, I. 1991. *Kant: Political Writings* (ed. and Intro. by Hans Reiss). Cambridge: Cambridge University Press.

Kapstein, Ethan B. 1999. *Sharing the Wealth: Workers and the World Economy*. New York: W.W. Norton.

Kastoryano, R. (2000), '*The Reach of Transnationalism*', Social Science Research Council, . http://essays.ssrc.org/sept11/essays/kastoryano.htm

Kelly, P. (ed.). 2002. *Multiculturalism reconsidered*. Cambridge: Polity Press.

Kepstein, B.E. 1999. *Unipolar Politics: Realism and State Strategies after the Cold War*. Columbia: Columbia University Press.

Khadria, B. 1999. *The Migration of Knowledge Workers: Second-Generation Effects of India's Brain Drain*. New Delhi: Sage Publications.

Khadria, B. 2007. Diasporas in Development: From 'Social Parasites' to 'economic boon'? *Asian Population Studies*, 3(2), 103–114.

Khadria, B. 2009. Adversary Analysis and the Quest for Global Development: Optimizing the Dynamic Conflict of Interest in Transnational Migration. *Social Analysis*, 53(3), 106–122.

Kirshenblatt-Gimblett, B. 1994. Spaces of Dispersal. *Cultural Anthropology*, 9(3), 339–344.

Koslowski, R. 1998. European Migration Regimes: Emerging, Enlarging and Deteriorating. *Journal of Ethnic and Migration Studies*', 24(4), 734–744.

Kymlicka, W. 1990. *Contemporary Political Philosophy: An Introduction*. Oxford: Oxford University Press.

Kymlicka, W. 1995. *Multicultural Citizenship: A Liberal theory of Minority Rights*. Oxford: Oxford University Press.

Kymlicka, W. 2001. *Politics in the Vernacular: Nationalism, Multiculturalism and Citizenship*. Oxford: Oxford University Press.

Kymlicka, W. 2007. '*Multicultural Odysseys: Navigating the New International Politics of Diversity*. Oxford: Oxford University Press.

Laden, S.A. and Owen, D. (eds). 2007. *Multiculturalism and Political Theory*. Cambridge: Cambridge University Press.

League of Nations, Treaty Series. 1930. Convention on Certain Questions Relating to the Conflict of Nationality Laws. 12 April, *Treaties and International Engagements Registered with the Secretariat of the League of Nations*, 179 (4137) (1937–1938).

Levitt, P. and Jaworsky, N.B. (2007), 'Transnational Migration Studies: Past Developments and Future Trends', 33; *Annual Review of Sociology*, 129–56

Levitt, Peggy and B. Nadya Jaworsky (2007). Transnational Migration Studies: Past Developments and Future Trends. Annu. Rev. Sociol. 33: 129–56.

Mahler, S.J. and Pessar, P.R. (2006), 'Gender matters: ethnographers bring gender from the periphery toward the core of migration studies', 40; *International Migration Review*, 27–63

McCorquodale, R. 2001. International Law, Boundaries, and Imagination. In David Miller and Sohail H. Hashmi (eds), *Boundaries and Justice: Diverse Ethical Perspectives*, Princeton, NJ: Princeton University Press.

Michelman, F. 2001. Morality, Identity, and 'Constitutional Patriotism'. *Ratio Juris*, 14(3), 253–271.

Musgrave, T. 1997. *Self Determination and National Minorities*. Oxford: Oxford University Press.

Nayyar, D. 2002. *Governing Globalization: Issues and Institutions*. New York: Oxford University Press.

Nussbaum, M. 1997. Kant and Cosmopolitanism. In Bohman and Lutz-Bachmann (eds), *Perpetual Peace: Essays on Kant's Cosmopolitan Ideal*. London: The MIT Press, 25–58.

Ong, A. 1999. *Flexible Citizenship: The Cultural Logics of Transnationality*. Durham and London: Duke University Press.

Osteraard-Nielsen, E. (2003), 'Sending Countries and International Migration: Key Issues and Themes', 3–33; In Ostergaard-Nielsen, E. (ed.), *'Sending Countries and International Migration'*, Basingstoke: Palgrave.

Ostergaard-Nielsen, E. (ed.). 2003. *'Sending Countries and International Migration'*, Basingstoke: Palgrave.

Panizzon, M. 2010. International Law of Economic Migration: A Menage A Trois? GATS Mode 4, EPAs and Bilateral Migration Agreements. *Journal of World Trade*, 44(6). Society of International Economic Law (SIEL), Second Biennial Global Conference, University of Barcelona, 8–10 July 2010. Available at: SSRN: http://ssrn.com/abstract=1633993

Parekh, B. 2000. *Rethinking Multiculturalism: Cultural Diversity and Political Theory*. New York: Palgrave.

Pfister, T. 2012. Citizenship and Capability? Amartya Sen's Capability Approach from a Citizenship Perspective. *Citizenship Studies*, 16(4), 241–254.

Pogge, T. 1989. *Realizing Rawls*. Ithaca, NY: Cornell University Press.

Pogge, T. 2001. Rawls on International Justice: Critical Study. *The Philosophical Quarterly*, 51(203), 246–253.

Pogge, T. 2002 (2008). *World Poverty and Human Rights: Cosmopolitan Responsibilities and Reform*. Cambridge: Polity Press. (Second Edition, 2008).

Portes A. (2003) 'Conclusion: Theoretical Convergences and Empirical Evidence in the Study of Immigrant Transnationalism', 37: *International Migration Review,* 874–92.

Pries, L. (2004), 'Determining the Causes and Durability of Transnational Labour Migration between Mexico and the United States: Some Empirical Findings' 42; *International Migration,* 3–39

Rawls, J. 1999. *The Laws of Peoples*. Cambridge: Harvard University Press.

Richmond, A.H. 1994. *Global Apartheid,* Toronto: Oxford University Press.

Rives, V. Borregon. 1952. *'La Emigracion Espanola a America',* Vigo, 335–347

Robeyns, I. 2003. Sen's Capability Approach and Gender Inequality: Selecting Relevant Capabilities. *Feminist Economics*, 9(2/3), 61–92.

Sassen, S. 1999. *'Guests and Aliens',* New York: New Press.

Scheffler, S. 2007. Immigration and the Significance of Culture. *Philosophy and Public Affairs,* 35(2), 93–125.

Schlereth, T. 1997. *The Cosmopolitan Ideal in Enlightenment Thought: Its Form and Function in the Ideas of Franklin, Hume and Voltaire*. Notre Dame: University of Notre Dame Press.

Schmitt, C. 1996 [1932]. *The Concept of the Political* (Trans. George Schwab). Chicago: University of Chicago Press.

Sen, A. 2009. *The Idea of Justice*. Cambridge: Harvard University Press.

Sen, A.K. 1999a. *Development as Freedom*. Oxford: Oxford University Press.

Sen, A.K. 1999b. *Commodities and Capabilities*. New Delhi: Oxford University Press.

Sen, A.K. (1992), *'Inequality Re-examined',* Oxford: Clarendon Press.

Soysal, Y.N. 1994. *Limits of Citizenship: Migrants and Postnational Membership in Europe*. Chicago: University of Chicago Press.

Sp'ang, M. 2007. Pragmatism All the Way Down? The Politics of Dual Citizenship in Sweden. In Faist, T. (ed.), *Dual Citizenship in Europe: From Nationhood to Societal Integration*. London: Ashgate, 103–126.

Spiro, P. 2007. *Beyond Citizenship: American Identity After Globalization*. Oxford: Oxford University Press.

Spiro, P.J. 1997. Dual Nationality and the Meaning of Citizenship. *Emory Law Review,* 46(4), 1411–1485.

Spiro, P.J. 2002, 'Embracing Dual Nationality', pp: 19-33; In Hansen, R. and Weil, P. (eds), *Dual Nationality, Social Rights and Federal Citizenship in the US and Europe*, Oxford: Berghahn.

Stevenson, N. 2002. Cosmopolitanism, Multiculturalism and Citizenship. *Sociological Research Online*, 1(1). Available at: http://www.socresonline.org.uk/7/1/stevenson.html.

Susan Strange. 1996. *The Retreat of the State: The Diffusion of Power in the World Economy*. Cambridge: Cambridge University Press.

Taylor, C. 1992. *Multiculturalism and 'The Politics of Recognition'*. Princeton: Princeton University Press.

Trepanier, Lee. 2012. Darrida's Hope and Despair for Globalization. *Essays in Anamnesis*, 27 April. Available at: http://www.anamnesisjournal.com/issues/2-web-essays/49-lee-trepanier (accessed on 23 June 2012).

United Nations, Treaty Series (UNTS). 1963. Convention on the Reduction of Cases of Multiple Nationality and Military Obligations in Cases of Multiple Nationality. 6 May, Treaties and International Agreements Registered or Filed and Recorded with the Secretariat of the United Nations, Vol. 634, No. 9065.

Vertovec, S. (2004), 'Cheap Calls: the social glue of migrant transnationalism', 4; *Global Networks,* 219–24.

Vertovec, S. 2009. *Transnationalism*, Oxon: Routledge.

Vertovec, S. 1999. Conceiving and researching transnationalism. *Ethnic and Racial Studies*, Vol. 22, No. 2 (447–462).

Vertovec, S. and Cohen, R. (eds). 1999. *Migration, Diasporas and Transnationalism*. Cheltenham, UK: Edward Elgar Publishing Ltd.

Vertovec, S. and Cohen, R. (eds). 2003. *Conceiving Cosmopolitanism: Theory, Context and Practice*. Oxford: Oxford University Press.

Villamil, Jose Joaquin. 1979. *'Transnational capitalism and national development: new perspectives on dependence'*, Vol. 2 of Humanities Studies in Development, New Jersey: Humanities Press.

Willis, K.D. 2000. 'Gender and Transnational Household Strategies: Singaporean Migration to China', 34' *Regional Studies,* 253–64.

Wong, L.L. 1997. Globalization and Transnational Migration. *International Sociology*, Vol. 12(3), 329–351.

World Bank. 2011. *Migration and Remittances*, Issue Brief.

World Bank. 2000. *Migration and Remittances*. Issue Brief.

World Bank. 2006. *Global Economic Prospects: Economic Implications of Remittances and Migration*. Washington, DC: International Bank for Reconstruction and Development.

Zappala, G. and Castles, S. 2000. Citizenship and Immigration in Australia. In Aleinikoff, T.A. and Douglas Klusmeyer, D. (eds), *From Migrants to Citizens: Membership in a Changing World*. Washington, DC: Carnegie Endowment for International Peace.

6

Tracing Transnational Networks in Amitav Ghosh's *In an Antique Land*

Anindita Shome

This chapter attempts to do an analysis of Amitav Ghosh's nonfiction, *In an Antique Land* (1992), to bring out the possibilities of medieval era transnationalism. By drawing analogies between the present era transnational trends and the traces of medieval era linkages amongst India, Egypt and Aden – that Ghosh brings out in this text – I wish to study these linkages as medieval era transnational phenomena that share several similarities to what is now known as transnationalism. Abiding by Nina Glick-Schiller's definition of the *Transnational Process* as the political, economic and cultural practices that transcend the borders of a particular state and comprising transnational individuals (Glick-Schiller 2007: 123), this chapter tries to study the findings of Ghosh through the transnational lens. Trade, languages, culture and personal relationships in host land and homeland are the important parameters through which this chapter will try to assert the presence of different kinds of transnational trends existent during the medieval era. While trying to draw similarities between the new and the old transnational trends, this chapter takes into account Ghosh's own travels and experiences that form an important part of this non-fiction.

Amitav Ghosh, an Indian-born author, has lived in India, Bangladesh and Sri Lanka, during his growing years. An illustrious writer of several novels and essays, and a recipient of many literary awards, he has pursued his studies in Delhi, Oxford and Alexandria, and has also taught in several universities in India and the United States. Beginning with *The Circle of Reason* (1986), Ghosh, in his work, has dealt with the issues of migration, alienation, travel, exchange of people and cultures amongst nations through the histories of commoners, especially the subaltern, that are generally considered to be insignificant (Srivastava 2015). Ghosh uses his training in social anthropology with fiction 'My essential interest is in people and their lives, histories and predicaments … fiction is my proper metier' (quoted in Srivastava 2015). According to James Clifford, a moral puzzlement over borders is to be found in Ghosh's novels and their entangled worlds, making his novels intricate and travel writing, a critical aspect of these novels (1994: 1). This chapter takes up Ghosh's nonfiction, *In an Antique Land*, as it is a unique work that strives to trace the bizarre history of shared connections between two countries, Egypt and India, through almost ten centuries of closed-mindedness as well as compassion, prejudices and affection.

Transcending Genres to Trace Transnationalism

Amitav Ghosh's historical nonfiction, *In an Antique Land: History in the Guise of a Traveler's Tale* (1992) could be considered a travelogue, a non-fiction, a historical non-fiction – all merged into one and each genre being complementary to the other. Ghosh uses the tool of narrative to create an alternate as well as a parallel history, which defies the Eurocentric view that there were no thriving trade relations of India with other nations before its colonization by the European powers. Clifford writes that the aim of Ghosh's narrative is to make space for a counter-history of modernity (1994: 7). Ghosh, through this text, narrates and sheds light on the supposed insignificant life of an Indian slave to a Tunisian Jewish merchant in the medieval era (1100s) and his possible transnational adventures amidst grander historical events that have the privilege to get recorded in the pages of history (1992: 17). This text could be read as an endeavour to document a non-Eurocentric view of pre-colonial India's transnational links with other nations and vice versa on the Indian Ocean trade routes.

On Travel

To begin with the narration of the text, Ghosh narrates his own modern-day travel account across Egypt-Lataifa, Nashawy and Cairo and medieval era travel accounts of Ben Yiju and his slave, Bomma, in alternative chapters, mostly. Ghosh's own travel account is in first-person narrative and it can be deduced as a transnational account of a modern or postmodern individual, who has been trying to trace the phenomenon of transnationalism in a medieval, pre-colonial age around 1100s. By transnationalism, this chapter takes into account the argument that a migration can be theorized as transnationalism when the migrants give rise to and nurture multiple connections – familial, economic, social, organizational, religious and political – transcending borders (Glick-Schiller 2007: 123). Similar to present day studies on transnational migration, which focus on how economic, religious, political and social relationships, that entrench people in two or more societies, operate and how they have an impact on the people directly or indirectly involved in transnationalism (Glick-Schiller 2007: 120), Ghosh throws light on all such aspects through this non-fiction. While narrating his own travel adventures, Ghosh brings out the stark similarities between the cultures and history of India and Egypt, and tells us how, with the advent of colonialism, the shared history of the both the nations has been lost to such an extent that now it seems implausible that such a shared history ever connected the two nations in the past (1992: 80–81).

It is interesting to note the ways in which Amitav Ghosh's own travels and time spent in a host land for his research work reflect the pangs of reminiscences one goes through when one is away from their homeland in another land, be it in the ancient eras or in the contemporary times. For example, Ghosh reminisces, 'in the manner that women hitch up their saris during the monsoons in Calcutta' (1992: 51). While writing about an incident in which he found it difficult to communicate about a tenet of his homeland with a native of the host land, Ghosh realizes that he was entrapped by language (1992: 62). Such situations are common with people in host lands or their new homelands and must have also been common with Ben Yiju and Bomma during their travels to distant lands. Drawing similarities between India and Egypt, Ghosh writes what Ustad Sabry, a native of Egypt and a school teacher, and also a part of Ghosh's narrative, had to say about their nations – that both India and Egypt have had long traditions of alliance (1992: 134). Ustad Sabry goes on to inform how India and Egypt were similar as predominantly agricultural nations; that Indians had villages like the fellaheen in Egypt; the common history of European imperialism that both the nations faced and so on. (1992: 134). Ghosh writes that a friend of his in Nashawy, Egypt, named Khamees, also a part of his narrative, reminds him of 'coffee-houses in Delhi and Calcutta ... to a familiar world of lecture-rooms, late-night rehearsals and black coffee' (1992: 167).

Ghosh set about finding the name of this Indian slave of Ben Yiju, which was written as 'Bama' in one of Khalaf ibn Ishaq's letters to Ben Yiju. Ghosh after going through several hurdles and sources came to the conclusion that 'Bama' came from 'Bamma', which used to be a common name in Tulunad, the region around Mangalore, during the medieval era. Ghosh now sets about to establish that Bomma's travels to lands far from his homeland. In a letter from Ben Yiju's friend, Madmun, from Aden, Bomma is mentioned and Ghosh writes that from the outline of Madmun's narrative, it could be possible to deduce that Bomma was actually present, on his very first appearance in the Geniza, at the enactment of a vigorous historical event, far away from his home in Mangalore (1992: 255). It was on a business and shopping trip on behalf of Ben Yiju that Bomma was in Aden around that time. From the letter, we come to know of Bomma's drunken histrionics in Madmun's office in Aden demanding more money. This incident did not matter much to Ben Yiju, as from the letters and the study of other sources and circumstances, Ghosh tells us that Ben Yiju and Bomma shared a unique bond which went past the master–slave connotations of the modern times (1992: 259), and gradually Bomma held a significant place in Ben Yiju's trade and Khalaf (one of Ben Yiju's friends) began to add the title 'Shaikh' to Bomma's name in his later letters (1992: 266).

On Subaltern

Amitav Ghosh, through his writings, attempts to bring into focus the lives of people in the margins or those people whose histories were never considered important enough to be properly recorded.

Ghosh's novels have always focussed on the subaltern and their histories. In his *Sea of Poppies* (2008), 'a high caste widow from Ghazipur … elopes with an untouchable' (Singh 2012). His *In an Antique Land* is primarily about tracing the life of 'Bomma, the Indian slave to the Tunisian Jew …' (Singh 2012: 51). The lives of these individuals are brought into central focus by the use of archives and fiction by Ghosh, for whom, if history is of interest, it is because it provides instances of unusual and extraordinary predicaments (Singh 2012: 51). Binayak Roy considers the narrative of 'the slave of MS H.6' in *In an Antique Land* to be a reconstruction of an 'obscure, fragile subaltern subject' and the slave to be a 'paradigmatic subaltern' (2011: 60).

Amitav Ghosh's *In an Antique Land* could be summed up as an endeavour to trace the history of the slave of MS H.6, who lived during the precolonial era. Amitav Ghosh refers to the first documented proof of the slave's existence in an article by E. Strauss, the 1942 issue of a Hebrew journal, *Zion*, which was published in Jerusalem (1992: 13) and that made the slave of MS H.6 to emerge from long-neglected history into modern times. This article consisted of a letter, from the year 1148 AD, sent from Aden to Mangalore, by a merchant, Khalaf ibn Ishaq, in Aden to another merchant named Ben Yiju in Mangalore. In this work of his, Ghosh intends to, through Ben Yiju and the Indian slave's life, unearth those undocumented or poorly documented threads of history that goes on without much interruption by the greater, documented historical events. This letter of Khalaf ibn Ishaq does not mention any of the greater historical events taking place around him; instead he focuses on the day-to-day events of their lives. He sends the Indian slave of Ben Yiju 'plentiful greetings' (1992: 16) before finishing the letter. Ghosh attaches immense significance to this mere mention of the slave in a letter because at the time of Ben Yiju and his slave's existence the only people whose lives went down in history were the rulers, chroniclers and other elites, those powerful people who had the means to etch their lives physically upon time (1992: 17). This letter is testament to the history of ordinary lives, whose lives were not considered important enough to be documented – those scarcely noticeable traces that ordinary and common people leave upon this world (1992: 17). Thus, this letter, unintentionally, conserves one of the many neglected strands in history, that talk of alternate, undocumented histories.

The next letter of Khalaf ibn Ishaq, in which the slave has been mentioned, was also from the land of Aden to Ben Yiju in Mangalore. This letter, although published 31 years later to that of the first one, is estimated to have been written earlier than the first one, that is, in the year 1139 (1992: 17). The letter contains the same essence of an indifference to greater historical events taking place around Khalaf ibn Ishaq, and a concentration on the daily, real lives of ordinary men – the issue of buying a 'frying-pan of stone in a case' (1992: 18). In this letter, too, the slave is only merely mentioned, but this time with a footnote as being Yiju's Indian 'slave and business agent, a respected member of his household' (1992: 18). This letter also provides with some information about Ben Yiju – a Tunisian, Jewish merchant, who had stayed in India for 17 years for trade.

Talking of Ben Yiju's origins, Ghosh talks about the world that existed in Egypt at that medieval era. He mentions that Ben Yiju did not join an ordinary congregation in Masr, but one which comprised people – whose range of travels, experiences and education seem bewildering even in our contemporary times, where our planet is considered to be newly shrunken due to incredible advancements in communication and technology (1992: 55). Ghosh while continuing to talk about the congregation writes that they had a chamber, 'Geniza', which literally means a storehouse, and they used this for preserving their writings with the idea of disposing them later on with rituals. Ghosh further informs us that this term Geniza originates from the Persian root 'ganj' and can even be found in the names of places in India – Ballygunge – as the British named it (1992: 57). The reader is also informed that the last paper to be sent to the Geniza was in 1875 – a divorce settlement written in Bombay (1992: 57). Ghosh informs us that although the synagogue has undergone outwardly changes through the centuries, yet its position remains the same, it is the same place that stored the ultimate single collection of medieval documents to be ever revealed (1992: 59), and it is the same neglected place of Masr where the histories of the lives of Abraham Ben Yiju and his Indian slave awaited to be discovered exceeding seven centuries. Binayak Roy writes that by digging up Ben Yiju's and his Bomma's origins, Ghosh discovers a vital medieval, cosmopolitan world that outdates our present ideas of cosmopolitanism (2011: 61).

On Transnational Networks

Talking about Cairo, Ghosh mentions that Cairo and Egypt are both known by the same name *Masr*, across the country, and even in India, Masr is known as *Mishor* in Bengali and *Misar* in Hindi (1992: 32). Ghosh is trying to re-establish the ancient connections of Egypt with other nations, including India. Contrasting this with the Eurocentric view, Ghosh writes that it is only in most parts of Europe that Egypt is not known by the term it prefers, but by terms such as 'Egyptian darkness' (1992: 32) and so on. This is one instance of how Ghosh implies that the Eurocentric views failed to understand the indigenous essence of all those places and cultures that were colonized and robbed of their ancient links and histories for centuries. While further talking of an interesting fact to the name 'Masr', Ghosh compares the modern day Fustat, Old Cairo, with the Fustat Masr of Ben Yiju's lifetime (1992: 33–34). Ghosh writes that the medieval age Fustat was the central point connecting innumerable commercial routes that linked almost the entire world and was considered to be the heart of one of the most prosperous and most diverse and cosmopolitan cities on earth (1992: 38). He compares the medieval era's incredible prosperity of a place like Fustat to the modern day Fustat that 'it is a gigantic refuse pit, an immense rubbish-dump' (1992: 38). He further informs us that it is in this decaying Fustat that traces of ancient era trade links with other far-off nations have been discovered, for example, pieces of Indian textiles that were of utmost worth (1992: 39). This could be an instance of medieval era 'broad' transnationalism, which include transnational activities on a regular as well as occasional basis (Vertovec 2012: 52), and it could also be placed under 'core' or 'expanded' transnationalism, depending on whether or not these transnational trade links led to other social linkages (Vertovec 2012: 52).

Binayak Roy writes that the possibility of a *trading argot* or an *elaborated pidgin language* (Ghosh 1992: 281) is a sign of multiculturalism in the mercantile world of Ben Yiju in Mangalore (2011: 65). Ghosh deduces that trade in the Indian Ocean could not have taken place without a pidgin, as use of any single language belonging to any one community of traders would have made trade very difficult amongst such a varied group of traders. He infers the possibility of the existence of a pidgin, probably made up of Perso-Arabic and north Indian features, especially used by the traders operating along the Malabar Coast region. Talking of language, linking up the past with the present and how the study of the origin of certain words in a language can lead to hidden connections between different languages and cultures is an incredible realization. Ghosh gives such an example of the modern world in his text that implies Indo-Egyptian ancient connections. The English word 'sugar' has its origins in the Arabic word 'sukkar', which has further origins in Sanskrit sources. But in various parts of the subcontinent, sugar is commonly known as 'misri', which is supposed to have been named after 'Masr' due to the medieval era import of sugar from Egypt to the subcontinent (1992: 269). Thus, the word sugar and names by which it is known in different parts of the world can imply some long-lost ancient connections existing between two different cultures that might have drifted apart through the centuries.

The medieval trade networks, that brought Ben Yiju to Mangalore and took Bomma to Aden, nurtured connections that surpassed the barriers of geography, religion, language and culture. Ben Yiju and his friends held strong connections with Gujarati merchants of India – who had a strong presence on the Indian Ocean trade routes from Aden to Malacca; and many other transmigrants, belonging to different religions and castes, who acted smaller or larger parts in this transregional Indian Ocean trade of the medieval era, ship owners, merchants, metal workers, agents, retailers and so on (1992: 278–279). Ghosh writes that the bonds made through trade were, sometimes, inseparable and unbreakable, as they were built on mutual trust and understanding, beyond the social barriers and differences. Implying a medieval period transnationalism that existed between Middle Eastern nations, India and few other nations, Ghosh writes that the Jewish traders of Fustat were for centuries connected to the Indian Ocean trade and several of them were frequent travellers between three continents (1992: 55). This could be placed under that kind of transnationalism where transmigrants are observed to travel repeatedly between specific sites (Vertovec 2012: 52).

Ghosh, while alternating chapters between his time in Egypt and the medieval time of Ben Yiju's, is drawing a similarity between his travels and Ben Yiju's and his Indian slave's travels. Summing up the loneliness of someone who stays away from one's homeland in a distant land, one of Ghosh's friends in Egypt, Nabeel, aptly asked him, if while making tea only for himself made him think of all the people he had left behind at home (1992: 152). Shaikh Musa, another of Ghosh's friends in Egypt, gave a reason behind why one leaves one's homeland and moves to another land 'The opportunity comes, and it has to be taken' (1992: 152). In a similar way, Ghosh writes that even for Ben Yiju, traveling to host lands away from his homeland, for better opportunities, would have been an obvious choice. This hints at the possibility of a kind of transnational community that is characterized by thick and dense linkages and networks across state borders shaped by immigrants in their search for economic progress and social recognition (Glick-Schiller 2007: 126) and that is similar to that of modern era transnational trends. For Ben Yiju, his friends and merchants like them, the trade relations and routes between India and the Middle East were very significant for them as travelling merchants, brokers or financiers. Ghosh writes that Ben Yiju stayed in the Malabar Coast for almost 20 years from around 1132 AD or slightly before that. For reasons of his own, Ben Yiju never made a trip back to Aden or Egypt in that time span; instead, it was his Indian slave, Bomma, who travelled to Aden for business on his master's behalf. While talking about the route Ben Yiju might have taken from Egypt to Aden and then to India, the text tells us of a town named Qus, north of Luxor, and it's description by Ibn Jubaîr, an Andalusian Arab, as the town was marvellously cosmopolitan, comprising several Yemeni, Ethiopian and Indian merchants using it to travel to other places (1992: 174). This traveller, who was travelling through these places almost 60 years after Ben Yiju's time, also expresses his surprise at the trade taking place around that area or the caravans that passed through around that area, as much of the goods were from India 'the loads of pepper ...' (1992: 175). Another port named 'Aidhâb, which Ibn Jubaîr reached, was one of the most used ports of the world, as Indian and Yemeni ships would regularly make use of it (1992: 175). These traces of a transregional trade between India and the Middle Eastern and African nations imply the frequent movement of people from these countries amongst themselves in the medieval era.

Clifford remarked that as Ghosh searched for traces of Ben Yiju's wife, a native of Malabar, he found a network of Indian,

Jewish and Arab traders, existing peacefully in spite of contradictory beliefs and cultures, and of trade and commerce in its truest sense (1994: 3). Further tracing these transnational links, Ghosh, in his chapter titled *Mangalore*, goes on to narrate the extraordinary history of the city in the past as a thriving cosmopolitan city, with a considerable expatriate merchant population consisting of around 4000 people, according to the Moroccan traveller, Ibn Battuta's report (1992: 242). It was with the advent of the European colonial powers, which were drawn to Mangalore due to its immense wealth and prosperity, that Mangalore slowly started losing the trace of its incredible history and trade relations with the Middle Eastern merchants and others (1992: 245).

While writing about the European colonial powers' forceful dominance and subjugation, Ghosh mentions that these trade connections that had made a bridge between the worlds of Ben Yiju, Bomma and Yiju's Indian wife, Ashu, fell into oblivion after the advent of European colonial powers in the fifteenth century, giving rise to a different age, where the existence of such shared networks and paths seem so questionable that their very possibility of existence have vanished from human memory (1992: 286). The culture of accommodation and compromise failed in front of the imperial powers in the battle of 1509 AD near the shores of Diu, India, and it was the last show of solidarity between the nations that had formed an integral part of this trade route – 'a transcontinental fleet ... Muslim potentate of Gujarat, the Hindu ruler of Calicut, and the Sultan of Egypt' against the Portuguese fleet of soldiers (1992: 288). Ghosh goes on to write that the rich transregional links over the Indian Ocean linking several nations during the medieval era were consumed and made extinct by that unquenchable, demonic thirst that has existed ever since, spanning over five centuries, over the Indian Ocean, the Arabian Sea and the Persian Gulf (1992: 288).

Conclusion

This chapter has dealt with 'transnationalism from below', that is, 'grassroots type of transnational connection', that is undertaken by common people out of economic as well as political interests (Glick-Schiller 2007: 124). I have tried to read the linkages amongst India, Egypt and Aden, found in the text, as transnationalism that existed in the medieval era, before the advent of the European colonial powers. Although all the features found in modern transnational trends might not be found in these older transnational social fields, yet there are several similarities that could be drawn from instances found in the text. This chapter has made an attempt to study Ghosh's nonfiction for those possible transnational networks, which flourished and declined without much trace. As Clifford (1994: 1) writes, this nonfiction stretches back to a medieval era, twelfth century, cosmopolitanism connected by Arabs, Jews and South Asians, and belonging to a world that was yet not shaped by centuries of Western imperialism.

Ghosh writes that Ben Yiju returned to Aden and then to Egypt after living in Mangalore for a considerable number of years, and as for Bomma, the Indian slave of Ben Yiju, letters of Yiju from the Geniza documents preserved in Philadelphia's Annenberg Research Institute testify that Bomma was with Yiju during the last years of Yiju's life in Fustat, Egypt – as a document survives which has Bomma's name among others in it to whom Ben Yiju owed money for domestic consumptions (1992: 348–349). Ghosh ends the story of Bomma by making a final connection between the past and the present by writing that 'the toddy-loving fisherman from Tulunad' belonging to the medieval era would have been surprised to know that the last proof of his existence and history now lay preserved in Philadelphia in the modern era (1992: 349).

References

Clifford, James. 1994. Looking for Bomma. *London Review of Books,* 16(6) (February), 26–27.

Ghosh, Amitav. 1992. *In an Antique Land.* New Delhi: Ravi Dayal Publisher.

Glick-Schiller, Nina. 2007. The Centrality of Ethnography in the Study of Transnational Migration: Seeing the Wetland Instead of the Swamp. In Ajaya Kumar Sahoo and Brij Maharaj (eds.), *Sociology of Diaspora: A Reader.* Jaipur: Rawat Publications, 118–155.

Roy, Binayak. 2011. Tiny Threads, Gigantic Tapestries, Amitav Ghosh's *In an Antique Land. Journal of Postcolonial Cultures and Societies,* 2(3) (July 2011), 58–80. Available at: http://www.jpcs.in (Accessed on 25 June 2016).

Singh, Omendra Kumar. 2012. Reinventing Caste: Indian Diaspora in Amitav Ghosh's *Sea of Poppies. Asiatic,* 6(1) (June), 47–59.

Srivastava, Pooja Raj. 2015. Amitav Ghosh Perspective on Subalternity and His Novels. *International Journal of English Language, Literature and Humanities,* II (IX) (January), 189–199. Available at: http://ijellh.com (accessed on 25 June 2016).

Vertovec, Steven. 2012. Trends and Impacts of Migrant Transnationalism. In Ajaya K. Sahoo, Michiel Baas, and Thomas Faist (eds), *Indian Diaspora and Transnationalism*. Jaipur: Rawat Publications, 48–106.

7

Mapping Diaspora Engagement through Entrepreneurial Perspective

Issues and Challenges

Rakesh Ranjan

Introduction

Entrepreneurship[1] is one of the very important prospects in serving the development of a society. A society with its interaction to other groups or societies and a process of exchange of goods is itself a state of entrepreneurial ideas. Entrepreneurs can be seen as the economic functionary, who forecast the wants of the consumers and leads to the two kinds of incomes: first is contractual income (wage, rent) and residual income (profit) of the entrepreneur (Knight 1921). Schumpeter (1934) with a little different perspective defined entrepreneur as a driver of economic development. Entrepreneurial activities can be seen as the introduction of new good or quality of a good, introduction of new methods of production, opening of new market, utilization of some new source of supply of raw materials or intermediate goods, and carrying out of some new organizational form of the industry (Schumpeter 1934). Broadly with observation of different theorists such as Hayek (1949), Kirzner (1992), Ricketts (1988), Casson (1982), Ripsas (1995) and other entrepreneurs can be seen as an innovative industry leader who assumes the risk associated with uncertainty and organize and coordinate economic recourse in order to fulfil the want of the society and equally drive the development as a whole.

The field of entrepreneurship is centrally concerned with understanding 'how opportunities to bring into existence 'future' goods and services are discovered, created and exploited by whom and with the consequences (Venkataratnam 1997). In modern management science, entrepreneurship is understood as a behavioural phenomenon, which can be described as the pursuit of business opportunities in the uncertain or risk-enabled areas. Entrepreneurship behaviour cannot be only explained by economic theory because there is equal importance of psychological, cultural and sociological factors (Campbell 1992).

In this chapter, with the preconceived notion of the relationship between diaspora and entrepreneurship and its other reflections, the argument tried to deviate from the analysis of diaspora networks at the macro-economic level to examine the extent to which diaspora facilitates entrepreneurship within India. In particular, this chapter, tries to answer some of the very specific questions about the diaspora-facilitated entrepreneurship in India. First, is to understand the volume and size of diaspora entrepreneurship. What is the trend of diaspora entrepreneurship in India? Is it possible to classify diaspora entrepreneurship in certain categories? Second, is the understanding the role and usage of remittances in entrepreneurship development. What role do remittances play? What reflections NSSO and census convey on usage of remittance particularly in context of entrepreneurship? Third, do policies related to diaspora investment give positive impact or negative impact on entrepreneurship development? Fourth and last question deals with diaspora entrepreneurship in different sectors and related stories.

This chapter tried to development insights with the help of three categories of diaspora entrepreneurship: First category is the large-scale investment by Indian diaspora, second is the investment by return migrants and the third is the entrepreneurial usage of labour remittances. There has been lack of direct literature on diaspora entrepreneurship. The most recent data related to NRI investment published by the Reserve Bank of India is about 1999–2001. Although the study used data pub, which was used by international organizations, periodicals and annual reports published by the Department of Industrial Policy and Promotion, it also used the reports published by

Reserve Bank of India, Ministry of Overseas Indian Affairs (MOIA) along with Census and NSS reports. This chapter will have two components. First, it will provide an overview of the diaspora emergence of entrepreneurship vis-à-vis development, and second, it will look into engagement of diaspora in five prominent sectors, that is, information technology (IT), science and technology, infrastructure, education and healthcare in the post-liberalized India.

Diaspora and Entrepreneurship

Diaspora entrepreneurship is often traced to as early as the fifteenth century, when traders of a single community migrate to other parts of the globe while maintaining their social and cultural network. There are evidences different diaspora ethnic entrepreneurs such as Jews, Greek, Japanese, Chinese and many others. However, the diaspora entrepreneur has become currency since the last three decades due to active state policies. Diaspora entrepreneurship and international networks have, to some extent, preceded the western European economic expansion. It appears that during colonial and the empirical expansion of Europe in the nineteenth century and the first half of the twentieth century, trade diaspora continues to play an important role in the service sector, namely trade shipping and finance (McCabe et al. 2005).

Diasporas investing in their home countries have advantages such as their understanding of cultural and social norms, familiar business cultures and social knowledge; such familiarities can help in developing trust and thereby open up opportunities closed or unknown to other investors and entrepreneurs. This results in helping them to venture into new areas and become enterprising in a given circumstance that they perceive having some opportunity. Emigration of one person or a group is a complex interplay of political-economic, cultural and psychological factors. Ethnic and social network has played an important role in promoting international trade for countries, by helping to overcome weaknesses in the informal and contracting environment faced by buyers and sellers across nations (Curtin 1984). In the case of transnational diaspora entrepreneurship, the cultural influence has played a vital role.

Institutions that facilitate the formation and growth of new businesses are either weak or completely missing in developing countries. Entrepreneurs based in developing countries, therefore, use a number of strategies to overcome these weaknesses, including a greater reliance on informal networks to help conduct business (McMillan and Woodruff 1999; Rauch and Casella 2001; Banerjee and Munshi 2004).

One set of informal networks that has received particular attention in recent years is diaspora, or cross-border networks, constituted by ties between expatriates from developing countries who are based abroad and entrepreneurs who live at 'home'. These studies have argued that expatriate networks seem to be vital in overcoming information barriers in cross-border business (Gould 1994; Rauch 2001; Rauch and Trindade 2002) and also an important channel for driving knowledge transfer across countries (Saxenian 2002, 2005, 2006;). Most of this research, however, has either focused on cross-country analyses or has used aggregate data that have made it difficult to shed light on the specific mechanisms underlying the functioning of these networks. In this study, therefore, we depart from prior work to focus on a single country and examine within-country variation in entrepreneurs' use of diaspora networks.

The Indian service sector provides a good setting to study diaspora networks for several reasons. First, the vast majority of businesses has flourished mainly after economic reforms and demands relatively higher investment. Since the output of software products and services is often hard to specify in advance or verify easily, and cross-border formal contracts are extremely hard to enforce, 'relational contracting' is especially important to generate business in these industries. While firms in the Indian service sector have been documented to use a number of formal mechanisms to overcome hurdles to business generation – such as the use of quality certifications (Arora et al. 2001) or choice of contract structure (Banerjee and Duflo 2000) – anecdotal accounts suggest that expatriate networks continue to play an important role in generating business and getting access to capital for entrepreneurs in India, especially because the industry is highly export oriented.

Devesh Kapur (2001) provides numerous examples where the diasporas from developing countries have played a role in either enhancing or vouching for the reputation of businesses in developing countries. Given the intensity of this industry, one such channel might be the diaspora network. The variation in the local institutional environment for diaspora entrepreneurs, thus, provides us with a natural testing ground to examine whether the difficulty of matching, referrals or monitoring within a city is related to entrepreneurs' reliance on diaspora networks to overcome hurdles to their business.

Indian diaspora is both extensive and varied, estimated at over 25 million people spanning 130 countries. A significant portion of the diaspora is composed of highly skilled immigrants who maintain strong ties to their home country. For example, a Saxenian's survey of Chinese and Indian immigrant professionals in Silicon Valley found that 80 per cent of the Indian respondents exchanged information on American jobs or business opportunities with people in India, 67 per cent served as an advisor or helped to arrange business contracts and 18 per cent invested their own money in start-ups or venture funds in India (Saxenian 2002). In addition, Indians from different regions in the country have different (and distinguishable) last names as it is possible to analyse whether people of different ethnicities – from different regions of the country – rely on the diaspora to different extents. The relationship and reflections derived from the above analysis allows us to study the extent to which ties between entrepreneurs and the diaspora are based on ethnicity, rather than 'professional contacts'.

Return Diaspora and Entrepreneurship

Is there any strong link between return diaspora and entrepreneurship? On the one hand, brain drain is often seen as a major setback for the developing countries such as India and China, especially in the case of IT and Health Professional during 1980s, a substantial share of the highly educated migrants to the United States come from China and India. Though only about one in 10 new arrivals are from one of these countries, they make up 28 per cent of college-educated new arrivals. Almost half of these migrants arrived in the last decade, and one in four come in just the last five years (Friedberg 2007). Recent analysis suggests that in the current global competitive environment, 'Brain drain' may provide a crucial advantage to these countries through return migration. Return migrants could play an important role in building innovation capabilities in these countries by filling knowledge gaps in critical areas of research and development (R&D).

Return diaspora not only denotes physical presence, but it can be through knowledge processing or entrepreneurial networks between host and home countries. As entrepreneurship is a process of risk, uncertainty and innovation (Knight 1921, Schumpeter 1934), cultural integration with home country influences workers to invest back home in order to get better security aspects since in the current global scenario where most of the developing countries' markets are still working with the protectionist mindset with a lack of innovation ecosystem based on collaborations between firms, universities, R&D institutes and financial institutions (Kale 2007). Diaspora entrepreneurs with global experience and innovative ideas helps to generate better livelihood and creation of the state development.

Diaspora integration towards home country is not a new concept, but it dramatically enhanced after globalization and the increase in cross-border entrepreneurial activities. Countries of origin are trying hard to attract diaspora's talents and resources while the countries of destination hope to increase the effectiveness of their development assistance and immigration and integration policies (Agunias and Newland 2012). Recent research suggests that diaspora entrepreneurship can contribute to economic development. Countries with higher levels of diaspora entrepreneurship tend to have promising prospects for economic growth, as well as proactive diaspora engagement policies, good governance, positive socio-cultural perceptions of entrepreneurship, a critical mass of human and social capital, and access to financial institutions and pools of capital (Newland and Tanaka 2012). Although conceptually diaspora entrepreneurship is an example of protected market hypothesis (Aldrich et al. 1985), which gives an entrepreneur market with less risk and uncertainty. But the attraction of diaspora needs to be addressed properly by government of the homeland through different relaxation and initiative, which can further lead to homeland development.

Understanding the motivations for remitting is necessary for analysing the wider economic consequences of remittances, for at least two reasons. First, the amount that a migrant transfers to family members remaining at home at any given time depends, among other things, on the migrant's underlying motivations to go abroad and to remit funds in the first place. The size and timing of remittance flows in turn determine their effects on economic activity in the receiving country. Second, the intended purpose of remittances affects the end uses of these funds, and the uses to which recipients put them is also an important determinant of their economic impact on the recipient economy. Remittances are the most important instrument for all country's diaspora-driven development. According to the World Bank, worldwide remittance flows, including those in high-income countries, reached $462 billion in 2010 and are expected to increase to $606 billion by 2017, in this $372.1 billion, with an increase of 12.1 per cent in developing countries (Ratha and Silwal 2012; http://blogs.worldbank.org/peoplemove/trends-remittances-2016-new-normal-slow-growth). Any diaspora entrepreneurial activities usually give effect to different dimensions of the society, it can create employment, develop infrastructure and increase economic capacity of stakeholders through financial as well as knowledge development.

Remittances and Investment

Remittance has proven to be one of the significant international financial flows in recent years. Worldwide remittances, including those in high-income countries, are expected to total $574 billion in 2012, and projected to grow to $606 billion in 2017, according to the latest issue of the Bank's Migration and Development Brief (http://blogs.worldbank.org/peoplemove/trends-remittances-2016-new-normal-slow-growth). Despite a constant rise in remittance earnings, the productive use of remittances has been the matter of concern. While the direct economic impact of remittances to alleviate poverty is not much controversial, the non-monetary significances of remittance, such as impact on health, education, gender issues, social participation, politics, women empowerment and cultural and social changes in origin societies, have been still unexplored areas. Remittances deserve strategic importance both in macro and micro level. On the macro level, the evidences confirm that remittance happens to be an increasingly important and relatively stable source of external finance for the countries afflicted by economic and political crisis (Kapur 2003). Such countries regard remittances as one of the most secure and reliable sources of foreign currency than other capital flows such as foreign direct investment and official development assistance. On the micro level, remittance has become a panacea for the marginalized poor people to enhance their livelihood by providing an alternative source of income. The remittance is believed to have direct impact on the poor and thus contributes to alleviate poverty in a more significant way than other sources of external finance. The remittance has been observed as a means to affect the well-being and capacities.

In contrary of generalized perspective that top remittance-receiving countries is also the most populous, with India and China receiving over USD 130 billion, Mexico over USD 22 billion, Philippines over USD 25 billion and Pakistan over USD 15 billion (World Bank 2014), countries such as Bangladesh (14 billion) and other small countries are appearing as important receivers. However, there are contrasting views on using remittances as a tool to promote growth and development. In some countries, remittances are considered as an important instrument for development because they drive the social and economic development of the society as well as country. For example, many countries such as Tajikistan, Samoa and Nepal are receiving remittances respectively as 52 per cent, 23 per cent and 25 per cent of GDP, which is helping in the total development of the state.

NSSO survey on employment and unemployment discusses about 12 purposes for which a household uses the remittance. Household expenditure is a prime use of remittance in both rural and urban areas. Nearly 95 per cent of the households in the rural areas and 93 per cent of the household in the urban areas reported using the remittance for household consumer expenditure. A study by the Reserve Bank of India (RBI) informs that most of these remittances are spent on household consumption. Though a bit dated to the period 2007–2008 and 2008–2009, it throws useful information. In 2007, India received $37.2 billion, $49.9 billion in 2008 and $49.2 billion in 2009. It is also interesting to find the trend towards the usage of remittance for entrepreneurial activities. An almost negligible portion of remittance used for entrepreneurial purpose. Although this data is not different from RBI, but RBI data show an interesting trend of usage of remittance in the urban sector, where it decreases from

15.15 in 2007–2008 to 2.19 in 2008–2009. This change appeared from 18.28 per cent in 2007–2008 to 42.40 per cent in 2008–2009 due to increase in other activities. Overall, there is negligible use of remittance towards entrepreneurship as shown in both the surveys of RBI and NSS.

Remittance with its multiplier economic effects always helped states such as Kerala. Remittance consists 31.2 per cent of total state GDP of Kerala (Zachariah and Rajan, 2012). The significance of remittance use is reflected in almost all studies on migration and development. Nevertheless, migrant remittances are used for different purposes at different stages of migration and their influence on the lives of family and household members will vary accordingly. The uses of money sent home has a capability and potential to extend along the whole spectrum of human development as it fosters business development, job creation and innovation; creates economic, political and social capital through global networks; mobilizes social capital through cultural and linguistic competence and positively correlates with economic growth. According to Migration Policy Institute, remittance-driven entrepreneurship can be understood in two ways. First, the necessity entrepreneurship, who opens a business for survival (such as a stall in the open market), is self-employed by default and concentrates in petty trade or personal services. Second, the opportunity entrepreneurs, who is directly helping the economy and introducing new forms of production, he/she contributes substantially to economic growth and often creates jobs outside the immediate family (Newland and Tanaka 2010).

Diaspora Entrepreneurs Network

Diaspora is itself a cultural category that reflects the idea of integration between homeland and host land through different approaches such as social, economy and culture. Most of the diaspora relations have a long history with various categories such as Jews, Armenian, African, Greek, Chinese, Indian and various others. The concentration towards diaspora facilitation and importance of diaspora entrepreneurship is not a very old phenomenon, broadly after globalization during 1980–1990, this side of diaspora relations came into existence through different technological innovation. Information technology did tremendous work in facilitation of diaspora entrepreneurship. Many things that are previously not seen as an object for commodity created a market, which can be further identified as an ethnic market. Indian ethnic products like Hindi cinema, mango, Indian snacks and saree created a huge market in different countries such as Mauritius and Malaysia. All these entrepreneurial activities demanded the need for social networks within diaspora communities as well as with homelands.

In order to guide the interpretation of our results, we first develop a simple model to examine how the institutional environment of the city where entrepreneurs are based might affect the extent to which they rely on informal channels such as expatriate networks and how this in turn would impact their firm's performance. In our model, revenue for entrepreneurs' firms is based on the extent to which they 'network' for their business. Our use of the term 'network' is aimed to capture the broader process of start-up financing, business generation and growth. For simplicity, we assume that entrepreneurs have the choice of either networking using local institutions or the diaspora. That is, entrepreneurs can choose to conduct business by relying on a mix of formal and informal mechanisms. Entrepreneurs choose the 'optimal mix' of networking using local institutions and diaspora networks in order to maximize firm revenue, a choice that is based on (1) each entrepreneur's own relative costs of accessing local institutions and diaspora networks and (2) a parameter, constant across all entrepreneurs, that determines the extent to which local institutions and diaspora networks serve as complements rather than substitutes.

This parameter aims to provide us with the flexibility to let diaspora networks serve as substitutes to the local environment, as would be the case if they served primarily to overcome institutional weaknesses. If, however, entrepreneurs in hubs use the diaspora networks more intensively, potentially an outcome of positive associative matching, then we would see the diaspora networks and the local environment as complements rather than substitutes. As we show in our model, the optimal investment in diaspora networks for a given entrepreneur varies considerably based on the extent to which the two serve as complements rather than substitutes. This allows us to generate specific predictions on the strength of diaspora networks, as well as firm performance for entrepreneurs based on different levels of complementarity between informal networks and the local environment. We then take these predictions to the data, gathered through a survey sent to domestic entrepreneurs, in order to shed light on which predictions fit best with the data.

Indian Diasporas: New Entrepreneurs at Home?

Migration has always been seen as a major characteristic of societies; the last two centuries have witnessed the mass mobility of populations, with millions of people moving across the planet to take up new lives in new places. In the post-Fordist era with increasing global competition and different technological innovation, the pattern of becoming mobile equally affected all over the world. With special attention on diaspora investment and entrepreneurial approach, liberalization helped in many ways, such as better transport facilities, involvement of information and communication technology, liberalization in state policies and others. Many countries started a separate overseas affairs ministry to facilitate the diaspora relationship with special focus on investment (India 2003, Greek 1983, South Korea 1997), it is a global phenomenon, one that is political, economic, social and cultural, which challenges the nation states and leads up to the birth of not only multiple networks, transnational or transcontinental, but also regional or local, bringing migration into the main world stakes (de Wenden 2009). But with the changing nature of state policy and liberalization of state regulation during 1990s it has helped migrant entrepreneur to invest and generate better development aspects.

Most of the return diasporas are the first time entrepreneurs, some of whom came to India post-1980 and many after liberalization to set up new ventures in IT and healthcare. These return diasporas were mostly professionals having considerable work experience and improved knowledge and skills, social contacts at the global scale and investment potential with the help of social networks. The entire concentration of diaspora entrepreneurship in India can be widely observed in five major sectors: education, healthcare, IT, infrastructure, and energy and environment. Foreign direct investment (FDI)[2] as a concept looks usual for investments in India, but with specific reference to diaspora entrepreneurship, there is something available, which needs to be addressed carefully. Information technology industry widely facilitated in India through overseas networks and trade expansion from developed countries after Indian economic liberalization and issues related to the 'Y2K' (Report of the High Level Committee on Indian Diaspora 2001) with interventions of Silicon Valley entrepreneurs such as TiE towards the expansion of IT firms in India. Although healthcare sector entrepreneurship in India entails similar preposition, but cultural ties can be seen more than any other industry with involvement of skill professionals, who are directly participating in this entrepreneurship approach either through economic entrepreneurship or knowledge entrepreneurship or both. Many examples, including establishment of Apollo Hospitals in different parts of India, the NRI Academy of Sciences, Narayana Hrudayalaya Hospitals in South India and many others, reflect involvement of strong cultural ties between health professionals towards the homeland.

We can initiate our discussion with the analysis of the healthcare sector. Indian doctors and health professionals are the backbone of the National Health Service in United Kingdom and playing influential roles in many other countries such as the United States, Canada and Australia. Not only in developing countries, but Indian healthcare professionals, particularly nurses, are also working in almost all parts of the world. Indian healthcare professionals as well as other NRIs and PIOs, have already made a valuable contribution to their homeland by establishing different health institutions. The Indian healthcare sector is predicted to reach US $280 billion by 2020. Government of India has permitted 100 per cent FDI inflows in healthcare sector in India.

Major diaspora-driven organizations in the Indian healthcare industry can be observed in Apollo Hospitals Enterprise Ltd., Fortis Healthcare Ltd., Doctor Z India Healthcare (Pvt.) Ltd., Translational Health Sciences and Technology Institute, Panacea Biotec and many others. Under consideration of diaspora activities in Indian healthcare sector, various roles can be seen, namely, physicians/medical professionals, professional medical organization, corporate sector, banks, financial institutions, chambers of commerce and industry, government, voluntary sector, medical tourism, Indian system of medicine and others. In an Indian healthcare sector, entrepreneurial activities can be facilitated through broadly two ways: first way is a direct investment by different diaspora-driven organization and second one is knowledge diaspora through different modes of communication such as tele-medicine, tele-consultation, through different workshops, training and medical research.

Another, which is getting high concentration from diaspora entrepreneurship, is science and technology or specially information technology enabled sector (ITES). The Indian diaspora has played an important role in the field of science and technology. The emigration of Indians in the nineteenth century to Fiji, Mauritius, Africa and the Caribbean countries consisted mainly of indentured labour However, from the mid-twentieth century onwards, emigration to the United States and some countries of the west was of a different nature. Part of the reason was because those countries were more receptive to highly qualified Indian/Asian immigrants. Indian emigrants thus increasingly consisted, among others, of highly qualified scientists, engineers and other professional, also termed as a brain drain. The opening up accelerated significantly in the wake of America's IT-led economic boom in the 1990s to which Indian IT professionals had made a visible, high profile and widely recognized contributions. Advisory panels with eminent NRIs and PIOs members set up by the Department of Biotechnology and the Ministry of Information Technology have catalysed technologies and investment into India and led to several IT and BT joint ventures, besides keeping Indian Research Initiatives up-to-date with global trends and policies in the biotechnology of information and computer sciences.

The higher education sector is expected to register a compound annual growth rate (CAGR) of 12 per cent from 2008 to reach a size of US$ 31.47 billion, according to reports released by Deloitte Touche Tohmatsu India titled 'Indian Higher Education Sector: Opportunities Aplenty, Growth Unlimited!'. The education sector in India is also considered as one of the major areas for investments as the entire education system is going through a process of overhaul, according to a report 'Emerging Opportunities for Private and Foreign Participants in Higher Education' by PricewaterhouseCoopers (PwC). The private education sector is estimated to reach US$ 70 billion by 2013 and US$ 115 billion by 2018, according to consulting firm Technopak.

Technopak sees enrolments in K-12 growing to 351 million, requiring an additional 34 million seats by 2018. This equals US$ 80 billion at US$ 2400 a seat. The government allows 100 per cent FDI in the education sector.

As per the existing FDI policy, NRIs and PIOs are allowed to invest directly up to 100 per cent in any Indian company in the housing and real estate sector without any approval. NRIs can directly set up companies in India, other than in the nature of venture capital in India and do business in India. NRIs/PIOs can also make direct investment under the FDI policy through an overseas entity into companies in the real estate Sector as per the terms of Press Note 2 of 2005 issued by the Department of Industrial Policy and Promotion, Ministry of Commerce and Industry, Government of India. This route allows investment in townships, housing, built-up infrastructure and construction-development projects (which would include, but not be restricted to, housing, commercial premises, hotels, resorts, hospitals, educational institutions, recreational facilities, city and regional level infrastructure). There are also certain restrictions on the repatriation of capital invested (subject to a lock in period of three years), minimum capitalization/investment requirements, minimum project area/size requirements and so on that have to be complied with. According to a report by JLL India and Assocham, NRI investment in Indian reality may rise by 35 per cent in 2014 (*Times of India* 2014).

Diaspora integration towards the home country is not a new concept, but it dramatically enhanced after globalization and the increase in cross-border entrepreneurial activities. Countries of origin are trying hard to attract diasporic talents and resources while the countries of destination hope to increase the effectiveness of their development assistance and immigration and integration policies (Agunias and Newland 2012). Diaspora entrepreneurship can contribute to economic development. Countries with higher levels of diaspora entrepreneurship tend to have promising prospects for economic growth, as well as proactive diaspora engagement policies, good governance, positive socio-cultural perceptions of entrepreneurship, a critical mass of human and social capital and access to financial institutions and pools of capital (Newland and Tanaka 2012). Although conceptually diaspora entrepreneurship is an example of protected market hypothesis (Aldrich et al. 1985), which gives an entrepreneur market with less risk and uncertainty. But the attraction of diaspora needs to be addressed properly by the government of the home country through different relaxation and initiative, which can further lead to homeland development.

Policy Impetus

Diaspora entrepreneurship has caught the attention of policymakers and researchers who recognize the most poor countries suffer from a deficit of entrepreneurship and that this is both a cause and a consequence of their poverty (Newland and Tanaka 2012). The emergence of the diaspora entrepreneurship has become a key resource for social as well as business development. These entrepreneurs are not only providing leadership and management skills, but also, and more importantly, bring sticky knowledge in the area of science and technology (Kale 2007). However, it is true that the transfer of knowledge is not a straightforward process and requires deliberate government policies and firm strategies for successful utilization of returnee resources.

There is an urgent need to change in the working style from the protectionist mindset of business to risk taker or innovator which includes innovation ecosystem based on collaboration between firms, universities, R&D institutions and financial institutions. State government should give importance to small and medium size enterprises as they are the most productive job creators. The state needs to address diaspora business forums and establish required policies specifically focused on attracting and retaining skilled returns for better entrepreneurial activities. The state should consider innovative programs and formulation of the sector- and technology-specific policies to encourage return migration of the skilled workforce in high technology areas. There is urgent need to support market firms to attract and retain returned engineers and scientists by improving social infrastructure and conditions so that returnees find it easier to adjust life in new places of work. As entrepreneurship talks about risk and innovation, there should be a risk sharing mechanisms such as loan insurance schemes, credit guarantee and so on as it is true that diaspora entrepreneurship is a process of development of homeland but it is also possible that local entrepreneurship can create problem for diaspora entrepreneurship with thinking like a threat or competitor. In this scenario, government needs to formulate policy to create better and sustainable diaspora investment and facilitate development.

Conclusion

Diasporas need not be in relation to any single host and home countries. They often work as a transnational community and the interaction becomes multidirectional. Transnational diasporas promote multidirectional flows of human beings, ideas, products, culture/physical interactions, negotiation and exchange of ethnic goods and services. The growth story in traditional way driven by energy and expertise of domestic entrepreneurs, but through the recent development in two to three decades the concept of diaspora and financial relations came into existence through diaspora entrepreneurship.

Diaspora entrepreneurship needs to be considered as a driver of economic as well as social development in the post-liberalized era. Through certain industries such as education, health care, infrastructure and IT, diaspora investment creates a better and sustained investment than others as there are a large number of human resources already available and well networked. Although there are two dynamics of diaspora involvement analysed in the study, that is, the knowledge and investment contributions of the diaspora, only the healthcare sector involves both these aspects. The role of knowledge diaspora is also reflected in IT industry, although the actual role can be seen in the form of 'mentorship'. The healthcare sector, however, involves a direct partnership of the diaspora. The survey of different hospitals observed that there is a good flow of return health professionals into many of these corporate hospitals as a result of many factors, culture being one of the factors.

Engaging diaspora entrepreneurs to pursue entrepreneurial ventures seems a matter of common sense as an element of development policy, but in many cases it creates a conflict between state run enterprises and diaspora ventures, as former thinks latter as a competitor. It is also true that just facilitating diaspora investment doesn't mean survival of the organization; in many cases because of failure of the venture it creates loss of capital and energy of both government and entrepreneurs. Even if an enterprise survives, there is again consideration of major problems, as it can go beyond the rules and regulation of state, and this is also possible that money flow to these organizations may have illegality which can destroy the economy of the state. As in many cases it is seen that the diaspora-driven investments usually happen in well-infrastructured countries, which are ready for developing further enterprises. A well-established diaspora enabled development can only be possible with the proper balance relationship between different stakeholders of the entrepreneurial procedure such as government, entrepreneurs, society, homeland, host land, manpower and available resources. If a state is possible to facilitate and interact with all required facilities and resources, then diaspora entrepreneurship can create more secure and better development.

The protectionist mindset of business to one of risk taking or innovation and collaboration between firms, universities, R&D institutions and financial institutions can give large-scale impact and inclusiveness in the health sector. The state needs to address diaspora business forums and establish required policies specifically focused on attracting and retaining skilled returnees for better entrepreneurial activities. The state should consider innovative programs and formulation of the sector- and technology-specific policies to encourage return migration of the skilled workforce in high technology areas. There is an urgent need to support market firms to attract and retain returned engineers and scientists by improving social infrastructure and conditions so that retirees find it easier to adjust life in new places of work. As entrepreneurship talks about risk and innovation, there should be a risk sharing mechanisms such as loan insurance schemes, credit guarantee and so on as it is true that diaspora entrepreneurship is a process of development of the homeland. However, it is also possible that the local entrepreneurship can create problem for diaspora entrepreneurship thinking them as threat or competitor. In this scenario, government needs to formulate policy to create better and sustainable diaspora investment and facilitate development.

Notes

1. A person who organizes and operates a business, taking on greater than normal risk in order to do so (*New Oxford English Dictionary*).
2. FDI provides a means for creating direct, stable and long-lasting links between economies. Under the right policy environment, it can serve as an important vehicle for local enterprise development, and it may also help improve the competitive position of both the recipient ('host') and the investing ('home') economy. OECD Benchmark definition: Foreign Direct Investment, Fourth Edition. http://www.oecd.org/daf/internationalinvestment/investmentstatisticsandanalysis/40193734.pdf

References

Agunias, D.R., and Newland, K. 2012. Developing a road map for engaging diasporas in development: A handbook for policymakers and practitioners in home and host countries. IOM/MPI.

Aldrich, Howard, Cater, John, Jones, Trevor, McEvoy, David and Velleman, Paul. 1985. *Ethnic Residential Concentration and the Protected Market Hypothesis*, 63(4) (June 1985), 996–1009: Oxford University Press.

Arora, A., Arunachalam, V.S., Asundi, J. and Fernandes, R. 2001. The Indian software services industry. *Research Policy*, 30(8), 1267–1287.

Banerjee, A.V. and Duflo, E. 2000. Inequality and growth: What can the data say? (No. w7793). National Bureau of Economic Research.

Banerjee, A. and Munshi, K. 2004. How efficiently is capital allocated? Evidence from the knitted garment industry in Tirupur. *The Review of Economic Studies*, 71(1), 19–42.

Campbell, C.A. 1992. A decision theory model for entrepreneurial acts. *Entrepreneurship: Theory and Practice*, 17(1), 21–28.

Casson, M. 1982. *The Entrepreneur: An Economic Theory*. Rowman and Littlefield.

Curtin, P.D. 1984. *Cross-cultural Trade in World History*. Cambridge: Cambridge University Press.

de Wenden, C.W. 2009. La globalisation humaine. Presses universitaires de France.

Friedberg, R. 2007. The economic impact of knowledge workers from India and China. Movement of Global Talent: *The Impact of High Skill Labor Flows from India and China*, 35–54.

Gould, David M. 1994. 'Immigrant links to the home country: empirical implications for US bilateral trade flows.' *The Review of Economics and Statistics*, 302–316.

Harris, Negel. 2005. Migration and Development. *Economic and Political Weekly*, 22 October.

Hayek, F.A. 1949. The intellectuals and socialism. *The University of Chicago Law Review*, 16(3), 417–433.

Kale, D. 2009. International migration, knowledge diffusion and innovation capacities in the Indian pharmaceutical industry. *New Technology, Work and Employment*, 24(3), 260–276.

Kapur, D. 2001. Diasporas and technology transfer. *Journal of Human Development*, 2(2), 265–286.

Kapur, Devesh. 2003. Indian Diaspora as a Strategic Asset. *Economic and Political Weekly*, 1 February.

Kirzner, I.M. 1992. *Entrepreneurship, Uncertainty and Austrian Economics. Austrian Economics: Tensions and New Directions*, Boston, MA: Kluwer Academic Publishers, 85–102.

Knight, F.H. 1921. *Risk, Uncertainty and Profit*. New York: Hart, Schaffner and Marx.

McCabe Ina Baghdiantz, Harlaftis, Gelina and Minaglou Ioanna Pepelasis. 2005. *Diaspora Entrepreneurial Networks: Four Centuries of History*. Oxford and New York: Berg Publication.

McMillan, J. and Woodruff, C. 1999. Interfirm relationships and informal credit in Vietnam. *The Quarterly Journal of Economics*, 114(4), 1285–1320.

Newland, K. and Tanaka, H. 2010. *Mobilizing Diaspora Entrepreneurship for Development*. Washington, DC: Migration Policy Institute.

Newland, Kathleen and Tanaka, Hiroyuki. 2007. '*Mobilizing Diaspora Entrepreneurship for Development*'. Migration Policy Institute and United State Agency for International Development, Diasporas and Development Policy Project, October.

Ratha, Dilip and Silswal, Ani. 2012. Remittance Flows in 2011: An Update, Migration and Development Brief, World Bank, 23 April.

Rauch, J.E. 2001. Business and social networks in international trade. *Journal of Economic Literature*, 1177–1203.

Rauch, J.E. and Casella, A. (eds). 2001. *Networks and Markets*. New York: Russell Sage Foundation.

Rauch, J.E. and Trindade, V. 2002. Ethnic Chinese networks in international trade. *Review of Economics and Statistics*, 84(1), 116–130.

Report of the High Level Committee on Indian Diaspora, 2001. Ministry of External Affairs. New Delhi (Chapters, 23, 29, 31).

Ricketts, E.R. and Sawhill, I.V. 1988. Defining and measuring the underclass. *Journal of Policy Analysis and Management*, 7(2), 316–325.

Ripsas, S. 1998. Towards an interdisciplinary theory of entrepreneurship. *Small Business Economics*, 10(2), 103–115.

Saxenian, A. 2002. Transnational communities and the evolution of global production networks: the cases of Taiwan, China and India. *Industry and Innovation*, 9(3), 183–202.

Saxenian, A. 2005. From brain drain to brain circulation: Transnational communities and regional upgrading in India and China. *Studies in Comparative International Development (SCID)*, 40(2), 35–61.

Saxenian, A. 2006. International Mobility of Engineers and the Rise of Entrepreneurship in the Periphery (No. 2006/142). Research Paper, UNU-WIDER, United Nations University (UNU).

Schumpeter, J.A. 1934. The theory of economic development: An inquiry into profits, capital, credit, interest, and the business cycle (Vol. 55). Transaction Publishers.

Times of India. 2014. City is a Preferred NRI Investment Destination, Available online at; http://epaperbeta.timesofindia.com /Article.aspx?eid= 31806&articlexml=CITY-IS-A-PREFERRED-NRI-INVESTMENT-DESTINATION- 31102014301019

Venkataratnam, C.S. 1997. Adjustment and Privatisation in India: Lessons from Privatisation.

Venkataratnam, C.S. 1997. Adjustment and Privatisation in India. In: *Lessons from Privatisation*, edited by R. van der Hoeven and G. Sziraczki, Geneva: International Labour Office.

Zachariah, K.C. and Rajan, S.I. 2012. Inflexion in Kerala's Gulf Connection: Report on Kerala Migration Survey 2011.

Websites

http://www.pravasitoday.com/

http://www.superbrandsindia.com/images/brand_pdf/consumer_3rd_edition/Apollo%20Hospitals.pdf

http://www.sebi.gov.in/dp/fortis.pdf

http://articles.economictimes.indiatimes.com/2011–05–27/news/29589845_1_net-wealth-wealth-tax-income-tax

http://www.migrationinformation.org/Feature/display.cfm?ID=833

8

State Strategies of Differentiated Citizenship

India's Diaspora Engagement Policy

Diksha Jha

Citizenship in the context of emigration can be understood in terms of both status and practice (Barry 2006). This chapter attempts to engage in a detailed discussion of both these aspects. The terms 'emigration', 'emigrants' and 'emigrant state' would be quite frequently used throughout. Emigration implies permanent or temporary movement from the state of origin. Emigrants are the category of population that move out temporarily or permanently from their state of origin, and emigrant states are the states from which this movement takes place. The reconfigured citizenship in the context of emigration may be called emigrant citizenship. This chapter attempts at presenting an understanding of emigrant citizenship in the context of the Indian state's varied nature of engagement with its different categories of diaspora. Using the conceptual frame of diaspora engagement policy provided by Alan Gamlen, an analytical assessment of the same would be undertaken in the Indian context. The Indian diaspora for the study has been classified into two categories, namely, the PIOs of the high-skilled order residing in the Western states and the temporary emigrant workforce possessing lesser skills and working on contract basis in the Gulf states.

The varied nature of state's engagement with both these segments of the diaspora results in what I call differentiated citizenship status in the context of emigration. While the PIOs experience a value addition in their citizenship status through the home state's efforts at extending benefits (such as Overseas Citizenship of India status), the migrant workers, from being the lesser citizens already at home, face further rights erosion in the context of temporary emigration.

The Global Indian Diaspora: Nature of Indian Emigration

India has the second largest diaspora in the world after the Chinese. The 25 million overseas Indians that constitute the so-called 'global Indian family' (popularly referred as in the annual diaspora meet such as the Pravasi Bharatiya Divas, PBD) is not a homogenous group either. It is vastly varied in terms of nature of migration, region, skill type and belonging to the homeland. The Indian diaspora, comprising PIOs and nonresident Indians, constitutes a global community 'representing diversity of forms, types, geographies and times of formation' and thus calls for an engagement that is distinct and diverse (Annual Report 2012–13).

The dispersion of people from India over the past hundred years may be divided into two phases. The first phase of migration that took place in the colonial era involved the involuntary, forced movement of people to fulfil the demand for cheap labour in the aftermath of the abolition of slavery. The second phase consists of two kinds of movement. The first includes the flow of highly skilled professionals, workers and students with tertiary and higher educational qualifications to the developed countries of the West. The second group includes the semi-skilled and unskilled workers going to the Gulf states and South East Asian states. It may be noted that the Government of India overlooks the category of such migrant workers into the fold of its global diaspora. This chapter seeks to include this segment of less skilled workers (in the Gulf countries) into the fold of the Indian diaspora and then analyse the state's diaspora policy. It may be argued that this inclusion is undertaken due to the fact that such categories of temporary migrant workers follow a pattern of migration that involves migration, return and re-migration (when their contracts get renewed). It may further be noted that they fall under the broader definition of diaspora as suggested by Vertovec (1997: 277) who defines the diaspora as 'any population that is deterritorialized or transnational, that is, which has originated in a land other than the one where it currently resides, and whose social, economic and political networks cross the borders of nation-state'.

Forms of Diasporic Belonging and Practices of Citizenship

The feeling of belonging to the homeland has manifested differently at various points of time in history. From undertaking revolutionary activities against British Imperial rule, while in exile (Zachariah 2013: 575), to being firmly rooted in Indian cultural traditions and customs (Graf 2008: 81), to being a significant contributor to the Indian economy (through remittances, investments, technological knowledge), the Indian diaspora has showcased from time to time its desire to connect with the homeland. The nature of belonging however remains varied for the different diasporic categories.

The categories of PIOs who are descendants of the older generation (who migrated in the pre-independence era) exercise a form of belonging that is primarily cultural in nature. For most of them, visiting India means renewing ties of culture, locating ancestral roots and learning about the country's history and culture. What remains pertinent in all this is the presence of a pervading hierarchy that these PIOs experience (vis-à-vis their counterparts who are recent migrants settled in the West) and at the same time speak at forums such as the PBD. Often, as it turns out from their experience during the visits they make to their cultural homeland where they are doubted to be the 'real' PIOs (Indians).[1] In one of the interactions I had on the occasion of 12th Pravasi Bharatiya Divas with a fourth-generation PIO (presently resident of The Netherlands, whose ancestors had migrated to Suriname in the early twentieth century), who felt that her belonging towards homeland was purely cultural, as, despite being away from India, her family had ensured that the religious and ritualistic practices in the Hindu tradition are adopted by every family member.[2] At the same time, she also believed in a strong presence of hierarchy among the PIOs, which meant that the Government of India had not much to offer to its older diaspora. She said, 'I don't think the Indian government treats people like us at par with the affluent and high class people coming from the Western countries. Most of the schemes that are for the diaspora are available not for all but few, who are close to the government'.[3] Another PIO shared a similar sentiment regarding cultural belonging to India. He said, 'My ancestral village is in Bihar ... I don't know exactly where, but I want to find out. People of Indian origin who are in Mauritius mostly have their ancestral roots in Bihar and they have kept the culture intact ... like everyone knows the Bhojpuri language'.[4]

The other category constitutes the recent (post-independence emigrants) PIOs of the high-skilled and professional class, standing tall in the hierarchical order, primarily due to their economic affluence, thus making them the most favourable diasporic asset for the state. Their belonging to homeland, it may be argued, is not just cultural and affective, but also economic and utilitarian in a number of ways. They are contributors to development processes in the state of origin in manifold ways. These include 'remitting money, investing, getting involved in trade or philanthropic projects, transferring knowledge, raising the country's tax income, spending as tourists, or by bringing about social change in the country or its bureaucracy' (Naujoks 2013: 83). This phenomenon of contribution not just exists at the individual level but at the level of organizations too. The Indus Entrepreneurs (TiE) recruits successful veteran entrepreneurs, corporate executives and senior professionals who have reached a stage in their professional life when they are ready and willingly able to contribute to the industry at large in both the countries of residence and origin (Sahay 2009: 205).

While the above category of the diaspora and its contribution is widely recognized and appreciated by the Indian state which regards them to be the diasporic heroes, the segment of temporary emigrants or migrant workforce in the Gulf countries constitutes that category of the Indian diaspora which the state exports in the form of cheap labour force requisite for the host state's construction industry, which is no less significant in terms of contribution through remittances, and also goes unnoticed in the eyes of the home state. The home state, in this case the Government of India, refuses to interfere and protect their rights, which get eroded in a huge way in the host states largely due to the labour unfriendly policies practiced in the Gulf countries. The already lesser citizens at home, the migrant workers, after emigrating to the Gulf states on contractual basis, find themselves trapped in a situation under mercy of the employers and inconsiderate host state governments. Under such a helpless scenario, they pin their bleak hopes on the Indian government, which to add to the already existing worries turns a blind eye to their problems.

The next section will provide a conceptual understanding of the Indian diaspora policy using the theoretical frame of Alan Gamlen's Diaspora Engagement Policy.[5] An attempt will be made thereafter to elucidate upon the differentiated state strategies towards the diaspora and the varied implications for citizenship for both the categories. Such an analysis will affirm the view that class and skill remain major indicators for state's engagement with the diaspora and that privileging of one diaspora over the other on grounds of higher degree of skill and economic affluence is a marker of Indian diaspora policy.

Indian Diaspora Engagement Policy: A Conceptual Understanding

The policy of engaging with the diaspora signalled a break from the past (till about the 1980s) when the Indian government made it amply clear that the diaspora was meant to show loyalty towards the state of residence and no attempt whatsoever was made from the part of the Indian state to reach out or involve the overseas Indians in any way with the issues of homeland. With changed global settings that included end of bipolar period and host of domestic factors such as the balance of payment crisis which led to a more open and liberalized Indian economy were some of the several reasons that resulted in the state's renewed interest in its diaspora. The Indian diaspora engagement policy must be understood in the light of this background.

The working of Indian diaspora policy and its varied implications for different categories of the diaspora (the two categories in this study) can be explored at the conceptual level by using the typology of diaspora engagement policy as proffered by Gamlen. There are two main underlying arguments. One, the diaspora engagement policies must be viewed as 'a constellation of institutional and legislative arrangements and programmes that come into being at different times, for different reasons, and operate across different timescales at different levels within home-states' (Gamlen 2006: 4). Second, such policies aim at '(re)producing citizen-sovereign relationships with expatriates, thus transnationalizing governmentality – the means by which a population is rendered governable, through the construction, machination, and normalization of a set of governmental apparatuses and knowledges' (Gamlen 2006: 5). In other words, such policies should not be necessarily considered as one homogenous strategy applied uniformly, but rather, as varied in nature.

The other point regarding the transnationalization of governmentality implies that the 'disciplinary apparatus requisite for the exercise of power constitutes three kinds of relationships, namely, relations of power, relationships of communication, and finalized activities'. Thus, the three components of the diaspora engagement policy (Gamlen 2006) include the following:

- Capacity building policies which aim at 'discursively producing a state-centric transnational national society, and developing a set of corresponding state institutions'.
- Extension of rights to the diaspora, thus 'playing a role that befits a legitimate sovereign'.
- Extraction of obligation from the diaspora, on the ground that emigrants 'owe loyalty to this legitimate sovereign' (Gamlen 2006).

Capacity Building Initiatives: Symbolic Practices and Institutional Building

Capacity building for the diaspora is achieved through the twin processes of institution and symbolic nation building processes (Gamlen 2006: 5). Thus, while institution building makes possible the exercise of power through putting in place the 'objective capacities', symbolic nation building allows the transmission of the exercise of power by establishing a 'relationship of communication' through a system of symbols and signs. Symbolic nation building policies consist of 'a broad range of initiatives and programmes to increase emigrant's sense of belonging to a transnational community of co-nationals and to boost the profile of the state within this community' (Gamlen 2006). The symbolic gestures are expressed during the high level rhetorical celebrations organized for the diaspora, where they receive 'national heroes' welcome and often even bestowed with prizes and accolades.

In India, such symbolic gestures are expressed during the annual diaspora meet called the 'Pravasi Bharatiya Divas'. Since 2003, India has been celebrating the PBD as an occasion to mark the contribution of the overseas Indian community in the development of India. Counting the diaspora to be an integral part of the global Indian family, the Prime Minister in his address at the Fifth Pravasi Divas said:

> We are one family. The whole world is our home. That is why I have often said that while the sun has set on many great empires of the world in the past, the sun will never set on the world of the Indian diaspora! From Fiji in the East to Los Angeles in the West, from Cape Town in the South to Toronto in the North, the people of Indian origin are the world's most globalized community.[6]

The rhetorical invocation of 'Mother India's Children' and 'One Global Indian Family' marks a crucial departure from a uniform stand (of leaving out the diaspora) that was held by the government for a long time. Such rhetorical imaginings and gestures assume a kind of uniformity and homogeneity in the diaspora by appearing to be difference blind towards the 'nature of migration, history of migration and class positions'. Events such as the PBD manage to consolidate such distinct categories such as NRIs and PIOs in order to 'produce a single history of cultural, economic and political affiliation to India' (Mani and Varadarajan 2005: 51). This Indian diasporic subject represented 'ancient histories of migration as well as more recent travels, that may be temporary or permanent; established residence and acquired citizenship in developing as well as industrialised countries; and accumulated wealth through manual as well as intellectual labour' (Mani and Varadarajan 2005).

The trend of holding conventions such as the mini or regional PBD in the overseas states from time to time can be seen as continuance of the state's attempts to engage and interact with its diaspora and ensure their connectivity with the ancestral homeland (Annual Report 2012–13: 17). To add to the fervour of symbolism and gestures, the Pravasi Bharatiya Samman (Annual Report 2006–07: 14) award does contribute further to such imaginings. Since 2003, the government on the occasion of PBD confers these awards to 'honour distinguished overseas Indians in recognition of their achievements; their contribution in strengthening India's relations with other countries, promoting the honour and prestige of India and fostering the interests of overseas Indians' (Annual Report 2006–07: 16). Through events such as the PBD, the Indian state seeks to create a 'transnational network between diasporic populations that is nationalist in origin, character, and aspiration' (Mani and Varadarajan 2005: 62). Other symbolic initiatives include programmes such as the Know India Program, Study India Program and Tracing the Roots program in order to familiarize the Indian diaspora youth (the PIO children and also the PIOs) with the culture, traditions and modern day practices of their ancestral land. These are attempts primarily aimed at strengthening the bond at the cultural level.

Having a set institutional mechanism in place is a second crucial element of the capacity building initiative by the state of origin. India has in place an institutional framework to cater to the varied needs of its diaspora (the PIOs, nonresident Indians and the migrant workers). Such policies related to institutional building, Gamlen regards, 'furnish the state with technologies, systems, and institutions to govern diaspora populations'. Steps such as monitoring efforts through the Foreign Service department, having in place a dedicated bureaucratic structure, and consular and consultative bodies to help build transnational networks, assist in the preparation of the state's strategic techniques to govern the diaspora (Gamlen 2006: 8).

In India, the MOIA, established in 2004, functions as an umbrella institution to facilitate the above-mentioned motives (Annual Report 2006–07). As is evident from its functioning and the structural framework, the creation of two divisions, namely, 'Diaspora Services' and 'Emigration Management', caters to the needs of high-skilled diaspora (PIOs and NRIs) and the low-skilled emigrant workers respectively. Furthermore, the use of the terms 'services' and 'management' is indicative of the fact that how the state views the two categories of its diaspora (the high skilled and the low skilled) where the low-skilled emigrant is subject to management and control by the state, and the high-skilled and professional diaspora are seen as contributors to India's development processes. Under the diaspora services, there exist several think tanks that look to bring on one platform the best overseas Indian minds and make use of their skills. The Global Indian Network of Knowledge (Global INK) is one such platform that facilitates knowledge transfer with the objective of leveraging skills, experiences and expertise of global Indian diaspora. The facilitation of diaspora philanthropy is done through the India Development Foundation (Annual Report 2012–13: 9). The Prime Minister's Global Advisory Council that is headed by the Prime Minister himself looks to consider ways and means to 'access the skills and knowledge of the Indian diaspora so as to meet India's development goals and facilitate investments of the overseas Indians' (Annual Report 2012–13: 39).

The Protector General of Emigrants under the Ministry is the authority responsible for protecting the interests of the Indian workers going abroad. It is also the authority to 'issue registration certificate to the Recruiting Agents (RAs) for overseas manpower exporting business' (Annual Report 2012–13: 31). The main logic governing the emigration of low-skilled workers is the fact that due to the lower educational and skill levels, they remain prone to exploitation and thus need additional protection of the state. This results in a range of protectionist safeguards. The Emigration Act, 1983, regulates the recruitment for overseas employment and departure of the intending emigrants from India. Under Section 22 of the Act, 'no citizen of India shall emigrate for any work falling under Section 2(1)(o), unless he obtains emigration clearance from the Protector of Emigrants' (Annual Report 2012–13). These come under the Emigration Check Required (ECR) passport holders, whose educational qualifications are below matriculation and who wish to emigrate for employment to the 17 ECR countries.[7] This process of categorizing emigrants according to education and skill levels and nature of work is a continuation from the colonial past where 'indentured labourers' emigrating to work in the colonial plantations were not supposed to possess any document of citizenship and thus were left to face the brunt of local labour laws in the destination countries. The creation of ECR category of emigrants in a similar way attempts at dividing the citizenship governance regime by bringing the less skilled workers under a strong regulatory framework, and thus making their situation in the host states even more vulnerable (Rajan et al. 2010: 20–21).

Thus, from being lesser citizens at home, such laws and rules lead to further rights erosion for the less skilled ECR category Indian diasporic emigrants in the Gulf countries. This makes a strong case for the argument that this chapter intends at. The policies and state strategies work in a way that privilege the high-skilled professional category of the Indian diaspora over those possessing less skills and whose migration is temporary in nature. Moreover, attempts by the state to control and manage the category of overseas Indian workers on the one hand and ensuring the involvement of the high-skilled permanent emigrants (PIOs in this case) by rhetorical and symbolic practices and extending them certain rights and privileges from time to time is what acts as differentiating state strategies of citizenship, and which also constitutes the second element of the diaspora engagement policy that is taken up in the following section.

Extension of Rights: Rights and Benefits for High-Skilled PIOs and Legislative Measures and Regulations for Emigrant Workers

While in the last section, discussion on institution building was aimed at 'constructing objective capacities to realize relations of power and symbolic practices that produced relationship of communication', in this section, the extension of rights would 'constitute finalized activities or specific effects of the exercise of power' (Gamlen 2006: 10). The Indian state through its diaspora policy attempts at this transnationalization of citizenship by, on the one hand extending limited overseas citizenship rights to its PIOs (thus practicing extension of thin membership and thin rights) and on the other hand by extending instruments of control, regulation and protectionist measures for its overseas worker community (thus extending thin sovereignty).

The long standing demand of the Indian diaspora for dual citizenship was met in the form of 'Overseas Citizenship of India', which was a middle path that worked as a compromise solution in place of dual citizenship. The first step towards establishing connection with the diaspora (PIOs in particular) began with the formulation of the 'Scheme for Issuance of Person of Indian Origin Card'[8] or the PIO Card in 1999. According to Section 2(b) of the notification issued by the Government of India, a Person of Indian Origin meant a 'foreign citizen (not being a citizen of Pakistan,

Bangladesh and other countries as the Central Government may specify from time to time)'.[9] The benefits to a PIO card holder included getting visa free travel to India, with the card's validity being 20 years, non-requirement for registration with Foreigner's Registration Officer if the stay in India did not exceed 180 days, and enjoying parity with the NRIs with regard to facilities in the economic, financial and educational fields except for acquisition of agricultural/plantation properties.[10] The PIO card due to high fees (1,000 USD) and lack of adequate publicity failed to attract the attention of the diaspora.

The High Level Committee on the Indian Diaspora in 2002 submitted a report regarding the possibility of granting dual citizenship to the diaspora. It held that Sections 9, 10 and 12 of the Citizenship Act, 1955, could be suitably amended to provide for dual nationality, thus avoiding any kind of constitutional amendment that would have otherwise complicated matters (Singhvi 2001). It was also argued that the conferment of dual citizenship would not be automatic and that 'it would be confined to persons who were or were entitled to become citizens of India, as well as their children and grandchildren if they have taken the citizenship of the countries specified[11] in the schedule' (Singhvi 2001). The contents in the report therefore were indicative of the fact that unlike the PIO card scheme, this new scheme regarding dual citizenship would benefit only selective diaspora population (mostly resident in the Western states, who migrated in the post-independence period) and that meant overlooking the descendants of the pre-independence migrants (old diaspora).

The new generation of Indian migrants to Europe, North America and Australia, who had become naturalized citizens in those countries, had a sense of nostalgia while giving up their Indian passports and were eagerly awaiting the Indian government's offer of dual citizenship. This wait finally ended, when, on the occasion of the first PBD (January 2003), the Prime Minister formally declared to extend the facility of Overseas Indian Citizenship (which was not exactly dual citizenship) to the diaspora. Subsequently, suitable amendments were made in the Citizenship Act, 1955 (with an addition of Section 7A in the Citizenship Act 1955) to make room for the rights of the diaspora and it came to be known as 'Overseas Citizenship of India' or 'OCI' status. Often regarded as an upgraded version of the PIO card

(Singh 2005: 145), the benefits under the OCI scheme included the following:

> (1) Multiple entry, multi-purpose lifelong visa to visit India; (2) Exemption from reporting to Police authorities for any length of stay in India; (3) Parity with Non-Resident Indians in financial, economic and educational fields except in the acquisition of agricultural or plantation properties; (4) Registered Overseas Citizen of India shall be treated at par with Non-Resident Indians in the matter of inter-country adoption of Indian children; (5) Registered Overseas Citizen of India shall be treated at par with the resident Indians in the matters of tariffs in air fares in domestic sectors in India; (6) Registered Overseas Citizen of India shall be charged the same entry fee as domestic Indian visitors to visit national parks and wildlife sanctuaries in India; (7) Parity with Non-Resident Indians with respect to entry fees to be charged for visiting national monuments and museums; and in pursuance of certain professions, namely, doctors, dentist, nurses, pharmacists, advocates, architects and chartered accountants; (8) Parity with Non-Resident Indians to appear for All India Pre-Medical Test or such other tests to make them eligible for admission in pursuance of the provisions governing the relevant acts. (Annual Report 2012–13)

Harping on the immense success of the OCI scheme among the contemporary, high-skilled PIOs, the Secretary of Ministry of Overseas Indian Affairs states:

> There are about 15 lakh OCI card holders at this point in time. The largest numbers have been issued in London (about 2.5 lakh), New York (about 1.8 lakh), San Francisco (about 1.3 lakh), Birmingham and Houston (about 1 lakh each). OCI cards have been issued by about 148 countries. The number of card holders is increasing at great pace, nearly 1,000 cards are being issued each day. This gives us the confidence that those Indian brothers and sisters who are staying outside also want to have link with the home country. That link could be economic, cultural and social in nature. (...) We have the confidence based on the OCI cards that our engagements can accelerate in science and technology, finance, banking and economics. (Chakravarty 2014: 13)

With the access to overseas Indian citizenship, the PIOs experience an elevated citizenship status as in addition to the citizenship rights in the state of residence, the home state offers socio-economic benefits in the form of OCI. OCI status may be seen as a form of legal incorporation of diaspora. For the other category of the Indian diaspora, that is the less skilled migrant workers, the state strategies work towards regulation and protectionism rather than rights and status. The Act of 1983 introduced a licensed recruitment regime by bringing about a new system of 'emigration clearance' where 'no citizen was allowed to emigrate without the prior approval of the POE (Annual Report 2012–13). By subscribing to the logic of 'protection by exception', emigration clearance was made mandatory only for the ECR category passport holders, leaving the ECNR passport holders out of the regulatory framework. The ECNR status was conferred by virtue of higher educational status of the passport holder, and initially, persons who were graduates and above were exempted from ECR; this was subsequently reduced, first to the intermediate level and recently to matriculation level (Rajan and Percott 2011: 229). The purposive division of citizenry on the basis of educational levels and making emigration extremely difficult for those with lesser skills appears to have a strong resonance with the colonial treatment of the indentured workers.

A review of the management of foreign employment system suggests that there exist four kinds of practices around the world. The laissez faire system, the regulatory system, the state managed system and the system of state monopoly (Sasikumar and Hussain 2008: 12). Under the laissez faire system, the decision regarding labour employment overseas is left completely to the market forces. In a state managed system, the state doesn't simply regulate, but sets up state enterprises to send workers abroad. Under the system of state monopoly, the state assumes full responsibility of labour migration. The emigration management system in India is regulatory in nature. In a regulated system, the state of origin adopts laws and regulation governing overseas employment. The regulatory nature of the Emigration Act, 1983, is evident from the manner in which the persons intending to migrate annually for temporary employment in the unskilled and the semi-skilled categories are subject to the procedures of getting emigration clearance (Sasikumar and Hussain 2008).

As per the law, employment contracts of the workers in the ECR category have to be scrutinized. However, there exist divergences between the letter of the law and the actual experiences of the migrant workers. In a large number of cases, the emigration authorities do not undertake proper verification of the employment contracts. The existing infrastructure in most of the POE offices is grossly inadequate to perform the functions efficiently (Rajan and Percott 2011). Along with this, there is hardly any system in place to monitor the conditions of workers in the destination countries. As a result, the unskilled and semi-skilled migrants encounter problems such as premature termination of job contracts, changing of clauses of the contract to their disadvantage, delay in the payment of salary dues and violation of minimum wage standards. Thus, the ECR status that was intended to provide protection to its holder, in practice has, become 'a stamp of vulnerability of its holder exposing him/her to various forms of exploitation at every stage of emigration and expatriate life' (Rajan and Percott 2011: 230).

The women emigrants falling under the ECR category constitute the most vulnerable category. The low-skilled women in general and domestic workers in particular are put under 'structures of governmentality, where the exertion of power is more effective as it is exercised through seemingly benevolent institutions' (Rajan and Percott 2011: 231). The government of India has sought to undertake restrictive practices for the women emigrants in the ECR category. Following the principle of 'protection by exception', such practices, it is believed, would offer protective cover to the women. In 1999, the government banned the migration of Indian workers as housemaids to Kuwait due to the post-war turmoil scenario. In 2002, the Ministry of Labour fixed 30 years as the minimum age prescribed for the deployment of Indian citizens as housemaids in the Gulf states. At the behest of the National Commission for Women, the Ministry of Labour, in 2003, directed all the POE offices to not grant emigration clearance to women who are below 30 years of age and wish to get employed as domestic workers in any foreign country (Rajan and Percott 2011). Such practices tend to attach stigma with the kind of work emigrating women in the less skilled/ECR categories want to take up. The government through an order issued in 2007 declared that women below the age of 30 years and seeking employment as housemaids, domestic workers, hair dressers, beauticians, dancers, stage artists, labourers and so on in any foreign country would be denied clearance from Protector's office (Rajan and Percott 2011).

After the creation of the Ministry of Overseas Indian Affairs in 2004, a concerted effort has been made towards signing labour-related memorandum of understandings (MoUs) with several host states where labour force from India emigrate in large numbers. Some broad underlining principles governing most of these agreements include working towards enhancing employment opportunities and ensuring worker's welfare and protection; recruitment and terms and conditions of employment must be in conformity with the laws of both the states; establishment of joint working groups to ensure the implementation of MoUs and bilateral agreements (Annual Report 2012–13). With regard to these agreements between the Indian government and the Gulf countries, there is no clarity about what sort of protection and welfare provisions exist for the workers.

All the provisions remain largely ambiguous without addressing the specific issues. These and many issues remain on a contested terrain and raise serious citizenship concerns with regard to the less skilled emigrant workforce in the Gulf states. The continued practices of regulation and control for this segment of the diaspora presents in front of us a scenario where India virtually has no emigration policy in place. As the following section will describe, while the Indian state wants the remittances and money from the unskilled manpower, but at the same time prohibits emigration in a number of ways.

Extraction of Obligations: Diaspora's Contributions through Remittances, Investments and Knowledge

Through the process of extension of rights (which also is equivalent to extending 'thin rights'), the sending states can expect to demand obligations from the diaspora, that is start asserting 'thin sovereignty'. The states may begin by attempting to 'assert thin sovereignty by extracting obligations without extending rights, but if these attempts are sustained, the extension of reciprocal rights becomes inevitable (Gamlen 2006: 13). During a parliamentary debate, a prominent Rajya Sabha MP said:

> It is advantageous to us that we expect FDI because a large number of our diaspora are very well off and are at very high position. It is a great potential which we should tap. It's a deposit there and therefore is brain bank. Moves like granting of OCI right to our diaspora is part of the larger attempt to draw from that deposit. Everyone says China gets much more FDI than India. If you analyse that, then you will find that they are getting the FDI mostly from the overseas Chinese. (Rajya Sabha Debate)

The states have often courted their emigrant population most extensively in the economic sphere. According to Kim Barry, the state's efforts at capturing a part of emigrant earnings fall under three broad categories, namely, sustaining or increasing the inflow of remittances; seeking to coerce economic contribution through taxation and offering a wide array of benefits and incentives to attract capital and investment inflows from them (2006: 35).

According to a World Bank estimate, the total volume of financial remittances to the developing states rose from 57.5 billion USD in 1995 to 240 billion USD in 2007 (Kapur 2010). The movement of semi-skilled and unskilled workers to the Gulf states increased in the light of the Gulf oil boom of the 1970s. A steady increase from 15.8 billion USD in 2001–2002 to 70 billion USD in 2012 has been noted (Annual Report 2012–13). Another way of demanding obligations from the diaspora is by floating attractive investment incentives. The 'Resurgent India Bonds', also called 'diaspora bonds', can be termed as one such initiative taken by the Indian state towards economic incorporation of its wealthy emigrant population. A term coined by Anupam Chander, 'diaspora bonds' are 'debt instruments offered by sovereign governments to raise capital principally or exclusively from their diasporas'. The reason that homeland states find the diasporas attractive to raise capital is that, even a lower rate of return on the capital than offered in general market is acceptable to them, and they are willing to supply capital at reasonable rates even when the country's economy is in bad shape (Chander 2001: 534).

The first time that India turned to its expatriate community was in 1991 by offering the 'India Development Bonds' during the balance of payments crisis. It helped in raising 2 billion USD in 1992 and 1993. Again in 1998, during the economic crisis following the international sanctions imposed on India after it had conducted the Pokhran nuclear tests, it once again turned to its diaspora 'sons and daughters' (Chander 2001). The Resurgent India Bonds (RIBs) launched in 1998 had the following features:

- India asserted that these instruments offered by its state bank were certificates of deposit and not debt securities.
- The instruments specified that the suits under them could be brought only under Indian law and courts.
- They were available only to the diaspora.

It may also be noted that these instruments were sold to the expatriates residing in Europe, the Middle East and the United States through Indian and foreign commercial banks that specialized in providing services to Indian expatriates. The sale was overwhelmingly successful raising 4.2 billion USD, almost more than double the initial expectations. Interestingly these diasporic heroes or 'departed sons and daughters' (Chander 2001) were selectively identified by the state whereby a large section of Indian overseas population (belonging to the older diaspora) was categorically overlooked.

Conclusion

After an analysis of the Indian diaspora policy through the conceptual lens of the diaspora engagement policy, one can conclude that it tends to have a differentiated and varied impact on the diaspora. On the one hand, the policy of Overseas Indian Citizenship provides a value addition in the citizenship status of the diaspora. Through OCI, the diaspora practices the idea of dual nationality. The OCI may not be a formal fulfilment of the aspiration of dual citizenship for the Indian diaspora, but it does offer them recognition as they 'embrace this new status with overwhelming national pride (Naujoks 2013: 214). Many of them even go to the extent in saying that they would not have naturalized (taken foreign citizenship) if OCI had not been available. The presence of a status such as OCI provides the diaspora with emotional comfort while they decide to forego the Indian citizenship and naturalize and become permanent emigrants. They came to view it as a 'replacement of their Indian passport and saw a lot of tangible and intangible benefits to it' (Naujoks 2013).

On the other hand, citizenship status that is already minimal in the homeland undergoes further erosion in the emigration context with regard to temporary migrant workers in the Gulf countries. It begins with seizing of the workers' passport by the employer, which is their basic proof of identity (as a citizen of India) in a foreign state. In extreme cases of harassment at workplace, the workers run away from the employer and as a result become illegal migrant in a foreign country and thus more vulnerable (Rajan et al. 2010: 49).

During the special Gulf Session at the 12th PBD held in January 2014, a nonresident Indian residing in Bahrain brought up the issue of Indian prisoners languishing in deportation cells even after finishing their jail term. He said:

> Once the Indian prisoners finish their jail term, they are moved to the deportation cell thus facing travel ban after ending the jail term. In order to get this ban lifted, the prisoners are required to get a no objection notice from their first sponsor. It is extremely difficult for them to go back and find the first sponsor and as a result they have no chance to escape from the deportation center and return home.[12]

To this query, an Indian Embassy official replied that, 'it is not easy to negotiate with the Bahrain authorities on issues like the travel ban as we have a lot of resource constraint'.[13] This clearly brings to light the apathy, an attitude of indifference of the Indian government towards the problems of its migrant workforce in the Gulf. Under the mechanism of the MoU, the role of joint committees or joint working groups become significant as they are responsible for monitoring the implementation of the MoUs.

Negotiations regarding such practices need to be undertaken on a high pitch by the Indian government. According to a social worker residing in Bahrain whom I met during the 12th PBD, 'It is not a big issue for the Indian government to take up the issue of its worker's rights one on one with the Government of Bahrain. After all it's a very small island nation and India can have a strong negotiation with them. But the political will is often lacking' (Anecdotes from 12th PBD 2014). The Government of India believes that it has been doing what is required and cannot go beyond a point in the negotiation process. I would end with a statement from a former official in the Ministry of External Affairs and this would sum up the Indian state's stand on the issue of the migrant workforce in the Gulf:

> Given the resources available, I believe the Government has done all it could have. It is a well-known fact that the Arab countries treat the workers coming from the developing states very shabbily. However, given our vulnerability on the energy security front, we cannot weigh this issue as a central point.[14]

Notes

1. Anecdotal evidence from the 12th PBD held in New Delhi during 7–9 January 2014.
2. Ibid.
3. Based on an e-mail interview taken with a PIO residing in The Netherlands. I met her during the 12th PBD.
4. Anecdotal evidence from the 12th PBD 2014.
5. The typology of diaspora engagement policy has been originally provided by Alan Gamlen in 'Diaspora Engagement Policies: What Are They, and What Kinds of States Use Them?' Centre on Migration, Policy and Society Working Paper No. 32, University of Oxford, 2006.
6. Prime Minister's address at the Fifth PBD held on 7 January 2007.
7. The 17 countries for which an emigration check is required includes Afghanistan, Bahrain, Indonesia, Iraq, Jordan, Kingdom of Saudi Arabia, Kuwait, Lebanon, Libya, Malaysia, Oman, Qatar, Sudan, Syria, Thailand, United Arab of Emirates (UAE) and Yemen (Annual Report 2012–13).
8. Ministry of Home Affairs Notification F.No. 26011/9/98-IC of 30 March 1999. http://indiandiaspora.nic.in/diasporapdf/chapter24.pdf
9. Ibid., 371.
10. Ibid., Under Section 8 and subclauses (i), (ii), (iii) and (iv).
11. The High Level Committee on the Indian Diaspora mentioned that dual citizenship would be applicable to citizens of select countries such as the United States of America, the United Kingdom, countries of the EU, Canada, Australia, Singapore, Malaysia, Thailand, Japan, New Zealand and such other countries mentioned in the schedule to the Citizenship Act, 530.
12. Based on anecdotal evidence from the Special Gulf Session during 12th PBD held on 9 January 2014 and in an e-mail interview conducted during the course of this research.

13. Gulf Session, PBD 2014, Anecdotes.
14. Based on an interview conducted during the course of this research with former Member Secretary, GOI.

References

Rajan, S. Irudaya, V.J. Varghese and M.S. Jayakumar. 2010. Overseas Recruitment in India: Structures, Practices and Remedies. *Working Paper 421*, Centre for Development Studies, Trivandrum, India.

Chakravarty, S. 2014. *'We want our bonds with Overseas Indians to strengthen': Interview with Mr Prem Narain, Secretary, Ministry of Overseas Indian Affairs*. Available at: http://indiaempire.com/article/380/we_want_our_bonds_with_overseas_indians_to_strengthen (accessed 15 January 2016).

Sasikumar, S.K. and Zakir Hussain. 2008. 'Managing international labour migration from India: policies and perspectives.' *ILO Asia-Pacific Working Paper Series*, International Labour Organisation.

Annual Report 2006–07. Ministry of Overseas Indian Affairs, New Delhi, Government of India.

Annual Report 2012–13. Ministry of Overseas Indian Affairs, New Delhi, Government of India.

Annual Report 2012-13. Ministry of Overseas Indian Affairs, Government of India, New Delhi.

Barry, Kim. 2006. Home and Away: The Construction of Citizenship in an Emigration Context. New York University Public Law and Legal Theory Working Paper. New York University School of Law.

Chander, Anupam. 2001. Diaspora Bonds. *New York University Law Review*, 479–573.

Gamlen, Alan. 2006. Diaspora Engagement Policies: What Are They, and What Kinds of States Use Them? Centre on Migration, Policy and Society Working Paper No. 32 1–32.

Graf, Carmen Voigt. 2008. Transnationalism and the Indo-Fijian Diaspora: The Relationship of Indo-Fijians to India and Its People. *Journal of Intercultural Studies*, 81–109.

Kapur, Devesh. 2010. *Diaspora, Development and Democracy: The Domestic Impact of International Migration from India*. Princeton: Princeton University Press.

Mani, Bakirathi, Latha Varadarajan. 2005. The Largest Gathering of the Global Indian Family: Neoliberalism, Nationalism and Diaspora at Pravasi Bharatiya Divas. *Diaspora: A Journal of Transnational Studies*, 45–74.

Naujoks, Daniel. 2013. *Migration, Citizenship, and Development Diasporic Membership Policies and Overseas Indians in the United States*. New Delhi: Oxford University Press.

S. Irudaya Rajan and Marie Percot. 2011. *Dynamics of Indian Migration Historical and Current Perspectives*. New Delhi: Routledge.

Sahay, Anjali. 2009. *Indian Diaspora in the US: Brain Drain or Gain*. Lanham: Lexington Books.

Singh, Shubha. 2005. *Overseas Indians: The Global Family*. Delhi: Shipra Publications.

Singhvi, L.M. 2001. *High Level Committee on the Indian Diaspora*. New Delhi: Government of India: Government Report.

Vertovec, Steven. 1997. Three Meanings of Diaspora Exemplified among South Asian Religions. *Diaspora: A Journal of Transnational Studies*, 6(3), 277–299.

Zachariah, Benjamin. 2013. A Long, Strange Trip: The Lives in Exile of Har Dayal. *South Asian History and Culture*, 574–592.

9

Diaspora on the Margin

Contextualizing Partition Diaspora and Abdul Ghani Sheikh's 'Two Nations, One Story'

Angshuman Kar

In a transnational and globalized world, diasporas are becoming more and more important to the homelands than they have ever been. 'As long as the homeland recognizes, patronizes, and praises its diasporans', writes Sahoo, 'the diaspora not only remains connected with the homeland socially and culturally but also becomes an economic and political asset' (2015: 43). Sahoo's observation seems to be more than true in the context of India's relationship with its diaspora. In the recent past, Indian government has taken a number of steps to patronize and celebrate Indian diaspora in the hope of getting substantial support to its project of socio-economic growth and development. The introduction of the PIO card,[1] the celebration of 9 January (the day on which Gandhi returned to India from South Africa) every year as the PBD, the introduction of the Pravasi Bharatiya Samman Award and steps like these have undoubtedly strengthened the links between India and its diaspora.[2] One may, however, question whether India treats its diaspora in the United Kingdom at par with its diaspora in the UAE or whether the Indian diaspora in Pakistan is as important as the Indian diaspora in the United States. In short, one may question whether some Indian diasporas are more equal than others. Beyond the governmental level, in academia and the literary world too, some Indian diasporas are pushed to the margin while others are at the centre.

Books on Indian diaspora usually include Indian diaspora writers of countries such as the United Kingdom, the United States, Australia, Canada and seldom some of the Asian countries such as Malaysia and Singapore. The absence of some other Indian diasporas and their writers in such books needs serious examination. As an academic who has written on Indian diaspora in the United Kingdom and the United States and as an editor who has produced a volume on contemporary Indian diaspora excluding 'minor' Indian diasporas, I felt disturbed by these issues while reading Abdul Ghani Sheikh's short story 'Two Nations, One Story'. This essay, the result of that disturbance, is an attempt at self-introspection. In that attempt, the essay will also try to see how diasporas created by partition are different from diasporas of other kinds.

Abdul Ghani Sheikh (born in 1936) is not an Indian diaspora writer. He is an Urdu writer of Ladakh. Twelve short stories of Sheikh have been translated by Ravina Aggarwal and published in the form of a book, *Forsaking Paradise* (2001), by Katha. Sheikh is a representative of Argon group of Muslims who are 'descendants of Kashmiri and Yarkhandi traders who had settled in Ladakh and married locally' (Aggarwal 2001: 25). In her long and insightful introduction to *Forsaking Paradise*, Ravina Aggarwal underlines the hybrid upbringing of Ghani Sheikh in a 'multicultural' Ladakh which is 'a land which borders Pakistan, Occupied Tibet and the Kashmir valley, where Buddhism, Islam and even Christianity have found homes' (Aggarwal 2001: 8). The history of Ladakh is interesting and unique. It was under the rule of the descendants of the tenth century Tibetan King, Skyid de Nyima Gon, till the mid-nineteenth century. This rule ended when, in 1834, Zorawar Singh, the general of the Dogra King of Jammu and Kashmir, Maharaja Gulab Singh, conquered both Ladakh and Baltistan.[3] To settle the disputes between the Dogras and the Tibetan about the possession of Ladakh British General Cunningham drew the Indian–Tibetan demarcation line in 1942.[4] Ultimately, Ladakh was handed over to Maharaja Gulab Singh in 1846 by the British, though they retained control over its economy to make the best of the highly profitable pashmina trade. The changes that took place in Ladakh around this time had long-lasting socio-cultural effects. Aggarwal writes: 'The roots of ecclesiastic and monarchic power were shaken and the extensive patronage once extended to

Ladakhi language and literature was to end forever. During this colonial period, a new kind of literature came to dominate the landscape. Tools of modernity, such as census records, economic statistics, area maps, and land surveys, were deployed by imperial agencies for documenting the region' (2001: 10). The region saw peculiar development after independence. In 1947, immediately after Independence, Ladakh became a part of India but Baltistan was still under Jammu and Kashmir. After one year, Baltistan 'ultimately became a part of Pakistan and the people of Ladakh, whose kith and kin were still living in Baltistan, tasted partition' (Kar 2014: 52). During the post-independence era, Ladakh saw rapid changes due to the development in tourism that resulted in the construction of new roads and a radical growth in education. India's wars with Pakistan and China in the 1960s and 1970s also re-shaped the territorial boundaries of Ladakh and badly affected the lives of the Ladakhi people. Ghani Sheikh's 'Two Nations, One Story' is a good testimony to all these changes and their impact on the lives of the people of that region.

As the very title of the story suggests, 'Two Nations, One Story' is a story of two brothers who have become part of two nations after Indian independence. One of these two brothers is the unnamed narrator of the story and the other is Kaga Din Mohammed, who was the clerk of Lala Amarnath, the last Wazir, the chief administrator of Dogra administration in pre-independent Jammu and Kashmir. Before independence, Lala Amarnath used to divide his time between Leh and Skardo, which was 'the biggest town of Baltistan' (p. 68). Kaga Din Mohammed, who went to Skardo with the Wazir in the autumn of 1947, ultimately became a citizen of Pakistan, as, in 1948, Skardo became a part of Pakistan. Initially, of course, Kaga's family members, including his wife, expected him to come back to Ladakh. But Kaga, like so many other unfortunate Ladakhis, could not come back home and had to settle down in Pakistan as an Indian diasporan. 'Two Nations, One Story' tells the sad tale of separation and the hope of a re-union of Kaga and his brother, the narrator of the story. Since the story is narrated by Kaga's brother who is a non-diasporan and is written by Ghani Sheikh who is also not a diaspora writer, it could be questioned whether 'Two Nations, One Story' be at all called a diaspora story. The story, one has to admit, is primarily a partition story. But since the partition of India produced diaspora communities on both sides of the border, stories on the partition of India are embedded with diasporic layers. I admit that there could be debates on the validity of reading such stories under the rubric of diaspora studies and it could be strongly argued that such stories should be studied only as partition literature. I have something to say on this and I shall come back to this issue towards the end of the chapter.

Ghani Sheikh begins the story with an observation on the plights of those families that have got separated due the partition of India:

> The partition of India has affected more than just the destiny of a nation. It has split apart towns, villages and homes that were once one. At the Line of Control there are, they say, such villages where a brother can see his brother on the other side – ploughing the fields, watering them, harvesting and threshing the crops. But if he wants to meet his brother on that other side, he has to trek several kilometers from his village and cross the forbidding Khardong pass, eighteen thousand feet high, to reach Leh. From there he can fly to New Delhi. After several months of struggle and waiting in the capital, should he acquire a visa, he can travel to meet his brother in Islamabad or Lahore, but not in his brother's own village in the trans-Himalayan territories. In spite of being so close to his brother's home, he is so far away. Like a star in the sky which he can see but not touch. (p. 68)

Such a beginning of a story makes one re-think about two issues: first, the relationship between partition and diaspora, and second, the nature of 'partition diaspora' and its similarities with and/or differences from other diasporas. Partition has been one of the causes of the *creation* of diaspora all over the world. Movements, group or individual, voluntary or involuntary, have been considered as key factors in giving birth to diasporas. Partition of a country, however, can *create* diasporas which are not the results of movements of any kind. This is something that Ghani Sheikh perhaps hints at when he writes that at the line of control there are villages where a brother can see his brother on the other side but cannot meet him. A line drawn on the map of a country in a closed-door, high-profile political meeting can make someone living in his/her own village the resident of a new country, and hence, a diasporan. Kaga, of course, is not a diasporan of this kind. He becomes a diasporan due to a movement, which was involuntary and governmental. As the clerk of Lala Amarnath, he had to go to Skardo and unfortunately this movement coincided with the partition of India and converted Kaga into a diasporan. His situation is somewhat different from that of one who becomes a diasporan in spite of staying at home. Both, however, become part of diaspora due to partition of their country. Partition, therefore, does *create* diasporas and diaspora thus created – which I would like to call partition diaspora – is different from other kinds of diasporas.

I know that many eyebrows would be raised at the use of the term partition diaspora. Diasporas are usually described in terms of homeland/region, religion, language, race, ethnicity, profession and markers like these; the cause of the diaspora is not usually used to describe a diaspora community. But, I would like to ask whether it is unjust and unwise to make the cause a part of the nomenclature for a diaspora community if the cause is that important as to make the diaspora (created by that cause) distinct from other diasporas? The cause of the diaspora has, indeed, been – as is evident in the use of the term 'indentured diaspora' – (a) part of the nomenclature in some cases. In an article, 'Dilemmas of Diaspora: Partition, Refugees, and the Politics of Home', Pablo Bose has used the term 'refugee diaspora' to examine the nature and consequences of the Hindu-Bengali exodus to India from the then East Pakistan (later an independent country, Bangladesh) during and after the partition of India. While I do not reject Bose's use of the term 'refugee diaspora', I consider partition diaspora a better term to study diaspora created by partition. This is because of the 1951 UN definition of the word 'refugee',[5] which underlines two important things about the refugees. It underlines that a refugee (a) must be outside *the country of his nationality* or his/her *formal habitual residence* and (b) must suffer from a persecution fear for reasons of race, religion, nationality, membership of a particular social group, or political opinion. As I have already argued and as has been hinted at by Sheikh in the first paragraph of his story, partition can make one a diasporan even in his/her own country, which, after partition, however, ceases to be his/her own and can make him/her an unwanted stranger in the newly born country. The issue of nationality is also highly problematic in this regard. Was not a Pakistani citizen, who lived through the partition, an Indian before the partition? What should be his/her nationality after partition? Thus, if we go by the UN definition of the word 'refugee', the use of the term 'refugee diaspora' for diaspora created by partition might seem problematic. Hence, my vote for the term partition diaspora, which is gaining slow currency in usage.[6]

Certain features of partition diaspora unquestionably distinguish it from other diasporas. Usually, for a diasporan, the geographic distance from the homeland – which is believed to produce a strong back pull on the diasporan that not only makes his/her acculturation process in the host land difficult but also creates what Rushdie called the 'imaginary homeland' – might eventually act as a blessing in disguise in that the impossibility of return can help the diasporan settle down in the host land through intelligent, realistic negotiations with its new socio-politico-cultural dynamics. But the situation of the partition diasporan, who lives close to the border that divides the two countries after the partition, is somewhat different from other diasporans. She/he sometimes, as pointed out by Sheikh, might see his brother on the other side of the border 'like a star in the sky which he can see but not touch'. For meeting his/her brother he/she needs to trek several kilometres, fly to the capital city of his newly born 'host land' and unquestionably go through what could be called a bureaucratic trial. For a partition diasporan living close to the border, the geographical proximity with and the bureaucratic distance – as suggested by Ghani Sheikh – from the homeland might make life extremely painful, almost unbearable.

I know that scholars might, again, raise two objections here. First, they might dismiss my arguments regarding geographic distance by reiterating that the cyber explosion has re-defined and re-mapped distance, which is no more a monolithic category as virtual proximity has contested and subverted geographic distance. True. In the age of Skype, cheap air fares and ISD calls, geographic distance between the homeland and the host land has become less important than it was, say, 30 years back. But can there be any generic conclusion on this? The middle-class and higher middle-class Indians are in continuous touch with the homeland and can afford to visit the homeland at least once a year. But what about those Indian taxi drivers in Australia or Canada who earn that much as is needed for their mere survival?

We do – though we should not – forget that diaspora means not only stories of success but also stories of failures. So, Ghani Sheikh is right in pointing out that the geographical proximity with and the bureaucratic distance from the homeland keep a partition diasporan living close to the border in a continuous fix, in a permanent flux.

The second issue that could be raised here by the scholars is about the problem of the blurring of the identities of the homeland and the host land for a partition diasporan. They would argue that for a non-partition diasporan, the homeland is clearly distinct from the host land, but such a clearly identifiable distinction between the homeland and the host land perhaps does not exist for a partition diasporan. For him/her, a part of the homeland suddenly is converted into the host land. True. But I would like to argue that, with time, a partition diasporan gradually becomes aware of the difference between the homeland and the host land. Of the several factors that contribute to this growing awareness, two are clearly visible in Ghani Sheikh's story. One of these two is the role of the government and bureaucracy in controlling the movement across the border, and the other is the notion of 'home', which, as we know, is more than an arrangement of bricks and sand. In fact, if the family of a partition diasporan remains on the other side of the border, and if he/she is unable to easily meet his/her family members due to the immigration laws and rules of the newly separated countries, he/she is bound to be aware of the difference between the homeland and the host land. Such a partition diasporan, of course, is different from a non-partition diasporan in that he/she seldom receives a culture shock as either he/she is not at all spatially dislocated or – as in case of Kaga – even if he/she is dislocated spatially, he/she is not, usually, dislocated culturally. Since the homeland and the host land were one before partition, the partition diasporan lives are transported from a cultural environment he/she has grown up with. So, the issue of acculturation is actually less important to a partition diasporan than it is to a non-partition diasporan.

'Two Nations, One Story' can act, indeed, as a very good proof in favour of our arguments cited above. The narrator, who had never been to Skardo and desperately wanted to meet his brother there, writes:

> I have always wanted to visit Skardo. Not only because my brother lives there but also because Skardo has been a vital part of our heritage. Ladakhis who have visited both places, or those who know about the relations between the two regions, have a great desire to see Skardo.
>
> Racially, culturally, and linguistically, the people of Baltistan and Ladakh are one. The disposition of their inhabitants are also very similar. The history and geography of Skardo and Leh bear striking resemblances. ... Baltistan gave Ladakh butter, dried apricots, apricot seeds, and earthen pots and we gave Baltistan pashmina, wool, and salt. Baltistan gave Ladakh polo, musical instruments, and ghazals. Ladakh gave Baltistan songs and epics. (pp. 76–77)

This inseparable link between Ladakh and Baltistan comes to the fore in the story when the narrator got a chance to visit Pakistan as a member of Indian delegation for participating in a seminar. The seminar was organized in Islamabad by the Pak-German Research Project and Lok-Virsa Institute on 'the cultural and geographical links between the Hindukush, Karakoram and Himalayan regions' (p. 77). In the seminar, the narrator and his Ladakhi compatriot Nawang Shakspo presented a joint paper comparing the cultures of Ladakh and Baltistan. They received a warm welcome from the Baltis who even organized a farewell party for the narrator and Nawang on their last day in Islamabad. Interestingly, the narrator, who had always been dreaming of meeting his brother in Skardo, could not go to Skardo, though a trip to Skardo had been originally a part of the programme. Actually, the Home Ministry of Pakistan, for unknown reasons, did not allow the Indian delegation to visit Skardo. A 'distinguished professor and historian of the Lok-Virsa Institute' and the Chair of the Pak-German Research Project appealed on behalf of the Indian delegation but the appeal was not entertained (p. 78). The narrator was advised to write separately to the Home Ministry informing them his desire of meeting his brother in Skardo as, the historian and the Chair of the Project thought, he might get the permission on humanitarian ground. But the permission was not granted. This incident clearly shows that bureaucratic suspicion and resultant intervention into the lives of the Indian diasporans in Pakistan and their kin have badly affected the residents on both sides of the border. In fact, such a role of bureaucratic intervention into the lives of a diasporan and his/her family is underlined by Ghani Sheikh in this story almost from the beginning.

From the beginning of the story, it is indeed reiterated that after Baltistan formally became a part of Pakistan, despite his attempts, Kaga could not come back to Ladakh. Initially, there was even no news of Kaga. Then the narrator's family somehow came to know that Kaga was faring well. Kaga himself, however, could not come back home. He even asked his wife Saffiya not to waste her time in waiting for him and to begin life anew as he himself was preparing for a new marriage and thinking of settling down in Pakistan. Kaga then sent the divorce papers to Saffiya, married for a second time and also had children from this marriage. The readers are shocked to know that Kaga was not even allowed to go to India when his father died. He could just send a letter:

> A month and half later, we received a letter of condolence. 'If only I myself could come to Leh to share this pain', he had written. But Kaga was a government employee. The state of Jammu and Kashmir was a sensitive border area. It was difficult to obtain permission to visit Leh. (p. 70)

A paragraph like this obviously makes one think whether it was possible for Kaga to have a visa for India had he not been a government employee. It also hints at the difference between a diasporan who is a government employee in the host land and one who is not, particularly, in terms of bureaucratic treatment.

Kaga, however, ultimately could come to Leh 38 years after he had left Ladakh. Kaga's visit created tremendous enthusiasm in his family and friends. They went to the airport to receive Kaga boarding two taxies. If Kaga's kith and kin found a sea change in Kaga, who 'had left as a bridegroom and returned as a grandfather' (p. 72), Kaga was surprised to see a changed Leh:

> The taxi made its way to towards Leh. 'Leh has changed a lot', Kaga observed, looking at the houses on both sides of the street beyond the airport. 'This place used to be totally deserted. People said it was haunted. They were afraid to walk here after dark' … . Kaga had been hearing about the changes in Leh for a long time. Now he could see them with his own eyes. (p. 72)

Kaga's confrontation with a changed Ladakh reveals a diasporan's complex engagement with the imaginary of 'home'. Interestingly, when Kaga's brief period of stay in Ladakh was over, he became anxious about going back to Skardo:

> It hardly takes any time for a month to pass. Kaga's visa was about to end and he was anxious to go back to Skardo. He loved his new country where his children were and where his new relatives and friends lived. (p. 75)

Such passages strengthen our claim that with time a partition diasporan becomes aware of the divide between the homeland and the host land and has a sense of belonging to both. In fact, if at the end of his stay in Leh, Kaga was anxious to go back to Skardo where his new family lived, his parting words to his brother in Islamabad prove that he was equally anxious to come back to Leh, the residence of his old family. During the narrator's trip to Pakistan, since the narrator could not go to Skardo, Kaga came to meet him in Islamabad. In this meeting, Kaga told the narrator that before his (Kaga's) death, he would wish to 'come to Ladakh once again' (p. 79).

Kaga's brief period of stay in Leh was marked by the visits of people who wanted to have information 'about their loved ones in Skardo' (p. 74). Kaga, in fact, acted as carrier of letters and gifts between the diasporans in Pakistan and their relatives in India. He brought in letters and gifts from Ghulam Mohammed for his brother Munshi in Ladakh and also promised Sonam Tshering's father that he would take a letter and a gift for his son in Skardo. The story, in fact, adequately foregrounds the role of communication in maintaining the relationship between a diasporan and his family of the homeland. In the pre-email era, communication was mainly dependent on letters. 'Two Nations, One Story' clearly shows how important the letters in the lives of the Ladakhi people on both sides of the border were. After partition, there was no news of Kaga for some time, as there was 'no channel for sending letters' (p. 69). Then news started trickling down from Skardo to Ladakh and after some time even correspondences between the two countries began. Kaga and his family did not receive letters written to each other during the two Indo-Pak wars of 1965 and 1971. Letters became irregular again when Kashmir got turbulent in 1995. During this time, Kaga in

Skardo and his family in Ladakh started receiving letters long after the letters were actually sent to each other. Some of the letters were not even received by them and they wondered 'where these straightforward and simple letters disappeared' (p. 76). Learning from these experiences, the narrator started handing over letters to the European tourists with the request to post these letters from their respective countries for Pakistan. 'Ironically', the narrator states, 'these letters reached Skardo safely after travelling thousands of miles from London or Birmingham or Copenhagen or some other European city. And letters sent from Skardo, situated only two hundred and three miles away from Leh, disappeared mysteriously' (p. 76). The continuous bureaucratic monitoring and controlling of the means of communication, which is apparent in the story, again brings us back to the issue of the effect of bureaucratic intervention in the lives of the diasporans and their kith and kin.

So, 'Two Nations, One Story', on the one hand, makes us re-think about the relationship between partition and diaspora and, on the other, calls for the need for examining partition diaspora's similarities with/differences from other kinds of diasporas. A careful reading of the story, for instance, reveals that the role of bureaucracy in mediating the life of the diasporan is more important in partition diaspora than it is in non-partition diaspora. In case of non-partition diaspora, a diasporan needs to continuously negotiate both alien culture(s) and bureaucratic interventions of the host land. But, 'Two Nations, One Story' shows that in case of partition diaspora because of the similarities between the cultures of the homeland and the host land, a diasporan is mainly in need of negotiating bureaucratic interventions. Negotiations with such interventions – which reveal that despite the geographic proximity between the homeland and the host land, a partition diasporan is actually as far away from the homeland as is a non-partition diasporan – are difficult and painful. Such negotiations, as 'Two Nations, One Story' further proves, become more difficult and painful if the homeland and the host land are the creations of partition and are in perpetual conflicting relations like India and Pakistan. Difficulty and pain, again, for partition diasporans such as Kaga, increase particularly during moments of political crises such as wars.

'Two Nations, One Story' also obliquely points out the presence of a hierarchy in the treatment/reception of Indian diasporas. Indian diasporas in the United Kingdom or the United States have always had the attention of the governments, writers and scholars. But this cannot be said about the Indian diasporas in Pakistan, Bangladesh or Sri Lanka. Again, are Punjabi diaspora and Ladakhi diaspora in Pakistan treated alike both by the host land and homeland governments? What about an Indian diasporan who is a government employee and one who is not? Are there any differences between those Indian diasporans who live close to India/Pakistan, India/Bangladesh borders and those who do not? These questions make us think about a few, what I would call larger political questions. Some Indian diasporans are assets to India. True. What about those diasporas which are not assets but liabilities? How are these diasporas treated by Indian government and Indian intelligentsia? Are contemporary Indian English diaspora writers or Indian English writers in general interested in writing stories on the Indian diasporas which are not assets but liabilities? If they do so, will these stories have market? While reading Ghani Sheik's 'Two Nations, One Story', one is bound to think that a writer like Ghani Sheikh, words written by whom bear the mark of experiences which are authentic, does not bother about the marketability of a story. In fact, the subject position of Ghani Sheikh, who is neither a diaspora writer nor an Indian English writer but a Ladakhi Urdu writer, makes me think aloud about another issue. Are we the Indian academics teaching English literatures in different Indian universities and colleges paying proper attention to Indian Bhasha writers in general and contemporary Bhasha writers of Indian diaspora in particular?

One last question before I conclude is, where should we place a story like 'Two Nations, One Story'? Should we place it under the umbrella term of diaspora studies or under the generic rubric of partition literature? It could be said that such a question on nomenclature should not bother a diaspora critic at all as diaspora itself implies multiplicity of experiences and intersectionality of disciplines. True. But naming has always been a political act and the marginalization of the Indian partition diaspora in diaspora studies – which, to me, is also political in nature – perhaps underlines the need for a separate term to highlight the study of the unique experiences of the Indian partition diasporans. In this spirit, I would like to argue that within diaspora studies we should think of creating a subcategory, 'studies of Indian partition diaspora', for reading stories such as 'Two Nations, One Story', which examines the links between the partition of India and its diasporas scattered in different parts of the subcontinent.

Notes

1. A PIO card is issued to any person of Indian origin living outside India, except few countries. Even a fourth-generation Indian diasporan might apply for such a card. A PIO card enables an Indian diasporan to come to India and to stay in India without a visa if the stay does not exceed six months. Sahoo writes: 'Thus, the PIO card made the journey of people of Indian origin back to their homeland much more simple, easy, flexible, and hassle-free' (p. 56).
2. Devesh Kapur's *Diaspora, Development, and Democracy: The Domestic Impact of International Migration from India* (2010) shows that Indian diaspora contributes to India's economy through three routes: remittances, bank deposits and foreign investments. Kapur has shown that FDI in India was around $5 billion per annum between 2000 and 2005 but increased to $19 billion in the financial year 2006–2007.
3. For more information, see Aggarwal and Kar.
4. For more information, see *How Buddhism was brought to Ladakh* and Kamala Mukherjee's 'Cultural History of Ladakh, Part I'.
5. This is the 1951 UN definition of a refugee: 'As a result of events occurring before 1 January 1951 and owing to well-founded fear of being persecuted for reasons of race, religion, nationality, membership of a particular social group or political opinion, is outside the country of his nationality and is unable or, owing to such fear, is unwilling to avail himself of the protection of that country; or who, not having a nationality and being outside the country of his former habitual residence as a result of such events, is unable or, owing to such fear, is unwilling to return to it'.
6. Of late, the term 'partition diaspora' is being used by some scholars. See Papiya Ghosh's book, *Partition and the South Asian Diaspora: Extending the Subcontinent* (2007).

References

Aggarwal, Ravina. 2001. Introduction. *Forsaking Paradise: Stories from Ladakh*. By Abdul Ghani Sheikh (ed.) and Trans. Ravina Aggarwal. New Delhi: Katha, 7–37.

Bose, P. 2006. 'Dilemmas of Diaspora: Partition, Refugees, and the Politics of Home'. *Refuge*, Vol. 23 (1). Available online: http://refuge.journals. yorku.ca/index.php/refuge/issue/view/1266

Convention and Protocol: Relating to the Status of Refugees. *UNHCR: The UN Refugee Agency*. UNHCR, n.d. 21 August 2015. Available at: www.unhcr.org/pages/49da0e466.html.

Ghani Sheikh, Abdul. 2001. *Forsaking Paradise: Stories from Ladakh*. Ed. and Trans. Ravina Aggarwal. New Delhi: Katha.

Ghosh, Papiya. 2007. *Partition and the South Asian Diaspora: Extending the Subcontinent*. New Delhi: Routledge India.

How Buddhism Was Brought to Ladakh. n.d. 21 August 2015. Available at: www.rinpoche.com/stories/ladakh.htm.

Kapur, Devesh. 2010. *Diaspora, Development, and Democracy: The Domestic Impact of International Migration from India*. New Delhi: OUP.

Kar, Angshuman. 2014. Partition and After: Situating Abdul Ghani Sheikh. In Basudeb Chakrabarti and A. S. Chandel (eds.), *Gender Perspectives: South Asian Writings in English and in English Translations*. New Delhi: Today and Tomorrow, 51–60.

Mukherjee, Kamala. 2015. Cultural History of Ladakh, Part I. *Bulletin of Tibetology* 3 (1996), 23–27. 21 August 2015 Available at: http://himalaya.socanth.cam.ac.uk/collections/journals/bot/pdf/bot_ 1996_03_cover.pdf

Sahoo, Ajaya K. 2015. Globalization, Diaspora, and Transnationalism: Challenges and Opportunities for the Indian Diaspora. In Angshuman Kar (ed.), *Contemporary Indian Diaspora: Literary and Cultural Representations*. Jaipur: Rawat Publications, 43–64.

10

Religious Fundamentalism and Indian Diaspora

M.G. Vassanji's *The Assassin's Song*

Arnab Kumar Sinha

Among the Indo-Canadian diasporic writers, M.G. Vassanji is a figure of significant repute, who has, till date, written eight novels, two short story collections and two non-fictional collections. Vassanji's novels, interestingly, offer an insightful study of the migrant subjects' problematic engagement with the culture of the host nation, and in doing so, these subjects do not seem to completely delink themselves from the cultural markers of their original homeland. In fact, Vassanji's novels are closely linked to the author's diasporic life and his evolution as a writer in the West.[1] His novels are structured like growing-up narratives that often project the journey of a protagonist in search for a definite goal in life. *The Assassin's Song* (2007) is the sixth novel of Vassanji, and it is a diasporic *Bildungsroman* as it attempts to present the growing-up of the chief protagonist, Karsan within an environment of the clash between tradition and modernity. Set in the communally sensitive state of Gujarat in India, this novel charts the growth of a Muslim boy Karsan in a family that happens to be an ardent devotee of the ancient Sufi shrine in Gujarat. The whole narrative of the novel is seen from the perspective of Karsan who is trapped between the traditional Sufi lineage of his family and his individual desire to play cricket or to do something in life which would give him freedom from the suffocating religious doctrines embedded in his family roots. Though Karsan migrates to America for studying in university, and he even finds a job there, yet his alienation from his cultural and religious roots does not render him ultimate happiness in life. The Gujarat riots in 2002 changes the whole course of Karsan's life as he ultimately comes back to India to witness mass destruction and genocide. The impact of this communal violence on his family posits Karsan in a problematic situation that ultimately leaves no option for him but to follow the family tradition and become a saint of the Pirbaag. Vassanji's novel is therefore an interesting take on the issue of religious fundamentalism and its impact on a diasporic Muslim subject like Karsan. This chapter will seek to interpret the interface between religious fundamentalism and Indian diaspora in the wake of events such as 9/11, 7/7 and Gujarat riots. In doing so, this chapter will also make an attempt to interrogate the problematics of equating religious fundamentalism with Islam across the globe.

I

The emergence of religious fundamentalism as a significant aspect in the contemporary social and cultural context has drawn the attention of many critics, who have in various ways theorized the impact of this aspect on different races and nations. Speaking in general terms, Claudia Derichs and Andrea Fleschenberg state:

> Amidst growing uncertainties in a globalized world, fundamentalist convictions have been gaining ground in many religions. Reinforced by the threat from international terrorism, this renaissance of religious fundamentalisms has created ideological conditions for polarization between 'us' and 'them', from community to transnational level. (2010: 5)

Though Derichs and Fleschenberg attempt to read religious fundamentalism from a gendered perspective, yet their analysis of the concept of fundamentalism is remarkable. Sylvia Estrada Claudio's essay in Derichs and Fleschenberg's book locates the root of religious fundamentalism in Islam, and this has become more obvious especially after the 9/11 incident. She argues that the very term 'fundamentalism' has been associated with Islam in the wake of different terrorist activities in the West during the last decade and this has contributed to making the term 'fundamentalism' 'politically charged' (2010: 14). Moving from these broader ideas that define religious fundamentalism and associate it with Islam, if we focus on the particular context of Indian diaspora and the role of religion in it, then a reference to the seminal essay written by Parvati Raghuram and Ajaya Kumar Sahoo must be made. They observe, 'Less fully explored is the role of religion in the Indian diaspora in shaping politics within India. In particular, each religion is treated separately rather than together. Moreover, religion too gets rescripted through its travels abroad' (Raghuram and Sahoo 2008: 16). Apart from emphasizing on the need to address the issue of religion in Indian diaspora, Raghuram and Sahoo quote from Bhatt and Mukta's article 'Hindutva in the West: Mapping the Antinomies of Diaspora Nationalism' to highlight the emergence of 'Hindutva' as an ideological denominator both within India and in the West among the minority Hindu diasporic community: 'These are pressing issues for the Indian diaspora as a "powerful diaspora Hindutva ethnic nationalist discourse of the homeland, and equally powerful Hindutva ethnic nationalist discourses of minorities within both the homeland and in the West" jostle for space' (Raghuram and Sahoo 2008: 16). Of late, this emergence of 'Hindutva ethnic nationalist discourse' has impacted upon the mindset of the majority of Hindu citizens in India and this has led to violent Hindu-Muslim communal riots across India. An illuminating example of this kind of communal violence is the Godhra riots of 2002, where an attempt was made by the Hindutva forces to demolish the Muslim community. In the next section of this chapter, the narrative of Vassanji's novel *The Assassin's Song* will be critically analysed from the point of view of the interface of religious fundamentalism and diaspora.

II

The narrative of Vassanji's text traverses through different time frames moving from the reference to the thirteenth century great Sufi saint and mystic, Nur Fazal, to the childhood days of Karsan, which refers to the India of 1960s and 1970s, and finally the action of the novel culminates in the circumstances that lead to the change of mind of Karsan in the aftermath of Gujarat riot of 2002. As mentioned earlier, the narrative progresses in the pattern of a bildungsroman which helps us to see the growing up of Karsan in a village named, Haripir located in the state of

Gujarat. Karsan's forefathers are dedicated devotees of the great Sufi saint, Nur Fazal. During his early childhood days, Karsan becomes aware of the religious heritage of his family: 'My father was the Saheb – the lord and keeper – of Pirbaag, the Shrine of the Wanderer, in our village of Haripir, as was his father before him, as were all our ancestors for many centuries. People came to him for guidance, they put their lives in his hands, they bowed to him with reverence' (*The Assassin's Song*). A large portion of the textual narrative presents the history of Pir Bawa, his wanderings around the world, propagation of his wisdom and his final settlement in the village of Haripir. Karsan's father, being a representative of Sufism[2] in Haripir, acquires a demigod status as people from different parts of India visit the house of Saheb – Karsan's father is addressed as Saheb by the visitors and local people – to pay homage to the shrine of Pir Bawa and also to the representative Pir Bawa. This knowledge regarding the religious status of his father makes Karsan feel privileged, because being the eldest son of Saheb, people in Haripir expect him to carry forward the tradition of Sufism. But, this privileged position of Karsan does not make him a blind follower of Sufism. He is intrigued by the spiritual aura that surrounds his family, and since his childhood days he is sceptical of his devotion to Pir Bawa. Whether he can become an ardent follower of Sufism like his father is a big question that he often asks himself:

> Sometimes when I watched him sitting before a bunch of white-clad devotees in the pavilion, imparting spiritual wisdom in his high, tremulous voice, or acting out a ritual as a Saheb of the shrine, I would wonder who my father was. Who was I, then? Was I different, deep inside me, from what I seemed to myself? (*The Assassin's Song*)

Questions like these make Karsan critical to the preaching of Sufism, and in the later years of his childhood, he gradually discovers his diminishing interest in following the religious tradition of his family. Karsan's lack of interest in religious affairs of his family lead him to the world of books and during one of his regular visits to a library in Ahmedabad he meets George Elias. Elias is a stranger with whom Karsan meets in the city of Ahmedabad, and later Elias also becomes a good friend of Karsan. Elias advises Karsan to apply for studying a course in America.

This advice triggers the imagination of Karsan as he realizes that if he is able to shift to an abroad location for studying, then the familial obligation of inheriting the Sufi tradition of preaching will not be his responsibility any more. Without informing anybody in the family Karsan applies for studying a course in America. His application is approved by the American government. The American government also grants a scholarship to Karsan. However, when Karsan's father comes to know about Karsan's plan of studying abroad, he is highly depressed. For the first time in his life, Karsan gathers courage before his father to state his disinterestedness in following the religious heritage of his family:

> 'You are the future Saheb of Pirbaag, Karsan … you will be the light of our Pir Bawa, the father of our people'.
>
> That was when I said in frustration, 'But I don't want to be God, Bapu-ji!' …
>
> Bapu-ji simply said, 'You have taken your own decision. A Saheb is not supposed to have a heart. But you have broken this father's heart'. But he didn't refuse; he expressed his displeasure and gave me the choice. (*The Assassin's Song*)

After realizing that his son is not interested in becoming a preacher of Sufism, Karsan's father, quite reluctantly, makes arrangement for Karsan's study in America and bids farewell to his beloved son. However, before Karsan finally leaves home, his father secretly utters a 'bol' (a kind of mantra) in his son's ear, requesting him to remember it throughout his life. This 'bol' as Karsan's father states will guide and assist Karsan in difficult times, and as a 'special mantra' it must be kept secret. (*The Assassin's Song*). In fact, it is this 'bol' that keeps Karsan connected to his home and religious moorings.

Once Karsan sets his foot in America, his attitude towards his home undergoes significant changes. The American life and especially the education system greatly appeal him, transforming him into a kind of a diasporian who falls in love with the host land culture. Karsan's love for the multicultural environment of America eventually dissociates him from his native culture and tradition. In fact, the secular spirit of American life liberates Karsan from the deeply religious roots of his native culture. In one of the letters that Karsan writes to his father, he emphatically expresses his love for the American culture and his desire to lead an ordinary life in the secular environment of America:

> 'What do I desire from life? Simply to be an ordinary person. Can you understand that, Bapu? Someone who likes to find out about new things, marry the girl he wants, follow cricket and baseball. (Yes, I do like baseball now, and occasionally even American football.) Someone who likes to read for pleasure; for whom this world is not a miserable prison but a place in which to seek personal fulfillment and happiness, full of other ordinary people like me. (*The Assassin's Song*)

The new found happiness in an alien land provides Karsan the opportunity to break free from the religious chains of his homeland. He completes his study in the United States and then moves to Cambridge for higher studies. He falls in love with Marge Thompson, a second-generation Indo-Canadian diasporian. When Karsan is well set in the West, he receives a big setback after coming to know about his mother's illness. This news creates a dilemma in the mind of Karsan. Though Karsan wants to go to India to see his sick mother, but he knows that going back to his home will be detrimental to the freedom that he has earned during his stay abroad. Also, he knows it very well that once he returns home, his father may compel him to stay in Haripir and order him to follow the religious tradition of his family. Karsan desires that, in future, his younger brother Mansoor should take over the responsibility of Pirbaag, and thereby relieve him from the religious shackles of Sufism. Stuck in the midst of such an ambiguous situation, Karsan falls in love with Marge and this new relationship gives Karsan a fresh lease of life. He marries Marge, knowing very well that his father will never accept the marriage, and ultimately settles in Canada with Marge's family. But, Karsan in his desire to sever ties from his homeland does not become a 'rootless cosmopolitan'.[3] In fact, after staying for a long period in Canada, he could never completely dissociate himself from the native cultural and religious tradition:

> I would like to say then that Pirbaag never left me ... But the truth is that I did find another life there, in North America, one of personal happiness and freedom; a second birth in which I managed to leave behind the manacle that had been Pirbaag ...

> It seems that Bapu-ji always won; but his was the cosmic truth of transience, therefore a truism, mine that of the small and personal joys that defy the grand design, but inevitably must confirm it. (*The Assassin's Song*)

After staying for so many years in the West, Karsan realizes that his desire to completely detach from the religious heritage of Pirbaag is futile. This phenomenon can be critically read through the lens of diaspora criticism. Sudesh Mishra in his seminal text, *Diaspora Criticism* (2006) talks about three different trends of diaspora criticism. The first trend, which also happens to be the oldest one, focuses on the idea of 'dual territoriality' (Mishra 2006: 16). This concept of 'dual territoriality' is premised on 'reading of the homeland state as classically auto-centred, racially self-evident and ideologically homogenized. Suspended between two such terrains (living without belonging in one, belonging without living in the other), diasporas are seen to represent a new species of social formation' (Mishra 2006: 16). As a diasporic subject, Karsan is located in this zone of 'dual territoriality'.

The real crisis in Karsan's life comes when he visits Haripir after the 2002 riots in Gujrat.[4] The whole village of Haripir, as Karsan visualizes, has been burned down by Hindu fundamentalists. The lord and the keeper of Pirbaag, Saheb (Karsan's father), has been killed by the rioters and the Sufi shrine of Pir Bawa has also been reduced to a ruined heap of ash. These scenes of mass destruction and hate killings symbolize heinous acts of communal violence: 'But now the shrine lies in ruins, a victim of the violence that so gripped our state recently, an orgy of murder and destruction of the kind we euphemistically call "riots"' (*The Assassin's Song*). Due to the riots Karsan's brother has fled away from Haripir, and he is now a suspect terrorist. This whole scenario at Haripir strongly projects the communal divide, which also enables Karsan to sense the marginality of his existence. The Hindu fundamentalists, disregarding the glorious mystical tradition of Sufi saints, equate Sufism with Islam, and therefore demolish the very basis of Sufism in Haripir, 'This centuries-old neutral sanctuary had now been marked as a Muslim abode to wreak vengeance on' (*The Assassin's Song*). In spite of the wrath and vengeance directed against Islam in the state of Gujarat, in the post–2002 riots, Karsan takes a bold decision to follow the family tradition by asserting his Sufi faith. He becomes the next

Saheb of Pirbaag. In fact, this act of Karsan speaks volumes about the intercommunal relationship in Vassanji's novel and it also tempts us to raise a few critical questions/issues for discussion in the conclusive section of this chapter.

III

The first critical issue that I would like to point out is the need to see fundamentalism from a more general standpoint rather than seeing it from a parochial Islamic point of view. Whenever discussions and debates are organized across the globe, there is a general tendency to associate fundamentalism with Islam which, I believe, renders a very simplistic reading of the term. In fact, the Gujarat 2002 riots exemplify the dominance of Hindu fundamentalism. Actually, in the post-9/11 era, due to the American war on terror, Muslims around the world have become suspect terrorists, and Islam as a religion has become symbolic of terror. This obviously has put Islamic fundamentalism under the scanner since the 9/11 event. In this context, one may refer to Margaret Scanlan (2010: 267) who draws our attention to the American 'public rhetoric' of equating Islam with terror in the post-9/11 era. In the novel, Vassanji makes an attempt to seriously interrogate this particular issue of connecting Islam with terror. The second issue is related to the problematic idea of homogenizing Islam. Like other religions, Islam too consists of many different versions and the Sufi religious tradition is one particular version of Islam. Islamic faith is based on many different types of religious traditions: Shia, Sunni, Ahmadiyya, Ibadi, Quranism, Sufism and so on. These religious traditions define Islam from multiple perspectives, which produce a heterogeneous notion of Islam. Thus, the very tendency of the West to stereotype Islam as dangerous is part of a 'neo-Orientalist' strategy that ignores the rich and varied religious traditions of Islam. Asef Bayat, one of the noted scholars of Islamic studies, defines the 'neo-Orientalist' perspective of the West in the following words:

> In this current neo-Orientalist imagination, the Muslim Orientals are not only trapped in archaic traditions, a frozen history and irrational behaviour; they are, far from being exotic or benign, dangerous; they are threats to the cultural values, civilizational integrity, and the physical well being of the West. (http://futureswewant.net/asef-bayat-neo-orientalism/)

The Hindu fundamentalists, in Vassanji's *The Assassin's Song*, appropriate this 'neo-Orientalist' perspective of the West. They see Islam as a threat to their cultural values, and therefore they resort to violence. The inability of the Hindu fundamentalists to distinguish Sufism from Islam leads to the mass killings of innocent Sufi followers. In this context, I would like to argue that Vassanji's text is highly critical of the dominant Hindutva discourse in India. It makes a direct appeal to the Indian readers to be tolerant towards other religions. Instead of building a nation based on a particular religious ideology, India as a nation should assume a more secular outlook creating a space for communal harmony. Karsan's decision at the end of the novel to become the next saint of Pirbaag can be read as a significant move towards creating a tolerant society. Despite the fact that his familial and religious roots are destroyed by the Hindu fundamentalists, he does not seek vengeance for the communal killings. This standpoint of Karsan shows his critical attitude towards the 'neo-Orientalist' gaze of the Hindus. The third and final issue is related to the problematics of identity. In the contemporary scenario, Muslims around the world are identified through the lens of religion and this obviously foregrounds the fact that in the case of Muslims the religious/communal identity is prioritized over the other competing identities. A person's identity is composite of many different competing identities: class, caste, gender, nation, race, religion, ethnicity and so on. Instead of prioritizing a particular identity over the other identities, there is an urgent need in our times to conceptualize identity from a plural perspective. Addressing this need to theorize identity from a pluralist perspective, Amartya Sen in his book *Identity and Violence: The Illusion of Destiny* (2007) asserts:

> In our normal lives, we see ourselves as members of a variety of groups – we belong to all of them. A person's citizenship, residence, geographic origin, gender, class, politics, profession, employment, food habits, sports interests, taste in music, social commitments, etc. make us members of a variety of groups. Each of these collectives, to all of which this person simultaneously belongs, gives her a particular identity. None of them can be taken to be the person's only identity or singular membership category. (Sen 2007: 4–5)

Sen further argues that prioritizing a particular identity is not always matter of choice for an individual (2007: 5). In the case of communal identity, it is often the society or people around a particular individual or group that often decide how a person should be seen. For instance, a Muslim adult may wish to prioritize his love for cricket over his communal identity, but the society may restrict this right of choice and prefer to see the Muslim adult from a communal point of view:

> However, even when we are clear about how we want to see ourselves, we may still have difficulty in being able to persuade others to see us in just that way .... Our freedom to assert our personal identities can sometimes be extraordinarily limited in the eyes of others, no matter how we see ourselves. (Sen 2007: 6)

This argument of Sen is highly persuasive, but at the same time it is also very contextual. In fact, Vassanji's take on identity, as elaborated in his book, *A Place Within: Rediscovering India* (2008), seems to echo the ideas of Sen, 'Instead of asserting their essential and primary Indian-ness, shouting it from the rooftops and from their guts, (Muslims) had fallen into the trap of allowing themselves to be seen as minority and as outsiders, accepting a primary identity defined by faith ...'. (quoted in Gaurav Desai 2011: 188). Thus, Vassanji's *The Assassin's Song* is a richly loaded text that interrogates complex issues related to religious fundamentalism and its impact on a diasporic subject.

Notes

1. Vassanji was born in Kenya and he lived in different regions of East Africa for a long period of time. His family belongs to the group of the Ismaili Muslims in Gujarat. For his study, Vassanji migrated to the United States to study nuclear physics in MIT and then moved to Canada to work in a nuclear research department. Vassanji's career as a writer began after he settled in Canada. In his novels, Vassanji incorporates his experience of living in Africa, the United States and Canada.
2. Sufism is a particular religious tradition that exists in Islam and is often argued to be mystical in its outlook. For a detailed understanding of the term, please refer to the following web address: http://en.wikipedia.org/ wiki/Sufism<Publisher: Please check whether reference to Wikipedia is okay.>
3. In her dissertation entitled 'Imagining the Lives of Others: Revisioning Cosmopolitanism in Amitav Ghosh's *The Shadow Lines*, Michael

Ondaatje's *The English Patient*, and Mohsin Hamid's *The Reluctant Fundamentalist*' (2009), Shauna Hall-Coates defines the term 'rootless cosmopolitanism' in the following manner: 'Within contemporary culture, cosmopolitans are often seen as synonymous with global travellers .... those who cast off the burden of their rooted identities, characterized by their familial, cultural, national loyalties, in order to exercise their global citizenship'. (p. 6)

4. The Gujarat 2002 riots, which are generally considered as heinous acts of communal violence in India, were responsible for the killings of many Muslims and Hindus in the state of Gujarat. In fact, as the statistics shows, many innocent Muslims were killed in these riots. Please refer to the following website for knowing the details regarding the history of these riots: http://en.wikipedia.org/wiki/2002_Gujarat_riots

References

Bayat, Asef. 2016. Neo-Orientalism. 31 July 2016. Available at: http://futureswewant.net/asef-bayat-neo-orientalism/

Derichs, Claudia and Andrea Fleschenberg. 2010. *Religious Fundamentalisms and Their Gendered Impacts in Asia*. Berlin: Friedrich-Ebert-Stiftung.

Desai, Gaurav. 2011. Ambiguity Is the Driving Force or the Nuclear Reaction behind My Creativity: An E-conversation with M. G. Vassanji. *Research in African Literatures,* 42(3), 187–197.

Hall-Coates, Shauna. 2009. Imagining the Lives of Others: Revisioning Cosmopolitanism in Amitav Ghosh's *The Shadow Lines*, Michael Ondaatje's *The English Patient*, and Mohsin Hamid's *The Reluctant Fundamentalist*. M.A. Thesis. Dalhousie University.

Mishra, Sudesh. 2006. *Diaspora Criticism*. Edinburgh: Edinburgh University Press.

Raghuram, Parvati and Ajaya Kumar Sahoo. 2008. Tracing the 'Indian Diaspora' for Our Times. In Parvati Raghuram, Ajaya Kumar Sahoo, Brij Maharaj and Dave Sangha (eds.), *Tracing an Indian Diaspora: Contexts, Memories and Representations*. New Delhi: Sage Publications, 1–20.

Scanlan, Margaret. 2010. Migrating from Terror: The Postcolonial Novel after September 11. *Journal of Postcolonial Writing,* 46(3), 266–278.

Sen, Amartya. 2007. *Identity and Violence: The Illusion of Destiny*. London: Penguin.

Vassanji, M.G. 2007. *The Assassin's Song*. New York: Knopf Book.

11

A Search for Identity in Meena Alexander's *Raw Silk*

Sanjoy Malik

The 9/11 terrorist attacks on the United States, carried out by the Al-Qaida destroyed the Twin Towers of the World Trade Center, the US economic might, and left thousands of people dead. The entire nation suffered a huge trauma. Following the terrible attacks, a sense of insecurity gripped the nation. Besides declaring a war on terror, the US Government increased surveillance as part of counterterrorism measures. As the perpetrators of the 9/11 attacks were Muslims, the United States began to suspect the Muslim immigrants of having links to terrorist outfits and having knowledge of terrorist plots, and tried to rob them of their civil liberties. In the wake of 9/11, Louise Cainkar (2010) observes:

> Muslims were persons who, if not terrorists themselves, might be hiding terrorists or covering up their knowledge of brewing terrorist plots. So constructed, Arabs and Muslims in the US were symbolically reconstituted as people who were not really part of the American nation and they were the 'them', and thus not fully eligible for its package of civil and constitutional rights. (p. 184)

After 9/11, the perception of the United State was that if the terrorist strikes by some Muslims outside the United States dismantled the social and political structure of the United States, the Muslims within could be a serious threat to the nation. So, the

United States and the other Western societies began to see the Muslim immigrants as outsiders and even considered them to be their enemies. In fact, Islamophobia makes them think that the connections between the Muslims inside and the Muslims outside of the United States could put the nation in a vulnerable position. However, while combating the potential threat to the national security, the United States enacted certain legislations so as to cut-off the transnational links of the immigrant Muslims, revoke their citizenship and send them back to their own countries. As Mahmood Monshipouri (2010) says, 'The Patriot Act[1] and other counterterrorism measures have infringed upon the civil liberties of Arab and Muslim immigrants who have been detained in various investigations' (p. 58).

Arab and Muslim immigrants found themselves under the surveillance of the federal government. Louise Cainkar (2010) observes that 'Arabs and Muslims readily understood their position as the subjects of watchdogs in a panoptical world' (p. 181). In the immediate aftermath of 9/11, the United States and the other Western countries heightened their suspicion on the immigrant Muslims by considering them as part of the pan-Islamic terrorism. In the post-9/11 period, anti-immigrant sentiments erupted to a horrible extent and the United States began to mistake some South Asian Americans who resembled brown skinned Arabs to be Arabs and Muslims and, accordingly, suspected them and made them victims of hate crimes. The immigrant Americans, particularly the South Asian Americans, faced the intolerance vehemently expressed by the mainstream white Americans. The South Asians, particularly, the Sikh immigrants found themselves victimized to a great extent. In this connection, one can cite the case of Balbir Singh Sodhi, a Sikh American of Indian origin. He was killed by a white American near his gas station in Mesa, Arizona. He was mistaken for a Muslim (an Arab terrorist) because he had a beard and was wearing a turban. The white American who committed this crime in retaliation for the terrorist attacks on the United States did not know the differences between a Sikh and a Muslim in terms of their respective faith. In fact, the Westerners do not want to know the internal differences among the immigrants along with the religious, cultural or ethnic lines. They regard the immigrants of multiple ethnic and cultural backgrounds as an undifferentiated group so as to strategically exclude them from the mainstream Western societies.

It is against this background that Meena Alexander,[2] one of the most important contemporary Indian American poets, comes up with her *Raw Silk* (2004), a collection of lyric poems. Most of the poems in the first section of the collection make responses to the events of 9/11 and its impact on the South Asian immigrants. Like Chitra Banerjee Divakaruni, Imtiaz Dharker, Jeet Thayil and others, Meena Alexander also responds to the traumatic 9/11and to the ways the Western societies treat the diasporic communities. This chapter seeks to examine how she negotiates her identity as a representative of the South Asian immigrants in the diaspora space of the United States in the post-9/11 period.

When the 9/11 occurred, Alexander had been writing a prose. But the events of 9/11 shook her so much that leaving aside the prose work, she embarked on writing poetry. She chose lyric poetry in which she poured out her intense emotions in response to 9/11. She wanted lyric poetry to serve as an outlet for her emotions. Through lyric poetry she also wanted to perform a kind of moral duty by communicating a truth to the world, the truth about the horrendous nature and the traumatic effects of the 9/11 attacks. It was an 'act of testimony' on her part. As she says in an interview with Lopamudra Basu:

> I have put aside the longish prose piece I was working on, a piece about childhood. After what has just happened in New York City I did not want to be swallowed up in the past, with so much molten and flowing all around, the world I love in turmoil. I need to bear witness to what is now.
>
> The lyric poem allows me much better to catch the edginess of things, the sharp nervosity, the flaming, falling buildings. And I think I must work back from the pressure of the present into the past, for that is the only way I will reach into the real. (p. 32)

Alexander lives in close proximity to the towers of the World Trade Center and this has enabled her to witness the scenes of death and destruction. She is terribly haunted by the events of 9/11. The lyric poetry that she wrote in response to the 'tragic reality' of the 9/11 catastrophe could serve as an attempt to restore order in her diaspora space. As she puts it in an interview with Daniela Gioseffi:

> I walked out to the linden grove in Fort Tryon Park, near where I live, and I saw the trees, the brush of sky, and felt that words could not happen in that tragedy. Only little crystalline bits of sound could be let in. So, I went for lyric compression. I wanted that tight order to hold things together, when everything seemed, literally, to be falling apart.

However, Alexander has tried to catch the attention of the world to the United States that was left in utter disorder by the 9/11 attacks. In the poem 'Invisible City', she writes:

> *Tall towers, twin towers, I used to see*
> A bloody seam of sense drops free.
> By Liberty Street, on a knot of rubble
> In altered light I see a bird cry. (emphasis original) (pp. 9–12)

Here Alexander laments the fact that the Twin Towers of the World Trade Center are reduced to a rubble. The New York City is rendered invisible because of the loss of the towers that served as the markers of identity of the city. This scene of desolation leaves her heart languishing.

In the poem 'Aftermath', she points to the gruesome nature of the 9/11 attacks by presenting the natural world in the vicinity of the Twin Towers. This natural world is left traumatized in the aftermath of the 9/11 violence. As she writes in the said poem:

> There is an uncommon light in the sky
> Pale petals are scored into stone.
> I want to write of the linden tree
> That stoops at the edge of the river
> But its leaves are filled with insects
> With wings the color of dry blood.
> At the far side of the river Hudson
> By the southern tip of our island
> A mountain soars, a torrent of sentences
> Syllables of flame stitch the rubble
> An eye, a lip, a cut hand blooms
> Sweet and bitter smoke stains the sky. (pp. 1–12)

Because of the horrible 9/11 catastrophe, the objects of nature have ceased to be natural. 'An uncommon light' has engulfed the sky and etiolated it while the petals of flowers have gone petrified. The linden tree is horribly affected by the disaster and left extremely shocked and morose. The marks of death caused by the attacks are still prominent on the insects that have feasted on the blood of those killed and injured, the blood that has stained the site. The image of the wings of the insects covered with blood suggests the horrendous degree of atrocity perpetrated. One can take note of 'an eye, a lip, a cut hand', the parts of the human body; but here no part stands for the whole as in the case of a synecdoche. Rather the availability of only parts presents the blood-curdling image of mutilated bodies. The poet shows us the haunting image of violence in the linguistic terms such as 'sentences' and 'syllables'. So, the traumatic nature of the attacks has left the poet concerned over her existence, the existence of her fellow citizens, the white and the non-white, in the island city. Not only that the myth of national security has been exploded by the 9/11 attacks that killed both the mainstream white Americans and the Americans of various national origins. In the post-9/11 period, the fear for potential terrorist attacks leaves everyone utterly insecure.

If this is the one side of the coin that is pathetic, the other side is no less pathetic for the immigrants who suffered racial abuse. The post-9/11 situation in the United States proves so hostile and threatening that Meena Alexander prefers to stay ethnically invisible. In public, she stops wearing her sari, the marker of her cultural affiliation. She feels that the post-9/11 climate in the United States is pervaded by much hatred for the cultural practices of the immigrants. So, she is compelled to wear Western dresses while going to her academic institute. Otherwise, she will fall a victim of hate crimes. Despite the fact that she has found her space in the cohort of American intellectuals, academicians and artists, she is seen as the 'other'. Her identity is racialized. The United States believes that no immigrant, for that matter, no South Asian is going to harmonize himself/herself with the American society and his/her presence is likely to destabilize the United States. In fact, the Westerners think that the immigrants are likely to endanger the security of their nations. Although Alexander has integrated into the American society, her identity as an American citizen seems to be under question. She feels her position to be vulnerable in the dominant society. As she is a woman, a woman of colour, she has to bear to a great extent the brunt of racism. For fear that she might be a victim of racism, she gives up wearing the sari, the sign of her cultural identity, her ethnic identity during the post-9/11 times. She feels the compulsion to wear the Western dresses – a jeans and a shirt. Wearing these dresses, she outwardly seems to have given the impression of being assimilated into the American society, but inwardly she suffers as these dresses produce in her a feeling of alienation. Her body seems to be the other. As she says in her *Poetics of Dislocation*: 'Perhaps the most devastating effect of racism is to render one homeless in one's body' (p. 104). Compelled to make herself ethnically invisible, she suffers from the crisis of identity in relation to her culture. It is in this context that she has written the poem, 'Kabir Sings in a City of Burning Towers'. In the poem, the poet-persona in her vision gets rebuked by Kabir, the medieval Indian poet-saint:

> What a shame
> they scared you so
> you plucked your sari off,
> crushed it into a ball,
> then spread it
> on the toilet floor.
> Sparks from the towers
> fled through the weave of silk.
> With your black hair
> and sun dark skin
> you are just a child of earth. (pp. 1–11)

Interestingly, the words 'plucked' and 'smashed' suggest acts of violence. Having 'smashed' her sari into a ball, Alexander has committed a kind of violence against the thing that is considered an integral part of her body. This act is nothing but a sacrilege. The fact that she has invoked Kabir and allowed herself to be rebuked by him, shows her sense of guilt because she has failed to stick to her identity in relation to her culture. Actually, she is deeply influenced by the teachings of Kabir who saw all the human beings as the one. In a way she makes an effort to spread Kabir's message of equity in the West, thereby fighting intolerance and hatred. Though Alexander has integrated into the American society by beautifully balancing her ethnic culture with the mainstream American culture, she is afraid of wearing her sari, the visible sign of her cultural identity because of the hostile atmosphere whereas many Muslim women continued wearing headscarves even in the face of intense anti-Muslim sentiments in the post-9/11period and did not want to lose their identity based on religion, a spiritual anchor. Alexander finds herself vulnerable to a potential racial abuse. The fact is that racism latent in American society becomes most patent in the 9/11period. This makes her feel that she has suddenly been different in the eyes of the dominant society. Tolerance and recognition of difference in culture, race and ethnicity that are central to a multicultural society are completely absent in the United States during the post–9/11 times. As an immigrant individual, she is robbed of the freedom of choosing the ways of life specific to her culture in matters of dress, language, rituals and belief systems. However, Alexander's integration into the American society is put under question. She now feels that she has been the 'foreigner', the 'outsider', the 'other'. The dominant mainstream society seems to doubt her loyalty and allegiance to the United States as a New Yorker. On the one hand, the immigrants are left concerned over their safety in their country of adoption for the potential terrorist strikes; on the other hand, they find themselves victims of racialization. As a representative of South Asians in the United States, she expresses that predicament in an interview with Lopamudra Basu:

> there came a time of fearful fragmentation, being torn apart in so many directions: the fear here on this island, the condition of our lives not knowing what could strike next, fire, racial profiling, pestilence – that bitty white powder filled with anthrax spores (a floor of the Graduate Center, since we are next door to the Empire State Building, was shut down for a while). (pp. 32–33)

Actually the events of 9/11 exposed the racism inherent in the US psyche. Meena Alexander got disillusioned with the United States that maintained the facade of inclusive attitude to the immigrants. The initial impression that she had of the United States was really encouraging. In an interview with Daniela Gioseffi, she said, 'I was wild with excitement to come here from so far away, to live in another country. And I loved that this is a country that honours immigrant stories …'. Alexander speaks highly of the ambience that an immigrant in the United States finds conducive to the materialization of his/her new vision of life. What Meena Alexander says in an interview with Ruth Maxey is worth mentioning here:

> There's something in the culture of the United States that really forces you to invent yourself. There's no other country that I know of in the world that has an idea of immigration, layer upon layer of it, as part of the very structure of the nation. (pp. 28–29)

She has come to the New York City from Allahabad, India, and begun her new life in this island city on the bank of the river Hudson. Gradually she has developed an attachment to the country of her adoption and considers America to be her home. But the incidents of growing racial abuse in the post-9/11period hampers the process of her acculturation to the mainstream society. However, she does have a strong sense of belonging to the mainstream white Americans as evident in many of her poems. 'School Yard' addressed to her son Adam Kuruvilla is one such poem. The poem tells us that New York is not merely the city of her residence, it has become her home. Her son 'grew up in this city/by these walls (of the World Trade Center, New York)/played stickball by the river (Hudson)/leapt over a path into a playground/by Battery Park'. It is very interesting to see how Alexander brings up her son in this city and enables him to develop a strong sense of attachment. What pains her is the fact that now the very walls (of the World Trade Center, New York) are engulfed by the fire caused by the terrorist attacks. A large number of victims are instantly killed and those rescued are kept in places like a schoolyard. They are half dead with their skin smouldering. Alexander shows how grisly the perpetration of violence is and how heart-rending the images of its victims are. She also expresses her concern over the vulnerability of human life to any potential terrorist attack. A strong sense of insecurity grips them, her home and her family.

Alexander's sense of Americanness can be attested to by the moral duty that she shows on her visit to the graveyard for thousands killed in the 9/11 attacks. No less is her homage to the 9/11 victims than a white American. She tells Lopamudra Basu in an interview that she 'kept walking down to Ground Zero, as close as I could get, making returns, a pilgrimage, the site a graveyard for thousands, the stench of burning flesh and wires' (p. 33). So Alexander's allegiance and loyalty to the United States cannot be called into question. Rightly does Himadri Lahiri (2009: 106) say, 'The claim to Americanness must be accompanied by a commitment to national issues which is part of the relocation process'. One can have little or no doubt that she has a strong sense of belonging and commitment to the country of her adoption.

Though the fact is that Meena Alexander is a Christian living among the dominant white Christians, her religious identity is relegated into the background. For her host society, her racial identity is important, not her religious identity. As she is black, her skin colour arouses intolerance on the part of the white society and makes her a potential victim of racism. Due to the prevalence of racialization, she is seen through the orientalist lens and made to feel inferior. There is a tendency on the part of the mainstream white Americans to establish their hierarchically superior position in terms of race. Not only that, the United States and the other Western societies have a generalized view that the immigrants are not compatible with the Western societies. Though Alexander has integrated into the US society, she finds that the United States is posing a threat to the civil liberties that she is entitled to enjoy. She, therefore, struggles hard to come to terms with her life in the New York City in the post-9/11period. She finds at stake her identity in relation to her culture, her ethnicity due to the patent emergence of latent racism. She feels more tormented when the white Americans consider her as an unpatriotic citizen despite her strong emotional responses and commitment to the national tragedy. In the process, she finds her American identity denied by the dominant culture. So, Alexander's search for identity is yet to yield any result.

Notes

1. Officially the Patriot Act is known as the USA PATRIOT (Uniting and Strengthening America by Providing Appropriate Tools Required to Intercept and Obstruct Terrorism) Act of 2001. This act is a law that was passed as a counterterrorism measure in the wake of the 9/11 terrorist attacks.
2. Meena Alexander was born to a Christian family in Allahabad, India. She was brought up in Kerala, India, and also in Khartoum, Sudan.

She went to the United Kingdom for her doctorate. She came back to India for a job. She has been living in New York since 1979 with her husband David Lelyveld, a Jewish American scholar. She is presently a distinguished Professor of English at Hunter College and Graduate Center, City University of New York.

References

Alexander, Meena. 2004. *Raw Silk*. Evanston, IL: Northwestern University Press.

Alexander, Meena. 2004. Aftermath. *Raw Silk*. Evanston, IL: Northwestern University Press.

Alexander, Meena. 2004. Invisible City. *Raw Silk*. Evanston, IL: Northwestern University Press.

Alexander, Meena. 2004. Kabir Sings in a City of Burning Towers. *Raw Silk*. Evanston, IL: Northwestern University Press.

Alexander, Meena. 2004. School Yard. *Raw Silk*. Evanston, IL: Northwestern University Press.

Alexander, Meena. 2009. *Poetics of Dislocation*. Ann Arbor, MI: Michigan University Press.

Cainkar, Louise. 2010. American Muslims at the Dawn of the 21st Century: Hope and Pessimism in the Drive for Civic and Political Inclusion. In Jocelyne Cesari (ed.), *Muslims in the West after 9/11: Religion, Politics and Law*. London and New York: Routledge, 176–197.

Gioseffi, Daniela. 2006. In the Mercy of Time–Flute Music: An Interview with Meena Alexander. Available at: http://www.thefreelibrary.com/In+the+mercy+of+time-flute+music%3A+an+interview+with+Meena+ Alexander.-a0142683245 (Accessed on 23 March 2015).

Lahiri, Himadri. 2009. Dislocation and After: Indian Women Poets in America. In Anisur Rahaman and Ameena Kazi Ansari (eds.), *Indian English Women Poets*. New Delhi: Creative Books, 106–124.

Lopamudra Basu. 2002. The Poet in the Public Sphere: A Conversation with Meena Alexander. *Social Text,* 20(372), 31–38.

Maxey, Ruth. 2006. An Interview with Meena Alexander. *MELUS*, 3(2), 21–39.

Milton Edwards, Beverley. 2006. *Islam and Violence in the Modern Era*. New York: Palgrave MacMillan.

Monshipouri, Mahmood. 2010. The War on Terror and Muslims in the West. In Jocelyne Cesari (ed.), *Muslims in the West after 9/11: Religion, Politics, and Law*. London: Routledge, 45–66.

12

Identity Formation or Corrosion: A Tale of Diasporic Conversion

Reading Shani Mootoo's *Cereus Blooms at Night* (1996) and Ramabai Espinet's *The Swinging Bridge* (2003)

Neetu Devi

Identity is a complex epistemic prefecture to enquire; it is manifold, indefinite and a never-ending process. It has both objective and subjective aspects; in the contemporary era where every constructed ideologues is in the process of getting deconstructed further religious, historical and socio-political identity that is bestowed to any individual, group or community by birth has not only been subverted but also challenged. Hence identity in the existing world has become one of the vital area of inquiry to deal with and has also become one of the highly contested and debated terms.

Identity is a core issue in every culture and society but when it comes into the sphere of migrant communities and into domain of a diaspora, which itself is an exceedingly debated term, it becomes disputed, subjective and highly contested, which with time keeps on evolving into new forms and shapes:

> 'Identity' is at least as problematic and contested a term as 'diaspora' and can no longer be referred to without challenge. Ever since Barth's contribution in 1969, identity, in the shape of ethnicity, has been investigated in terms of the construction and

> maintenance of boundaries. The 'essences' of identity are seen by many anthropologists merely as the content of an ongoing process of boundary construction, being constantly re-invented and shifted according to the requirements of the situation. Nonetheless, these 'essences' are still deeply meaningful and existent for many of those we study and they may be put to use to stabilize existing conditions, as well as for subversive and critical purposes. (Kokot et al. 2004: 4)

The evolution of multiple diasporic identity does not only bring collide and conflict into the individuals of that diasporic community but also brings the community and its identity under an ambivalent position, where there is an unvarying struggle to prove its inimitability and distinctiveness.[1] Stuart Hall in his article 'Cultural Identity and Diaspora' claims that:

> Identity is not as transparent or unproblematic as we think. Perhaps instead of thinking of identity as an already accomplished fact, which the new cultural practices then represent, we should think, instead, of identity as a 'production' which is never complete, always in process, and always constituted within, not outside, representation. (Hall, cited in Vertovec and Cohen 1999: 299)

There are diverse diasporic communities spread throughout the world and the definition of diaspora gets its immediate lacuna when one tries to apply it for the heterogeneous multiply assorted communities throughout the globe. There is continuous deliberation among academicians who seem to disagree to accept that there is a uniform and well accepted definition of diaspora. Different academicians and theoreticians have tried to define the term diaspora in their own ways.

William Safran has defined diaspora by giving six characteristics to any expatriate minority communities whose members share several of the following characteristics: (1) they, or their ancestors, have been dispersed from a specific original 'centre' to two or more 'peripheral', or foreign, regions; (2) they retain a collective memory, vision or myth about their original homeland – its physical location, history and achievements; (3) they believe that they are not – and perhaps cannot be – fully accepted by their host society and therefore feel partly alienated and insulated from it; (4) they regard their ancestral homeland as their true, ideal home and as the place to which they or their descendants would (or should) eventually return – when conditions are appropriate; (5) they believe that they should collectively be committed to the maintenance or restoration of their original homeland and to its safety and prosperity; and (6) they continue to relate, personally or vicariously, to that homeland in one way or another, and their ethnocommunal consciousness and solidarity are importantly defined by the existence of such a relationship (Safran cited in Vertovec and Cohen 1999: 364):

> 'A Diaspora exists precisely because it remembers the "homeland". Without this memory ... these migrants and settlers would be simply people in a new setting, into which they merge, bringing little or nothing to the new "home", accepting in various ways and forms the mores and attitudes that already exist in their new country and society'.
>
> However these people 'do not merely settle in new countries: they recreate in their socio-economic, political and cultural institutions a version of that ... that homeland they remember'. (Lal et al. 2007:18)

The above definition does not only ignore the variety of experiences of multiple migrations but also exclude the experience of ideological assimilation of the migrant community. There are many instance where migrant communities are discursively expected to play the role as the host country expects them to play, for instance the cases of altering the identity of migrant communities by attracting them towards the privileges of assimilation into meta-culture, religion and language which as a migrant could not be availed by the community, thus altering the already problematic and ambivalent identity of diasporic community.[2]

There are different ways through which a diasporic community represents its distinct identity, for instance by asserting its religious, linguistic and cultural differences. The need to assert its distinct identity emerges from the diasporic politics of the marginalization experienced by the immigrants. Marginalization is an important contributing factor to the politicization of immigrants based on religious, linguistic and cultural lines. But it becomes even more challenging for a community which is deprived of its religious identity via conversion in majority religion of the host nation. It brings the diasporic individual into an ambivalent position where he or she forms a 'trishanku' position. Religious identity is one of the important markers of the identity of any community, where it is generally believed that preserving the religious identity of any community plays an important role for the community to assert its distinct ethnic identity.

The case of ambivalent identity by erosion of religious history is very explicit in old Indian diaspora who became the victims of manipulative colonial policies where labourers were deprived of any connection from homeland from a very long time, they were not allowed to take any religious education except Christianity and so were their children. They were cut off completely from the commercial, cultural, educational, religious and political ties with India. They were living in pitiable condition in plantation where certain portion of the population tried hard to hold on to their old identity but a high number of populations slowly and gradually are fallen easy prey into the colonial Christian ideologues and Western propaganda of conversion. The missionaries despised the religion, traditions, culture, language and food of the labourer by calling it to be the primitive, pagan and barbaric.

Thus, white Christian came to provide an escape to the indenture labourers from their misery (which was ironically imposed by them). In the disguised form of philanthropy, they spread Christian propaganda of mission civilization, to educate and 'civilize'[3] indentured labourers on the expanse of bartering their religious identity. Anand Mullo in his book *Voices of the Indian Diaspora* (2007) says that the Westerners put all sorts of ideological pressure on the Indians to convert them by any means 'So that they might remain for-ever dependant on them as they earlier had crushed the soul of the slaves. To be a Christian meant to be entirely dependent upon their sway. Afraid of their numbers the westerners fought back by suppressing them by denying them their basic needs' (2007: 284).

The conversion was made on promise of a new life full of success and prosperity away from the mucky barracks of indenture labourers, which often turned out to be the antithesis of success and prosperity and exposes the hypocrisy of Christianity in the form of internalize racism where the converted were considered as an inferior variety of Christianity filled with oddness and weirdity.

Conversion did not only curtail their historicity but also bring the converted into a 'nowherian' position of exile and dislocation, which brought their identity in further question and made it more complex due to the lack of preservation of their religious identity. In the context of diasporic religious identity, Martin Baumann in his article 'Diaspora: Genealogies of Semantics and Transcultural Comparison' argues that in the context of migration, religion and identity, the preservation and continuation and upholding of one's religious identity becomes a nucleus issue (2000: 326–327); further he states that perpetuation and alteration of a religious tradition in a diaspora situation becomes very important (2000: 329). In diaspora an original perpetuation or retaining of one's genealogically derived is not possible and mostly the identity is assumed. Change and alteration are integral part of diasporic experience but whatever is retained, for instance, one's culture, language, identity, religion and tradition is of course changed and transformed but what as an immigrant the diaspora has to grasp is the preservation of the plural and altered change, and if that is also curtailed as in the case of conversion, the preservation becomes more complex and problematic.

The explication of 'nowherian' self, multilayered identity and complex diasporic historicity is one of the important recurrent themes into the literatures that are emerging from old classical Indian diaspora, the writers from old Indian diaspora negotiate with this theme very potently in their writings. Mootoo and Espinet are one of the major authors of this genre and their novels *Cereus Blooms at Night* (1996) of Shani Mootoo and *The Swinging Bridge* (2003) of Ramabai Espinet respectively deal with these themes and issues very dexterously.

Cereus Blooms at Night (Mootoo 1996) glimpses the situation and the life of indentured labourer communities in Trinidad; she weaves the story around a place called Paradise, which is ironical because it depicts the life of the labours in pitiable condition. Religion is all pervasive and recurrent themes, which appears significantly in the novel. The very incident of religious conversion comes on to the fore right in the beginning of the novel as a symbol of colonization and imperialism, when the parents of

Chandin Ramchandin are asked to convert from Hinduism to Christianity in order to ensure a better education for his son Chandin. Reverend Thoroughly from Northern Wetlands towards his White Man's Burden is usually perceived as a compassionate and generous figure who plays the role of demi God in the eyes of the labourers and the native population. He is providing the opportunity to the children of these community and have himself migrated to the land of Trinidad to perform the philanthropic deed of educating the children by converting them, unaware of the repercussions of the conversion; when the natives speak of the Reverend, they say:

> Now, you see any schools set up for our children, besides the Reverend's school? We looking after our own self, because nobody has time for us, except the Reverend and his mission from the Shivering Northern Wetlands. All he wants from us is that we convert to his religion. (Mootoo 1996: 28)

The politics of conversion can very explicitly be seen into the novel where Tyler narrates the story of Mala Chandin, a mad woman in attic. It begins with Mala's father, Ramchandin who was adopted at a very early age by a person name Sir Reverend Thoroughly, a white man in exchange of his parents' conversion from Hinduism to Christianity.

The other instance is Sarah, in the missionary school who is the only Indian and addressed as 'other'. Here we observe the hypocrisy of conversion, where on the one hand, the converted are made to feel Christian and being part of the meta-narrative but at the same time one is excluded and marginalized as being racially 'other'. The glimpse of 'arrogant Christian theological and religious practices and internalised racism'[4] can easily be observed here.

Chandin who loves and admires Lavinia thought of confessing his love to Lavinia who without giving any thought to him straight away rejected his proposal and declared that she has a boyfriend in northern Wetland who was a white Christian and she is going to be engaged to him. The embedded internal racism could be subtly observed in the rejection of Lavinia, although Chandin is a devoted Christian but his identity as an Indian again makes him different from the white Christian population in Trinidad. Here position of Chandin as an allusion to 'trishanku'[5] could easily be understood, he is neither a Hindu with his ancestor's old Indian religious beliefs nor he is a Christian without being seen as the 'other' category of Christian; after the conversion he was neither an Indian Hindu nor a pure Christian.

Suresh K. Pillai, in the article 'Indentured Indians' argues on the conversions of Armenian-Indians in Trinidad by the Church, he says:

> For the church, the natives were a bunch of pagans, barbarians, heathens or worse than animals and therefore the church could not find any fault in the atrocities committed by the colonizers. Those who refuse to succumb to the will of Christian God were eliminated forthwith. Later when the population became almost extinct the church preached peace and converted the remaining population into Christianity. Those who had remained alive had to accept the church and its divine conceptions. The accommodation of these natives into the Christian faith was soon followed by the appropriation of natives' culture. Nothing was spared. The Gods and Goddesses became Christian. Their rituals and festivals had to bear the Christian stamp. Their ancestors and the rebels who fought against the colonizers were demonized. The colonizers invented several stories, which made the natives cannibals.[6]

Similarly Ramabai Espinet's *The Swinging Bridge* (2003) is replete with the instances of the contradictory and highly paradoxical nature of conversion. Mona, the Protagonist, migrates to Canada with her parents and siblings in 1970s. Although Canada, under Pierre Trudeau's coerce towards nationalism, multiculturalism and pluralism, created the opportunity for the people to settle in Canada and during this force of migration the middle-class Caribbean populace who were highly ambitious migrants came to Canada with lots of hopes and aspirations were coldly received by their new countrymen. Mona recalls her arrival to the Canada. She says:

> When I arrived in the early seventies, Canada was a white country. If multiculturalism was an idea, it never touched me. For Da-Da, the moment of truth came when he saw a wall covered with graffiti that read Keep Canada White. As if it ever was. (Espinet 2003: 243)

While Mona's younger brother, Johnnie, becomes meticulously Canadianized, satirized by Mona's continuous reference to his frosty respectability and his blonde wife's prairie whiteness (Espinet 2003: 214), the rest of the family hasn't fared it well. Her sister, Babs, has adopted a butterfly-like personality, filling her life with men and materialism in an attempt to hide her lack of ease with her identity (Espinet 2003: 26).

Mona, in her forties, finds it really hard to adjust in Canada and she has been struggling with feeling of unaccommodating self, from the time she has entered into her new assumed abode Canada; to her, accommodation in Canada and her belongingness is a complex domain and to make a new home in Canada for herself was still a remote thought. Even after decades of staying in Canada, she feels that she belongs to nowhere, she is neither a Caribbean nor a Canadian. Her home and belonging is not permanent, rather it is a temporary phenomenon like her identity, which has evolved from multiple histories and is like a swinging bridge connected to more than one ends but still not stable rather keeps on swinging; hence to feel at home for her is a shifting and evolving process.

Mona's present alienation and isolation in Canada has its genealogical roots in the role of Presbyterian missions in Trinidad who with their mission civilization via conversion of the native and indentured labour population created a new Indian Christian middle class. These people were not only deprived of their religious identity but they too were taught the Christian way of living, which was very different and alien to them. The converted people attained an odd identity where they were made stranger to their own history as indentured labourers, culture and society. Though they were converted and were following the religion of their colonial master, but their body too became stranger to them as they could not associate them with white population of Christian.

John Morton, the first Canadian Presbyterian missionary in Trinidad, established missions and a system of Western-style primary education rooted in Presbyterianism upon his arrival in 1868. This included a girls' training home 'for the protection and training of Indian girls' to become good wives for the converted Christian missionaries. Morton kept a written record of his dealings with and impressions of Indo-Trinidadian women, representing them as wanton, morally depraved and incapable of being elevated to Euro-American standards of femininity and civility. Morton's diary also reveals the close relationship not only of religion and education, but also of music and Christianization in the Indo-Trinidadian communities overseen by the missions (Myers 1998: 112).

In the novel, Mona talks about her childhood memories of going to church and her childhood innocence, when she did not understand the politics of conversion and assimilation. Recollecting her thoughts from Trinidadian life, going to church on Sundays with her family, for the adolescent Mona, was the pleasant experience. For Mona, Church hymns were source of elevated feelings and thoughts, that provided her sublime pleasure, after listening to the hymns she says she used to feel 'so happy! Happy, happy, happy!' (Espinet 2003: 33).

Yet, Mona later recognizes the irony of the representations in lyrics of the hymns and the concealed connotations, the hidden messages of hypocrisy of Christian conversion, not only the lyrics of the hymns but also the church seat arrangement, explicated about order of people which kept her 'at the edge of that circling sphere' (Espinet 2003: 30). She reminiscences her past and says: Her parents:

> Lifted themselves into a space free as air through the hymns they sang at church on Sundays, those old hymns wrought out of the stoicism required for life in a frozen land, peopled by hymn writers with eyes of cold blue steel. Inside the armour of those hymns they found repose: *O God, our help in ages past/our hope for years to come/our shelter from the stormy blast/and our eternal home.* The Canadian missionaries and their wives sat in special pews at the front of the beautiful Savana Grande church, one of the first buildings of their mission. … Our hearts flew up to heaven, and all the soot and flying dust of burning cane vanished into the smoke fires of hell while we ascended skywards, washed in the blood of the lamb. (Espinet 2003: 29–30)

This passage could be seen as an exemplar of the superiority complex that white Christians in Trinidadian society perused in their psyche, through the hymn the white Christian showed the converted Christians their place into the white Christian community.

Mona's family, like many others in Trinidad who have accepted and converted to Presbyterian religion, and abide by its education and values, is embarrassed of their Indo-Trinidadian history and culture. Mona remembers how 'newly educated people would throw out almost everything Indian at first, and would slowly gather back into their lives only those relics that were essential for survival' (Espinet 2003: 64–66).

Further, author describes the detrimental and ruinous consequence of Christian education and religious values on the Indo-Trinidadian consciousness. Although it had hazardous effect on the life of the whole community, but for the men the sacrifices were not much. It was only limited to the changing of their name from Hindu to Christian but the effect of Christian education and values on the psychology of women was far worse and damaging. It not only challenged their sexual identity and sexual roles that they were playing but also made the women suffer the aftermath of conversion in many ways: for instance in the novel we learn that Mona's grandparents' marriage is a result of conversion and was performed by the Presbyterian mission, which ruptured her grandfather's previous marriage with Etwaria who was his 'bamboo wife'. The term 'bamboo wife' was condescendingly used by the Christian community to describe about the traditional Hindu marriage rituals, according to which the marriages were performed 'under bamboo', which the white Christians considered to be primitive and a barbaric rituals. Further, Mona illustrates that though her grandfather married again but Etwaria, the traditional Hindu wife, waited for him for her entire life. The ruinous effect of conversion on the life of plantation women could be seen into the next instance where due to the Christian and Presbyterian respectability Joshua does not allow Gainder to sing chutney music since it was considered to be a lower form of art, which was practiced by the primitives.

Showing the effect of Christian religion, colonialism and patriarchy altogether, Mona recollects moral policing of her sexuality in her adolescent age. At the mission-run La Pastora Girls' School, where her female teachers exercise influence over young Indo-Trinidadian girls' sexuality by instructing them to think of themselves as sexually wanton, 'hot hot from small' (Espinet 2003: 144).

As Brinda Mehta (2004) in her book *Diasporic Dislocations* states, the intimidated migration to Trinidad not only ruptured traditional gender roles and facilitated new reconstitutions of families, but also allowed indentured women to renegotiate labour, gender and sexual economies on the sugar plantations. Consequently, Indo-Trinidadian male orthodoxy disparaged the presumed sexual freedoms of itinerant Indo-Trinidadian womanhood. Indo-Trinidadian women were caught between two competing readings of their sexuality: on the one hand, the chaste Indian woman in the guise of the Ramayana's Sita, and on the other hand, the suspicion that they were innately sexually loose and must be kept in check (Mehta 2004: 32–33).

Mona talks about the deleterious effect of Canadian neo-colonialism in making the Indo-Trinidadian community alien from their values and culture, she also talks about the repercussion of it by showing how it makes women like Mona strangers to their own bodies.

Revolting alongside the politics of Christian respectability for indentured women and the stiff and controlled watch over their bodies, Mona and her schoolmates engage in a unsaid combat with their school uniforms, which they call 'The Dirty Skirts Club' and keep a secret journal of 'hot things' where they write about their personal experience especially about their sexual desires and sexual experiences. In the journal writing we can observe the subversive potential of women writing which empowers the women characters in the novel to assert an Indo-Trinidadian female subjectivity that repudiates the restraints and curb placed on her individuality.

In other way, journal entry becomes a powerful tool that shows the reason of Mona's thought formation and her rant and rave against the orthodox education that the missionary and Church education system was imparting, it also shows how her mission-educated father bullied her to crawl on rock-strewn as punishment for her assumed 'wantonness', the mere confirmation of which is a dress that her father believes to be too sexually alluring for his daughter to put on in public, her father says: 'What the hell you doing again in that ho dress? You ain't find you attracting enough man already?' (Espinet 2003: 178).

The outcome his drunken rage is the public shaming of his daughter and humiliating her by publically burning her dress which she liked so much. This incident marks an important place into the heart of Mona and created a wrath and felling of insurgence into her heart and as an upshot of this incident Mona began to despise the marriage institution and the role of women into the domestic sphere. In other words, she is revolting against the Indo-Trinidadian orthodoxy, Presbyterianism and the religious and cultural values that she had been forced to internalize.

Conclusion

From the above illustration, it is explicit that identity in diaspora is multifaceted, contested and debated term, and in such a scenario life of migrants become extremely complicated and complex. Isolation and rootlessness is an embedded part of diasporic consciousness and diasporic identity where an individual does not stay in one personality rather wear multiple personality, which is hybrid and highly ambiguous. Further when it comes into the process of conversion by altering ones religious self, the individual attains more blurred identity which makes an individual estranged to his own history and origins.

If there is an end product of identity formation at all, as Avtar Brah states, it cannot be one homogeneous model of identity that equally serves for all members of a group. We must be as ready to ask for different and shifting levels of identity, as for conflicting and contesting designs. In the case of diaspora, the matter seems even more complex. Members of diaspora communities are confronted with a multitude of 'others', towards whom quite different designs of identity may be presented – be it the nation states of residence and their different requirements, globally dispersed communities of the same diaspora or the demands (on a symbolic or a political/economic level) of what is considered their true homeland. Any research into identity and diaspora must therefore take into account a great variety and heterogeneity of identities at any given point in time, among which 'diaspora identity' is only one, albeit formative, part (Brah 1996, quoted in Kokot et al. 2004: 7).

Notes

1. There is always continuous struggle from the diasporic community to display its distinctiveness from the host community basically due to the expectation of assimilation that the host society indirectly imposes

on the migrant communities, for instance the conversion of migrant population in order to assimilate them into the mainstream culture.

2. The instances could be seen into the conversion of the indentured labourers into Christianity by making them feel that they would be treated as the Christian population and would have all the privileges as the majoritarian Christian religion has. For further explanation, read the *Book Cereus Blooms at Night* by Shani Mootoo and *The Swinging Bridge* by Ramabai Espinet.
3. The term highly subjective when one takes an oxidant positioning because it is only the white elites who consider them to be civilized without even knowing the culture and social life of the other community. Further read the poem *White Men's Burden* by Rudyard Kipling from an Orientalist perspective to understand hidden Eurocentric racism and white men's aspiration to dominate developing world.
4. Read the article online available at: https://www.questia.com/library/journal/1G1-133685493/dislocation-and-desire-in-shani-mootoo-s-cereus-blooms (accessed on 20 February 2014].
5. Trishanku is a mythological figure from the Indian Hindu Mythological book *Vishnu Purana* who due to the curse of lord Vishnu is still into the hanging position between the earth and sky.
6. Go through the article on https://www.academia.edu/447217/INDENTURED_INDIANS (access date 20 February 2014).

References

Baumann, M. 2000. Diaspora: Genealogies of Semantics and Transcultural Comparison. *Numen*, Vol. 47(3), 313–337.

Brah, Avtar. 1996. *Cartographies of Diaspora: Contesting Identities*. London: Routledge.

Espinet, Ramabai. 2003. *The Swinging Bridge*. Toronto: Harper Collins Publisher.

Kokot Waltraud, Khachig Tölölyan and Carolin Alfonso. 2004. *Diaspora, Identity and Religion: New Directions in Theory and Research*. London: Routledge Press.

Lal, Brij V., Peters Reeves and Rajesh Rai (eds). 2007. *The Encyclopaedia of the Indian Diaspora*. New Delhi: Oxford University Press.

Mehta, Brinda. 2004. *Diasporic (Dis)locations: Indo-Caribbean Women Writers Negotiate the Kala Pani*. West Indies: The University of the West Indies Press.

Mootoo, Shani. 1996. *Cereus Blooms at Night*. Vancouver: Press Gang Publisher.

Mullo, Anand. 2007. *Voices of the Indian Diaspora.* New Delhi: Motilal Banarsidass.

Myers Helen. 1998. *Music of Hindu Trinidad: Songs from the India Diaspora*. Chicago: University of Chicago Press.

Pillai, K. Suresh. Indentured Indians: Emergence of Hindu Identity in Caribbean Countries. Available at: https://www.academia.edu/447217/INDENTURED_INDIANS (accessed on 12 March 2015).

Vertovec, Steven and Robin Cohen. 1999. *Migration, Diasporas and Transnationalism*. Cheltenham: Edward Elgar.

Index